FIRST PERSON SINGULAR:
Studies in American Autobiography

FIRST PERSON SINGULAR:
Studies in American Autobiography

edited by
A. Robert Lee

VISION PRESS · LONDON
ST. MARTIN'S PRESS · NEW YORK

Vision Press Ltd.
Fulham Wharf
Townmead Road
London SW6 2SB

and

St. Martin's Press, Inc.
175 Fifth Avenue
New York, N.Y. 10010

ISBN (UK) 0 85478 076 9
ISBN (US) 0 312 02425 8

Library of Congress Cataloging-in-Publication Data

First person singular.

(Critical studies)
1. American prose literature—History and criticism.
2. Autobiography.   3. Self in literature.   3. Authors,
American—Biography—History and criticism.   I. Lee, A.
Robert, 1941–   .   II. Series: Critical Studies series.
PS366.A88.F57   1988   810'.9'492   87-15504
ISBN 0-312-02425-8

Printed and bound in Great Britain at
The University Printing House, Oxford.
Phototypeset by Galleon Photosetting,
Ipswich, Suffolk.
MCMLXXXVIII

Contents

Introduction

by A. ROBERT LEE

> I know lives, I could miss
> Without a Misery—
> Others—whose instant's wanting—
> Would be Eternity—
> —Emily Dickinson

If ours indeed is an Age of Literary Theory, then few genres
have been more the testing-ground for debate and controversy
than Autobiography. Where as provocatively in literature does
the factual meet with the fictive, the actual with the invented or
mythicized? How, precisely, are we to judge the point of view on
offer, a Life of necessity told in retrospect and through all the
tilts and uncertainties of memory? How much accuracy, in
reality, do we as readers ask of the self-told account, subject as it
must be to massagings of fact, justifications and idealizations,
certain detail put to the foreground and other softened or
played down, in all the autobiographer set in his or her
preferred—which is not to say always favourable—light? These
to be sure express issues which have been in play for some
considerable time, not least with reference to the two great
beacons of classic autobiography, the *Confessions* respectively of
Saint Augustine and Jean-Jacques Rousseau. They are issues,
nonetheless, which of late have won a quite momentous new
round of attention. And nowhere more so, as the essays
gathered in this collection serve continuing notice, than with
reference to American autobiography.

Still other issues of a general kind press as hard. How
hospitable a genre can Autobiography be allowed to be? Does
it always include, to offer a familiar listing, not only the
Confession but the Memoir, the Apologia, the Diary, the

Personal Journal, the *Life* told as a sequence or exchange of correspondence? What, too, of the formal collaboration, the subject aided and articulated to one or another degree by the co-writer? What, indeed, of the transcription of a given individual's life or sayings at the hands of and for whatever reason an uncommissioned second party—with the upshot of an autobiography never intended or off-centre or even consciously made to falsify and distort? And what of the status of the novel or long poem which assumes a first-person, 'autobiographical' stance, the 'I' as an acknowledged persona? In addition, what are the implications of a life consciously shaped into narrative, given a sequence and measure which in the living it may never have seemed to possess?

One has only to ponder the sub-titlings of certain recent studies of Autobiography to recognize the elusiveness of any single or decisive formulation. Autobiography, for instance, has been construed as if anything an 'autobiographical *occasion*' (my emphasis), as more a 'metaphor of self' than the self in truth, and as a mode variously to be thought 'exemplary', 'confessional' or even 'prophetic'. Which, in turn, raises the issue of a genre which even as the very process of writing is taking place can 'create' the life at hand, the upshot a *Life* bound to have been told self-reflexively and thereby equally bound to signal its own fictionality, its own status as artifice or improvisation. And what in sober critical conscience *does* make a Literary Autobiography 'literary', as against, say, 'popular' or by intention simply inspirational or evidentiary?

Have we not, on a related tack, an obligation to historicize all autobiography, to recognize that whatever the endeavour to become the arbiter of one's own history, to bid at least to put history for a moment at bay, that in itself could not be more historicizing? Little wonder that of all literary kinds autobiography has been so frequently used as testament, evidence, witness, and often enough as an expression of counterpoint to or dissent from the perceived historical flow of things. Insofar as these and a still further round of contemplations can lay claim to any one renewed point of departure, there is good cause for it to be thought Roy Pascal's *Design and Truth in Autobiography* (1960), a model of awareness as to Autobiography's subtleties and challenge. Which is not for a moment to avoid recognizing that the debate has moved on, most especially at a time when structuralism, deconstruction and now their aftermath, have put virtually all literary activity under a new interrogation.

In the case of American autobiography, one recognizes from the outset a quite unique dispensation. For from its European settlement onwards America has shown itself subject to an endemic and at times positively startling self-consciousness. Not only has that centred on a wished-for general definition of Americanness (with its unhappy corollary of un-Americanness) but on the 'American' identity of the individual—men and women 'En-masse' and as the 'simple separate person' as Walt Whitman put it in his opening 'Inscription' in *Leaves of Grass*. Thus, too, when Ralph Waldo Emerson, listing the 'Peculiarities of the present Age' some two decades earlier in his Journal for January/February, 1827, spoke of the path of 'the first person singular', he like Whitman clearly saw it as essentially that of the sovereign self within a unique national selfhood, a heterogeneity within shared American ideals and aspirations.

Time and again America has pronounced itself a New World, a world at least to be newly won and named. Whether, accordingly, as a new-found land, a city upon a hill, a frontier, or no more than a beckoning future, America has seemingly always of its very being acted as a call to self-declaration in its citizenry, a profession of contributing identity. But however heeded, that call to the future becomes in autobiographical terms a past, a life now gone by and unfolded as its own American forward journey. If, too, the story in general has been one of up and onwards, it has also and not a little discomfortingly been the story of many for whom American history has not been benign, a bondage to be both endured and escaped from as reported in Afro-American slave narrative or a preexistent native culture ignorantly broken into and subsumed under white expansion westwards as told in Indian-American autobiography. Yet whichever the emphasis one fact overwhelmingly persists. Few nations have quite literally produced as much autobiography—estimates run to nearly 10,000 volumes—witness still further were it needed (yet all inside the one genre) of the unabating drama of identity in America.

It might in fact have been thought surprising in a nation so much about the business of self-definition, so eclectic in its ethnic and regional make-up, simply so large, had auto-biography *not* been one of its principal literary forms. How else to tell the one American life-story in the face of the many? How else to register individual difference against the assumption of a larger and determining national destiny? For from the Puritan foundation onwards, whether that of New England or Virginia, the stress has fallen upon the need always to enscribe one's own signature, to make permanent and literally graphic one's identity. Autobiography has accordingly been but one mode—though a most prominent one—of convenient response to all those circlings within the national culture and history to do both collectively and 'separately' with who one is and why so.

Given a body of autobiography as amply and diversely stocked as that of America, the present essays attempt essentially representative explorations and soundings. But by editorial design if nothing else, they have been commissioned to be both inclusive and particular. They also in the main observe historical order, though with considerable cross-historical reference as to issues of gender, ethnicity, 'period' influence, and differing kinds of autobiography. They also offer a mix of approaches. Two, for instance, explore the autobiographical impulse first in Puritan culture and then in its mid-nineteenth century Transcendentalist offshoot, a tradition of linking historical-cultural discourse. A second grouping explores some notable pairings in American autobiography, Benjamin Franklin and Jonathan Edwards in the eighteenth century, and perhaps less usually, the interesting contrasts of thought and inclination in Mark Twain and Henry Adams as contemporaries a century later. Others look to traditions of a more collective and ethnic kind—lines of autobiography within Afro-American, Jewish-American and Indian-American culture. A separate essay is given over to twentieth century women autobiographers, with Gertrude Stein as the touchstone. As to single authors, the collection includes a major modern and a major contemporary, Henry James and Norman Mailer.

In her analysis of the origins of an American autobiographical tradition, Elizabeth Kaspar Aldrich sets up a paradox: under Puritan writ 'autobiography' could only be vainglorious indulgence, a celebration of self at the expense of a celebration of the

Maker. Yet where other does the American tradition of intro-spection, self-scrutiny, the self anatomized and pursued begin? As we read through the inaugurating names—William Bradford, Increase and Cotton Mather, John Winthrop, Thomas Shepard, John Woolman, Robert Keayne, as well as more secular counterparts like John Smith, William Byrd and pre-eminently Mary Rowlandson—it is hard not to discern the emphasis which recurs in all American autobiography, that of the will to a self-account. So, too, one also discerns the crucial, subtle interplay between the wish to offer a generic story—the 'working' of God's purposes in the life of His creatures or the 'captivity' saga—and the wish to offer an account of the one sovereign or autonomous life. Out of that tension arises almost all subsequent American autobiography.

Most especially can it be said to be so in the cases of Jonathan Edwards's *Personal Narrative* and Benjamin Franklin's *Auto-biography*, both classic texts written in the waning shadow of the seventeenth century Puritan settlement. As David Seed under-scores, the parallels abound: a Puritanism in all its Calvinist intensity and prescription still fought for and urged, a Puritanism secularized into utility and the Protestant work-ethic; a Puri-tanism to be valued for its inward spirituality as against its secular, public and communal meanings especially in the winning of wealth; and a Puritanism which looks to a redemp-tion in the afterlife rather than in the present. In their different but utterly mutual ways, both Edwards and Franklin open up yet another enduring dialectic in the American soul—the ideal and the pragmatic, the self alone and the self among its fellows. As autobiography, both texts could not be more historically instructive.

'Be expert in home-cosmography' wrote Henry David Thoreau in *Walden*, one of the essential litany of texts which make up the mid-nineteenth century American Renaissance. It serves as an apt motto to the three autobiographical presences considered by Brian Harding: Ralph Waldo Emerson, Walt Whitman and Thoreau himself. 'Self-culture', 'Song of Myself', 'A community of one': each phrase typifies its author, their insistence upon the transcendentalist self as a dynamic, a process, an uncompletable becoming. For all three of them, no autobiography, however defined, could ever give the final

11

account. In Emerson's terms, as the universe circles dynamically outwards and inwards so the self equally enacts its own circling motions of growth and consciousness.

In comparing the *Education* of Henry Adams with the (unfinished) *Autobiography* of Mark Twain, Warren Chernaik looks to two writers again moved to seek the measure of their age in their own outwardly differing modes of experience. Yet equally and once again irresistible parallels arise: Adams as the Harvard-educated, patrician WASP scion of a Presidential line and Twain as the frontier-raised story-teller and one-time Mississippi riverboat pilot in whom the language of vernacular America rarely found a more decisive voice brought together as the incorrigible Easterner and the incorrigible Westerner. Both, too, saw a blackness in the American Dream, a lurking and even fatal flaw in the will to ever more and greater progress. Their autobiographies, as different in particulars as in irony, offer a most striking and unexpected convergence.

So determined and masterly a voice of 'the ordeal of consciousness' as Henry James almost inevitably, one is bound to think, had to be drawn to autobiography. Drawn to it, also, as David Ellis takes care to demonstrate, in a manner which continues those tactics of indirection and nuance which mark out his fiction—the major body of which when he composed *A Small Boy and Others*, *Notes of a Son and Brother* and *The Middle Years* lay behind him. James's autobiographies, too, look as much to his making as a writer, a creative consciousness, as they do to any 'external' notation of the history of his life. But they do so with a discretion which might well be thought exquisite, a handling of memory, desire, the sexual wellsprings of human energy in terms as engagingly equivocal as anything in his fiction.

The essays which follow take up more collective considerations. Faith Pullin argues for the discreetness of women's autobiography, the allaying of an imposed image and the finding and using of a self-made image. Beginning from Gertrude Stein, both *The Autobiography of Alice B. Toklas* and *Everybody's Autobiography*, and with stop-overs at H.D., Lillian Hellman, Mary McCarthy, Charlotte Gilman, Kate Chopin, Sylvia Plath and Maxine Hong Kingston, she suggests that the writerly path for these women has been one always of self-recovery, the usable creative self rescued from inutility or marginalization. My own essay similarly looks to a history of selfhood re-found and re-made through autobiography, that of Afro-America in the four decades since Richard Wright's *Black Boy*. With a backward glance both to slave-narrative and the autobiography of the Harlem Renaissance, I propose a mode of reading both the 'modern' and the 'contemporary' in black autobiography, an insistence upon the black self composing itself *as* a self in the face of the historic denial of that self. The essential reference I make, in turn, is to *Black Boy*, Zora Neale Hurston's *Dust Tracks on a Road*, Chester Himes's *The Quality of Hurt* and *My Life of Absurdity*, *The Autobiography of Malcolm X* and the five-volume *Life* of Maya Angelou.

David Murray also takes a broad sweep in looking to selective autobiographies within American-Indian, Hispanic and Asian tradition, three bodies of self-expression too easily designated 'ethnic'. He gives his emphasis especially to the authenticity and status of the American-Indian autobiographical 'text', the transcription and patterning of an essentially oral witness into an established Western literary form. For Michael Woolf the issue in Jewish-American autobiography is the paining conjunction between the Jew who survives into the wellbeing of America and those Jews whose tragic destiny took them to the Nazi death camps. For him, all Jewish-American autobiography, thereby, becomes a dialogue with the past, the haunting human presentness of the martyrs.

Eric Mottram rounds out the collection with a reconsideration of Norman Mailer, the begetter of an outpouring of autobiography which begins with *Advertisements for Myself* in 1959 and has continued militantly and even pugilistically through to work like *The Executioner's Song* (1979). However regarded, as the early hipster-beat figure of *The White Negro* (1957), the massive promissory voice of *The Naked and the Dead* (1948), the self-appointed counsel of *The Presidential Papers* (1963), the reporter—'Mailer' as he calls him—of *The Armies of the Night* (1968), or as any or all of his subsequent incarnations of the 1970s and beyond, few would deny him a unique autobiographical status. His, and one might have given a single focus to other American contemporaries, a Tom Wolfe, Gore Vidal, Adrienne Rich, Joan Didion or LeRoi Jones/Amiri Baraka, gives continuing evidence of the vitality, the compulsion possibly, behind American auto-biography. Of necessity, then, this newly commissioned collection of essays offers selective bearings, discreet but linking evaluations of a quite inescapable contribution to the history of American self-expression.

1

'The Children of these Fathers': The Origins of an Autobiographical Tradition in America

by ELIZABETH KASPAR ALDRICH

1

Let us begin indirectly, with a Pilgrim Father who, far from writing an 'autobiography' or any other form of personal account, produced what may be the most sublimely selfless of chronicles-of-his-time in American literature, and certainly one of that literature's few great Histories. In Book I, Chapter IX in *Of Plymouth Plantation* (1630–51), 'Of their Voyage and how they Passed the Sea; and of their Safe Arrival at Cape Cod', William Bradford (1590–1657) is brought to a moment of reflection and to a very rare instance of the first person singular:

> But here I cannot but stay and make a pause, and stand half amazed at this poor people's present condition; and so I think will the reader, too, when he well considers the same. Being thus passed the vast ocean, and a sea of troubles before in their preparation (as may be remembered by that which went before), they had now no friends to welcome them nor inns to entertain or refresh their weatherbeaten bodies; no houses or much less towns to repair to, to seek for succour. . . .[1]

This is a much-anthologized passage, sometimes cited as evidence that the seventeenth-century Puritans were not, after

15

all, nineteenth-century Romantics and neither idealized nor
pastoralized Nature or what was to become their children's
native land. Bradford continues:

> Besides, what could they see but a hideous and desolate wilder-
> ness, full of wild beasts and wild men—and what multitudes
> there might be of them they knew not. Neither could they, as it
> were, go up to the top of Pisgah to view from this wilderness a
> more goodly country to feed their hopes; for which way soever
> they turned their eyes (save upward to the heavens) they could
> have little solace or contentment in respect of outward objects.
> For summer being done, all things stand upon them with a
> weatherbeaten face, and the whole country, full of woods and
> thickets, represented a wild and savage hue. If they looked
> behind them, there was the mighty ocean which they had passed
> and was now as a main bar and gulf to separate them from all the
> civil parts of the world. . . . (62)

And it is of course cited often as evidence that the 'plain style' of
the Puritans could be aesthetically beautiful and complex. The
writer's enumeration of difficulties and dangers is at once
circumstantial in detail and epic in tone. His own response to
them, 'here' in his writing-present and still 'half amazed', is to
our own retrospect orthodox and inevitable—'What could now
sustain them but the Spirit of God and His grace?'—and then,
again to our retrospect, both inevitable and somehow unexpected:

> May not and ought not the children of these fathers rightly say:
> 'Our fathers were Englishmen which came over this great ocean,
> and were ready to perish in this wilderness; but they cried unto
> the Lord, and He heard their voice and looked on their adversity',
> etc. 'Let them therefore praise the Lord, because He is good, and
> His mercies endure forever.' (63)

'May they not', '*ought* they not . . . rightly say': there is surely
both a prospective and a prescriptive injunction here. According to the *prescriptive* injunction 'autobiography' for the later
generations will take the form (or formula) of a kind of
hagiography of the first.

Now we are accustomed to finding a state of fatherless-ness as
the identifying mark of the American literary tradition: Benjamin
Franklin of the *Autobiography* is the prototype and Jay Gatsby,
who 'sprang from his Platonic conception of himself' (albeit

using Poor Richard as model) one twentieth-century apotheosis.
But if American autobiography exists within and indeed at the
origins of this tradition, then the tradition itself may be haunted
by a paternal injunction unfulfilled: Hawthorne's 'Roger
Malvin's Burial' in literary history.[2] To formulate an account of
oneself and publish it to the world may strike us as the
quintessential American impulse, intrinsic to the national
experience, character, literature. But behind the self-creation
and self-celebration of classic American literature—Thoreau's
chanticleer bragging to wake his neighbours up, Whitman's
bard sounding his barbaric yawp over the roofs of the world—
we may also discover an Anxiety of Origins.

2

Strictly speaking, an account of the origins of 'American
autobiography' would properly begin with the prototype
Franklin—not simply because the term autobiography itself
comes into its first usage around the late eighteenth century
(the first listed by the *Oxford English Dictionary* is 1809), but
more importantly because Franklin's sense of what 'American'
means is probably the first to approach or coincide with our
own; he is in life and writings a creator of that modern sense.
Moreover, changes in terminology and usage aside, the textual
sources before Franklin, that is personal accounts written, as his
was, for some kind of public readership, are very scant. Most of
the now 'classic' personal accounts of early American writing
were published posthumously, often well into the nineteenth
century and sometimes still later (the most significant exception
to this rule is discussed below), a fact which does not necessarily
diminish their interest for us today, but which certainly
confuses the question of their influence on earlier generations of
writers, of their place within a literary tradition or canon.[3]
Finally, the overwhelming Puritan dominance of what has
become canonical for students and scholars of seventeenth- and
early eighteenth-century American literature has recently come
under challenge—most amusingly, perhaps, by James M. Cox,
who has remarked that 'the Puritan ascension could be
attributed to three causes: Harvard, Yale, and Perry Miller.'[4]
But *pace* Cox, and despite the lack of appeal intrinsic to received

wisdom (Perry Miller is a father against whom many American scholars are in revolt), we must look to the Puritans for the origins of an autobiographical tradition in America. Not only were they the most uniformly literate group to arrive on the shores of the New World; they were, it seems beyond dispute, collectively and individually the most *self*-conscious. Central to Puritan theology and culture was what we may call the life accounted for: consciously and conscientiously, the life examined, interpreted, justified, and shaped into a transmissible *account*.

Puritan history is the public account of the life of God's elect on earth, collective life as exemplary of that election and of the working out of God's design in earthly affairs. The self-consciousness of the group turns both inward and outward:

> ... for wee must Consider that wee shall be as a Citty vpon a Hill, the eies of all people are uppon vs; soe that if wee shall deale falsely with our god in this worke wee haue vndertaken and soe cause him to withdrawe his present help from vs, wee shall be made a story and a by-word through the world. . . .[5]

Story is paramount. Puritan biography, what Miller has called 'the preparation of case histories', offers to the world and to the community itself exemplary individual instances of the same election and favour. In both history and biography the life recounted has a shape in so far as it fulfils the design of God, and the account is didactic in that it both illustrates that design, and, in the case of biography, offers a model for emulation. Hence biography's special importance: paradoxically, the individual case provides confirmation of collective unity; it typifies, to however extraordinary a degree, the *collective* virtues, the subject is marked by his self-forgetful devotion and service to God and fellow-man. And in presenting his subject as a type the biographer both recapitulates the collective history and invites the identification and emulation of his audience across time, and hence through history itself.

Bradford's brief account towards the end of *Of Plymouth Plantation* of the life and death of the Reverend Elder Brewster (Ch. XXXIII), a father to him in age, example, and support, is a model of Puritan biography; Brewster embodies those virtues which underlie the survival and success of the community of saints, and the life in sum provides future generations with evidence of 'the marvellous providence of God' in preserving his servant, a lesson which He 'would have all men to behold and observe . . . that they in like cases might be encouraged to depend upon God in their trials' (329). Puritans of the first generations regularly produced biographies of their fathers, such as Increase Mather's *Life and Death of that Reverend Man of God, Mr. Richard Mather* (1670), which seem never to swerve from the didactic model.[6] Increase's eldest son Cotton (1663–1728) included in his ecclesiastical history of New England, *Magnalia Christi Americana* (1702), a series of biographies of colonial governors and Puritan divines which is hagiography pure and simple (they were all 'visible saints'), whether or not it fulfils the wish Bradford expressed.

Autobiography, the account of the self *by* the self, is more problematic. The Puritans' habit of journal-keeping is well-known, but with a very few deservedly famous exceptions, such as those by John Winthrop (1588–1649) and Samuel Sewall (1652–1730), these records are formulaic and so private as to be without any real or imagined readership other than the writer himself; to be without, it might be argued, the realm of literary if not historical texts.[7] But the Puritans of the first generations did sometimes act as their own biographers, and these auto-biographical acts occupy a curious borderland between the public and private realms. Never published in the author's own lifetime, the narrative (exemplary, didactic) of the life has nevertheless a carefully specified readership in the generations which spring from or follow its author. Here we find Bradford's prescriptive wish enacted in a most particular way.

A case in point would be a work first published in 1832 as *The Autobiography of Thomas Shepard*, probably the earliest-written (1646?) and certainly the best-known personal narrative of seventeenth-century America. It begins with an injunctive dedication to the writer's son:

> To my deare son, Thomas Shepard, With whom I leave these records of God's great kindness to him, not knowing that I shall live to tell them myself with my own mouth, that so he may learne to know & love the great & most high God, The God of his father.[8]

19

We must note one unexpected pronoun: Shepard's account of his own life is not presented as one of God's great kindness to himself, but to his offspring. The form of the work not only underlines this purpose but establishes—prescribes, if we like—the pattern for what will be the son's account of *his* life. In a quite artful-seeming violation of chronology, Shepard begins with an account of the moment when his infant son was near death and the father, as part of a bargain with God for his preservation (Shepard gives it as one of several reasons why the son *was* preserved) vowed that his child 'should be the Lord's forever. . . . Remember, therefore, my son, this mercy of the Lord to you' (10). This is an injunction to a form of life (within the Puritan ministry), but more immediately to the form of its 'records'. And it is an injunction re-enforced by what we would today most certainly if anachronistically brand as imposed guilt. So after the son's dedicatory baptism in the New World, Shepard writes, his mother dies, 'who did loose her life by being carefull to preserve thine; for in the ship thou wert so feeble and froward both in the day and night, that hereby she lost her strength and at last her life' (11).

The ship here mentioned is crucial to the principal, formally unconventional aspect of Shepard's narrative—that is, the use of the transatlantic passage, *rather than* his own moment(s) of religious conversion, as the central and transfiguring experience of the recounted life.[9] Shepard's 'life' proper begins ('In the yeare of Christ 1605', that is the year of his birth) only after the dedication mentioned and an introductory chapter on the crossing, the latter being for this text the beginning of the son's life and of the dedication of that life to the Lord.

Apart from the deviations from convention mentioned, Shepard's narrative of spiritual progress towards Grace is predictable enough in pattern: he is affected, he backslides, he is rescued and reforms but insufficiently; he is persecuted and resolute, he backslides again, he is chastened and awakened, and so forth. What seems to have awakened Shepard most effectively were not persecutions or independent moments of revelation so much as close shaves with death. After once nearly drowning, for example:

> . . . and the Lord made me then to professe that I now looked
> upon my life as a new life given unto me, which I saw good

20

reason to give up to him and his service, and truly about this time the Lord had only dealt gently with me fore, began to afflict me and let me taste how good it was to be under his tutouring. . . . (37)

Thanks to the order of his narrative, Shepard has endowed this moment in his life with a curious quality of repetition; the son is 'already' thus given up to the Lord.

The connection between the two parts or purposes of the narrative becomes explicit at a comparable occasion: the first attempted emigration to New England of Shepard and his family, along with 'diverse & godly Xtians, resolved to goe . . . if I would goe' (48). This attempt is sadly and almost cata-strophically ill-planned and executed. Shepard has considerable narrative gifts, and his account of the near-wreck of their ship is so dramatically exciting that full quotation is almost irresistible. We can only note in passing, however, that the action and suspense of the narrative are sustained within a properly Puritan rhetoric which attributes *all* action and event to a Providence whose ends are determined. Thus as the weather rises and the ship threatens to founder, 'the Lord directed one man to cut some cable'; later 'a wonderful and miraculous providence did appear' to those on board, when a seaman given up for lost is later rescued: unable to swim himself, he has been 'supported by a divine hand' (47). Later still, God chooses as his mysterious instrument a drunkard of no sailing experience or knowledge whose motives for going to New England have been throughout a mystery to Shepard ('whether it was to see the country or no I cannot tell'). This anomaly persuades the men to overrule a reluctant and 'besotted' captain and cut down the mainmast, whereupon hopes briefly rise. 'But the ship was driven away towards the sands still', Shepard writes,

> and the seamen came to us and bid us looke (pointing to the place) where our graves should shortly be. . . . I then did think if ever the Lord did bring me to shore agayne I would live like one come and risen from the dead. (54)

Thus after his deliverance he arrives at the ordained fulfilment of that inward vow: 'I desire this mercy may be remembered of my children and their children's children when I am dead, and cannot prayse the Lord in the land of the living any more.'

Whereas the records of his life are of God's kindnesses to his child, his child and *his* children shall record God's mercies to Shepard.

This is not egotism but its opposite. As readers of his autobiography have often noted, once Shephard joins his brethren in New England his personal account becomes a far more impersonal record of collective travail and accomplishment. The exceptions to this effacement of the 'I' occur only when the Lord seems to scourge and correct Shepard for private shortcomings, and even in these instances the individual life is indistinguishable from the lives of others. Thus all sufferings of the family Shepard records are 'afflictions' sent to him for his sins; he laments 'that I should provoke the Lord to strike at my innocent children for my sake' and indeed wonders at one point that the Lord persists 'in threatening me to proceed in rooting out my family' (67). We may see this as one of the paradoxes of Puritan piety, but we should recognize it as well as a paradox intrinsic to Puritan personal narrative itself. I refer to its *resistance to individuation*: of parent from offspring, of self from community, of personal history from that cosmic historical unfolding which, as indicated, is God's plan for his Chosen in the New World.

It may be that some such sense of history and the individual's place within it is prerequisite to the autobiographical impulse as we understand it. Hence the canonical status of the Puritans which I have been defending. Two aspects of the Puritans' sense of self-in-history certainly contribute to it. First, their emphasis on the inward state translates fairly readily into our concerns with the psychology, if not the personality, of the individual. And second, the determining significance with which they endowed the fact of migration and their position in the New World seems to anticipate that sense of national identity which we assume as underpinning to any account of an *American* life.

3

I have stressed the notion of account—of a written life retrospectively given shape and meaning—since without this minimal requirement we are left, it seems to me, with any and

all writing of a remotely personal nature as potential autobiography. This returns us to the question of the diary, a
common and obviously important form for the early period in
American letters of which two examples have already been
mentioned. The chief value of the diary is almost always to the
historian, I maintain, and indeed the self-conscious diarist often
writes, as did Winthrop, with a view of some future historical
record. The famous *Diary* of Samuel Sewall published 1878–82
(covering 1674–1729, with some gaps) is valued for its minutely
detailed record of the daily life of a Boston merchant and
magistrate, as well as for its patently honest (sometimes
troubling, sometimes quite funny) revelations of character. An
equally celebrated diary of this period, discovered and published
in 1941, is that of William Byrd of Westover (1674–1744), a
wealthy and extremely cultivated planter of Virginia who spent
more than half his life in England and numbered such distinguished men of letters as Wycherley and Congreve among
his friends. Byrd's diary points up once more, by contrast, the
peculiar and peculiarly modern-seeming tendency of the Puritan
to self-revelation. The work 'does for southern colonial life what
the journals of Sewall do for New England', according to one
textbook, and indeed the minutiae of early eighteenth-century
plantation life have their fascination. But Byrd's version of
introspection is entirely formulaic: 'had good health, good
thoughts, and good humour, thank God Almighty' is the
standard close to most entries (reminiscent of if less effective
than Pepys's 'and so to bed'). And the whole work is genuinely
secret; much of it was written in code.[10] It does not, finally, no
matter how loose our thematic or generic criteria, communicate
a life qua 'Life'.

But did anyone in the New World at this time write his Life
to be read outside of his own family? Dissenting religious groups
other than the Puritans (who were in New England, after all,
the Establishment)—notably the Quakers—used personal
accounts as a form of bearing witness, of public declaration of
faith sustained under persecution. These are of very limited
purpose and readership, however, and until the great *Journal*
(1774) of John Woolman (1720–72) none survives in the
literature.[11] Since Columbus, explorers and adventurers in the
New World have written not only journals but narrative accounts

of their exploits, and John Smith published his *True Travels, Adventures, and Observations* (1630) a year before his death (to widespread incredulity). Interestingly enough, it is this sort of 'episodic' account—of travel or military adventure, or of single events such as captivity or imprisonment—that Louis Kaplan omits from his *Bibliography of American Autobiographies*, although for this period I think the omissions are a mistake. What the student of seventeenth-century Lives quickly discovers is that autobiography consciously performed emerges from special circumstances and is devoted to special ends. And what is fascinating about this process in the case of the Puritans is that we can see the special purpose or end of the narrative as breaking down that resistance to individuation which is the mark of the saint. When is the Life conceived of as apart from or unique in God's design for the Elect? When does the 'I' assert itself apart from that chain of filial piety indicated by Bradford and Shepard?

Not surprisingly, in self-defence. One of the most curious documents of this period is 'The Apologia of Robert Keayne' (1653), the Last Will and Testament of a self-made merchant of Boston, disposing in lengthy and very complicated fashion of a fortune of some £4,000. In 1639 Keayne had been tried and convicted of usury before both the General Court and the elders of the First Church of Boston (who reprimanded him severely), and this evident trauma in his life left him with a pathological need for self-justification, not just before his family and his posterity, but in the eyes of his fellow townsmen as well, perhaps even of a wider public. The will runs to some hundred pages in the *Publications of the Colonial Society of Massachusetts*, where it was printed in 1952 (it was first published 1886), and it amounts to a life-story of remarkable fullness and self-consciousness, particularly about its own public nature: 'a will will be read and made known and may be perused, searched, or copied out by any when other writings will be more hid and obscured', Keayne assures himself and his readers.[12] Determined to address this public, he acknowledges openly that the text of his bequests is a pretext for the putting of his life into words: the Will is a double accounting. After a page describing his book-keeping system (inventory book, receipt book, day book, pocket book, two number books, three debt books, a farm book, a rent book, the list goes on), Keayne continues:

Happy yea more happy would it have been for me if I had been as careful and as exact in keeping an account of my sins and the debts I owe to God and of that spiritual estate between God and my own soul that I could as easily have made it appear to others or to myself when I gained or when I lost and to have taken as much pains this way as in the other, which, though I cannot say I have altogether neglected or omitted, yet comparatively I may justly say I have been greatly deficient in that one thing necessary. (322)

For which the present Will represents something of a remedy. The anticipation of Franklin—his expressed wish in the *Autobiography* for a 'second edition' of the life in which 'errata' are corrected, his literal bookkeeping system for moral perfection—points to the strong continuities in their shared culture. But the most striking difference between the two, the position of Keayne in relation to his readership, is the more suggestive point; here the 'I' emerges not in harmony with history and community, but at odds.

4

Another motive for self-publication we might term the pressure of experience—that need to narrate what the self has undergone from which the Ancient Mariner stoppeth one of three. One such work (also excluded from Kaplan's catalogue as episodic) is the *Narrative of the Captivity and Restoration of Mrs. Mary Rowlandson*, an account of the author's eleven weeks' captivity among the Wampanoag Indians in 1675, during King Phillip's Wars. Published in 1682, the *Narrative* was one of the most popular prose works of its time, in England as well as in the New World. And it is not difficult to account for its enduring popularity. Mary Rowlandson's story is a horrifically gripping one, and she herself has a natural gift as story-teller. The gift extends, moreover, beyond the effective recounting of a series of events. Surprisingly, considering its brief length and formulaic didacticism, the *Narrative* brings forth a character of flesh-and-blood reality, of a psychic reality both problematic and, to our modern sensibilities, fully credible.

Richard Slotkin has defined Rowlandson's Narrative as 'an archetype—that is, the initiator of a genre of narrative within

American culture, the primary model of which all subsequent captivities are diminished copies or types'.[13] The originator of a sub-genre (the captivity), the narrative may also be viewed as an early and seminal work in the American autobiographical tradition, for episodic and specialized as it is, it is also in distilled, almost synechdochical form, an account of a life, an *accounting for* the identity of the woman who writes it. The fact that Rowlandson is writing for publication—for public consumption, we could say—has an important influence on this accounting: why should the public consume? why should its attention be solicited? (This question becomes doubly vexed when the solicitor-for-attention is a woman—today as well as in the seventeenth century, perhaps, but I think it is safe to assume that the disparities inherent in female authorship were greater then.) Also of importance to the work and our appreciation of it is that, whereas it is an account of change in the self—traumatic change of condition, as well as lasting spiritual and psychological change in the person—it is *not* a conversion narrative, conventional or otherwise. Thus we are at greater liberty to follow the narrator's own liberty of choice: what to include, what omit, how interpret. This is worth doing in some detail, and I propose to devote the remainder of this essay to such an examination of Rowlandson's work.

Of course 'captivity and restoration' determine the boundaries of the narrative, and Rowlandson begins with a kind of unembellished directness we associate with newspaper report:

> On the tenth of February 1675 came the Indians with great numbers upon Lancaster: their first coming was about sunrising; hearing the noise of some guns, we looked out; several houses were burning, and the smoke ascending to heaven.[14]

This is reportage, but it represents as well a 'natural' gift raised to art. We 'see' in our minds sun and Indians together on the eastern horizon; we see with the narrator the scene of burning houses, through the window of one as yet but soon not to be secure; and finally that smoke, rising to a heaven which for this instant at least (if not for the duration of a narrative which insists the contrary) is so clearly blind. The reportorial style serves well for the scenes of carnage that follow. Of course there are the time- and convention-bound judgements we would expect ('thus were we butchered by those merciless heathen' and so forth), but in general we have with one exception the sense of an account given by someone in shock, an account *of* shock.

The exception involves her eldest sister's death, and it raises for the first time the question of self-justification. Watching the slaughter and hearing of losses in her family, the sister wishes aloud, ' "And Lord, let me die with them", which was no sooner said, but she was struck with a bullet and fell down dead over the threshold. I hope', the narrator goes on,

> she is reaping the fruit of her good labors, being faithful to the service of God in her place. In her younger years she lay under much trouble upon spiritual accounts, till it pleased God to make that precious scripture take hold of her heart, 'And he said unto me, my Grace is sufficient for thee' (2 Corinthians 12.9). More than twenty years after, I have heard her tell how sweet and comfortable that place was to her. But to return: the Indians laid hold of us. . . . (60)

and on to her own capture. These particular words, this death-as-answered-prayer, are not only selected and preserved in the account, but mused upon. Like Bradford, she interrupts her narrative to look backward at an earlier time and to anticipate the future—here, an afterlife. We sense some self-projection, however indirect, in the recollections of doubts comforted, perhaps some doubtfulness in the hopes of reward. But the more striking connection is with Rowlandson's acknowledgement of her own survival.

> I had often before this said that if the Indians should come, I should choose rather to be killed by them than taken alive, but when it came to the trial my mind changed; their glittering weapons so daunted my spirit, that I chose rather to go along with those (as I may say) ravenous beasts, than that moment to end my days; and *that I may the better declare what happened to me* during that grievous captivity, I shall particularly speak of the several removes we had up and down the wilderness. (61; emphasis added)

Several elements are of interest here, not the least of which is her evident assumption that death or survival might be a matter of choice for the victim. The passage is best understood as logically following on (as it is parallel to) the one recounting the sister's violent *but no less chosen* end. In effect, the writer's statement of intent works as a justification of her having been 'chosen' over the sister to survive, the agency of choice being simply, if partially, transferred to the self. This in turn becomes a *raison d'être* of the narrative: Mary Rowlandson has survived to declare what happened to her; for the greater glory of God, understood, but for whose benefit on earth?

Rowlandson does not mention the orthodox purpose of glorifying God until what is in effect Chapter 9 of the Narrative ('The Eighth Remove'): 'And here I may take occasion to mention one principal ground of my setting forth these lines: even as the psalmist says, to declare the works of the Lord . . .' (70), and so forth. But even though the psalm in question (118.17–18) has been pointed out to her by her son Joseph, unexpectedly met in captivity, she makes no mention of directing the praise to him or his surviving siblings or their children's children, who might, as in Shepard's case, transmit this praise through unbroken time. She makes no mention at all of future generations. The son is in fact on a later occasion the source of a lesson to her on her own self-centredness, one that she records with an intriguing lack of comment.

> Hearing that my son was come to this place, I went to see him, and told him his father was well, but very melancholy. He told me he was as much grieved for his father as for himself. I wondered at his speech, for *I thought I had enough upon my spirit in reference to myself, to make me mindless of my husband and everyone else;* they being safe among their friends. (77; emphasis added)

We might read a tacit admission of degradation here, but we might also read this as a largely unconscious expression of strength on the woman's part rather than as an expression of fault; after all, it may well have been that mindlessness of everyone but herself which kept her alive through the worst of the physical and mental ordeal. Its greater interest is in the way it suggests how Rowlandson's narrative tends to break through both the didactic mould and the generational rationale of the personal account.

Interestingly, it follows immediately on an anecdote which seems to have *no* point, confessional, didactic, or otherwise. An

Indian woman demands a scrap of Rowlandson's apron for her child; Rowlandson refuses, the other threatens to retaliate, and the quarrel goes on until Rowlandson's own mistress joins in, threatening her very life with a large stick. Rowlandson escapes just barely, gives away the entire apron, 'and so that storm went over.' Part of the appeal of the *Narrative* is that such anecdotes are not rationalized to fit a moral, or even necessarily tagged with pious reflection. Another part of the appeal, I believe, is the surprise we may feel at her own behaviour: why quarrel over a scrap with such obviously dangerous women? And one result is that the Indian women become human (indeed all-too-human) *along with* the Christian narrator herself.

This humanity is of a negative kind, but Rowlandson has a more serious problem, at least potentially, in dealing with the humanity of the Indians as manifest in their not infrequent acts of kindness to her. Some of these are simply acts of omission ('not one of them offered the least imaginable miscarriage to me' for one example); but many involve disinterested generosity, particularly in the matter of food. Now the solution to Rowlandson's receiving charity from the fiends of hell is that they be God's instruments, and her rhetoric, like Shepard's, accommodates this transfer of agency. But what if the Lord seem to favour his instruments over his faithful servant?

The first time Rowlandson asks her captors if she might be allowed to observe the sabbath, they answer that, as she reports, 'they would break my face.' By an easily discernible association, she at once interrupts the sequence of her narrative:

> And here I cannot but take notice of the strange providence of God in preserving the heathen. They were many hundreds, old and young, some sick, and some lame; many had papooses at their backs. The greatest number at this time with us were squaws, and they traveled with all they had, bag and baggage, and yet they got over this river aforesaid; and on Monday they set the wigwams on fire, and away they went. On that very day came the English army after them to this river and saw the smoke of their wigwams, and yet this river put a stop to them. God did not give them courage or activity to go over after us. We were not ready for so great a mercy as victory and deliverance. If we had been God would have found out a way for the English to have passed this river, as well as for the Indians with their squaws and children, and all their luggage. (68–9)

Trying to hold fast to her faith and its outward observance Rowlandson is 'punished'. This punishment (the refusal and threat) in turn leads her to thoughts of a far more severe one (the failure of the English), and as well to a kind of disturbance in the prose. Notice the pronoun confusion of 'over after us. We were not ready': 'us', most logically at least, the Indians and I; 'We' the English Christians. The covert resentment expressed here, particularly in the reiteration of the Indians' impedimenta, for example, is directed less at a strange providence than at an English army which has fallen short on its own responsibility. What? *All* those squaws and baggages across, and a troop of unencumbered armed men, clearly shown the strategic advantage of pursuit, put a stop to by the same river? What immediately follows is the strongest, most vivid image in Rowlandson's narrative of her *radical* isolation:

> I went along that day mourning and lamenting, leaving farther my own country, and traveling into the vast and howling wilderness. . . . The Indians were as thick as the trees: it seemed as if there had been a thousand hatchets going at once. If one looked before one there was nothing but Indians, and so on either hand, I myself in the midst, and no Christian soul near me. . . .
> (68)

The juxtaposition makes logical sense: she has been left to this fate by Christian men.

And rescued only by the Lord. Rowlandson's solution to this crux is a lesson in radical humility, or in the very extinction of the individual will, and it is here—in conveying this lesson— that she is most overtly didactic. In a summary enumeration of the five 'remarkable passages of providence, which I took note of in my afflicted time', Rowlandson reviews more than once that fatal halt at the river, records the Indians' evidently just contempt for English ineptitude, describes in detail their own capacity and methods for wilderness survival, and then concludes with 'the strange providence of God, in turning things about when the Indian was at the highest, and the English at the lowest'. God's purpose has been that his people see that there is no help but in Him; when they are fully surrendered to that reliance on faith, 'then He takes the quarrel into His own hand' and the enemy is destroyed (89–91). The lesson is orthodox or, as most readers point out, 'conventional'; but we should also note how the extreme, enforced passivity of a captive appears, transfigured, in it. No one knows better than the narrator that surrender of will; does she suggest that her readers be as she has been? Her position, albeit as captive, has been a privileged one; she has been both instrument of and special sufferer from that strange providence which has chastened and then raised up the community of saints.

All the more remarkable that she is not herself raised up or restored to that community in the fullest sense. Although Rowlandson's distinctive voice is all but lost in the crescendo of scriptural allusion with which she ends, a final and haunting image of the woman emerges to preside over the *Narrative* as a whole:

> I can remember the time when I used to sleep quietly without workings in my thoughts, whole nights together, but now it is otherways with me. When all are fast about me, and no eye open, but His who ever waketh, my thoughts are upon things past, upon the awful dispensation of the Lord towards us. . . . I remember in the night season, how the other day I was in the midst of thousands of enemies, and nothing but death before me. It is then hard work to persuade myself that ever I should be satisfied with bread again. But now we are fed with the finest of the wheat, and, as I may say, with honey out of the rock. . . . Oh! the wonderful power of God that mine eyes have seen, affording matter enough for my thoughts to run in, that when others are sleeping mine eyes are weeping. (95)

We would expect Rowlandson's recollection of her former ordeal of isolation in the midst of thousands of enemies to call forth a contrast with her present state, surrounded by Christian family and friends. Although this is the drift of the scriptural allusions, the effect of the entire passage is rather that of an echo: here too she is isolated and profoundly, spiritually alone. Here is the ultimate differentiation of the writer of her own Life, whose very readership is 'sleeping'—incapable of full understanding, much less of a pious re-enactment, of her experience—while she is 'weeping', and writing nevertheless. The resulting text, secondary in its surrender to a prior (scriptural) text, has the air of being posthumous as well.[15]

This brings us back to the sister whose death presages

Rowlandson's survival. There are two 'texts' in the account of her death: the quoted speech ('And Lord, let me die with them') and the remembered verse from Corinthians. The first is abruptly suicidal, it stops time ('no sooner said, but she was struck . . .'). The second restores time, linking the younger years of the sister whose trouble was eased by it, the 'more than twenty years after' that time which Rowlandson recalls, and the eternity in which the sister is to reap the fruit of her good labour. The first is individual and self-referential; the second is universal and theocentric. The sister is restored by the second text and in a sense restored *to* it.

This is the pattern of Rowlandson's narrative of her own experience. At once we have the individual voice, the 'text' of one woman's trials and sufferings, and at the same time, the scriptural text or (in its priority) pre-text to which the account of those sufferings will presumably be restored. We may consider the pretext as the strictures of orthodoxy, as the injunction, real or symbolic, of the fathers, or—as Bercovitch among others has argued—as the rising pattern which is the history of the new land and its people.[16] Such a prescribed pattern for the life is both burden and blessing for the autobiographer, as in Rowlandson's case, where the breathing life of her narrative arises from the always tragic, always generative gap between the two. And her anxiety about this failure of restoration, perceptible and moving however masked, is both inevitable and, for American letters, prophetic.

A Note on Texts: I have remarked above on the paucity of autobiographical texts for the period with which this essay is concerned, drawing not-always explicit distinctions among those published during the author's lifetime (such as Rowlandson's *Narrative*), those published after the author's death but in accord with his explicit or evident wishes (Keayne's *Will*, Woolman's *Journal*), those which became on first publication 'classics' of the nineteenth century (Shepard's *Autobiography*), and those known only to the twentieth (Byrd's *Diaries*). Any student with the desire (and the time) to confirm the near non-existence of the first group need only skim through Charles Evans's *American Bibliography* (12 vols., 1903–4), a catalogue of the nearly 36,000 titles published in America from 1639–1799. From my own uncomputerized review I conclude that with the exceptions mentioned above (and see below note 11), and according to any reasonable definition of the genre as first-person account of the writer's life, there is simply none published in America before the latter part of the eighteenth century. (For a contrasting view of the situation in the Old World see for example Paul Delaney, *British Autobiography in the Seventeenth Century* (New York: Columbia University Press, 1969).)

In his important and seminal work, *Spiritual Autobiography in Early America* (Princeton, 1968), Daniel B. Shea, Jr., makes no systematic distinctions such as are outlined above for the twenty works he has chosen to analyse, nor between that group and the one to which he refers, comprising the innumerable manuscripts preserved in various State Historical Societies which are awaiting future scholars. Similarly, in Louis Kaplan's *Bibliography of American Autobiographies* (Wisconsin, 1961), covering works written through 1945, contemporaneous or posthumous publication forms no part of the rather eccentric criteria for selection and exclusion, or of the system of classification followed in the book itself.

Fair enough, perhaps. But I think such questions have been long enough neglected, and this note is meant to indicate an area for study which present limitations of subject-matter and space must exclude. As Albert E. Stone has detailed in his useful review of work in the field ('Autobiography in American Culture: Looking Back at the Seventies,' in Jefferson B. Kellogg and Robert H. Walker (eds.), *Sources for American Studies* (Westport, CT, and London: Greenwood Press, 1983), pp. 389–400), there has been in the past fifteen years or so something of an explosion of critical interest in this hitherto neglected area of American letters—of which the present volume is presumably one instance. But it seems remarkable that in the copious commentary on this phenomenon so little account is taken of the possibility that the critical neglect of previous generations has been a function of what was or was not in print. Of course this is a two-way street, and critical fashions influence publishing decisions, as witness the novel preponderance of autobiographical writing in recent textbook anthologies of American literature, or the myriad discoveries, rediscoveries, and reprints (especially by unknown or forgotten women and minority writers) we find on the paperback shelves. But if autobiography as *genre* is in general critical fashion, then criticism in American Studies may need to catch up with itself. That is, many of the questions central to today's criticism, from the Marxist to the feminist to the whole range represented under the rubric 'reader response'—questions about the writer's sense of his audience (or market), the conditions under which he writes (or produces) for it, the conditions or expectations under which his work is received—all of these are also of intrinsic relevance to autobiography itself. Here is where much valuable and original work can be done.

NOTES

1. William Bradford, *Of Plymouth Plantation 1620–1647*, ed. Samuel Eliot Morison (1952; rept. New York: Modern Library, 1967), p. 61. Subsequent references in parentheses in the text.

2. Hawthorne's story of this title, first collected in his *Mosses from an Old Manse* (1846), is his most powerful, allegorical representation of just such a haunting; for his explicitly autobiographical reflections on the same theme, see 'The Custom House', his narrative Introduction to *The Scarlet Letter* (1850).

3. See above, 'A Note on Texts' for further discussion of this issue.

4. James M. Cox, 'Recovering Literature's Lost Ground Through Autobiography', in James Olney (ed.), *Autobiography: Essays Theoretical and Critical* (Princeton, NJ: Princeton University Press, 1980), p. 126. Cox makes the remark in the course of an exposition and defence of *The Autobiography of Thomas Jefferson* (first published 1830). Acknowledging its partial facetiousness, he goes on to offer other explanations of 'why the Puritans hold the field' for literary studies of the early period, ranging from the influence of the Civil War to the proclivities of academics. He does not mention the fact that for the seventeenth century (by the time of Jefferson's active life the term Puritan is already a bit anachronistic) they simply wrote and published more than their Southern cousins. Cox also has several pertinent and illuminating remarks to make about autobiography as *genre*, as do many of the articles in Olney's collection, which is the best I know on this subject.

5. John Winthrop, 'A Modell of Christian Charity' (1630), in Perry Miller and Thomas H. Johnson (eds.), *The Puritans: A Sourcebook of their Writings* (New York, Harper & Row, 1938), I. 199.

6. True to form, the Mathers established something of a family industry in this line. Increase wrote the biography (his first published work of some hundred and thirty) with the help of notes left him by his father; his son Cotton followed the same procedure in writing *Parentator* (1724), the biography of Increase; the biography of Cotton, *The Life of the Very Reverend and Learned Cotton Mather* (1729), was in turn produced by *his* son Samuel, the last, by all accounts the weakest, and no doubt the most tired out of the dynasty.

7. Kaplan excluded, rightly in my opinion, all diaries and journals from his bibliography. The editors who extended his work, however, reversed the judgement, see Mary Louise Driscoe et al. (eds.), *American Autobiography 1945–1980, A Bibliography* (Madison: University of Wisconsin Press, 1982), which includes sixty-two entries for the colonial period, most of them

journals and letters. Whereas these bibliographies reflect current debate about the definition of *genre*, corresponding bibliographies of diaries and journals reflect corresponding uncertainty about the definition of 'American'. William Matthews (ed.), *American Diaries: An Annotated Bibliography of American Diaries Written Prior to the Year 1861* (Berkeley and Los Angeles: University of California Press, 1945) begins with the diary of a Puritan minister written in 1629 (published 1846). The editors who expanded and revised his work—see Laura Arksey et al. (eds.), *American Diaries: An Annotated Bibliography of Published American Diaries and Journals* (Detroit: Gale Research, 1983)—begin with Columbus (1492–93; published 1893).

8. *The Autobiography of Thomas Shepard, The Celebrated Minister of Cambridge, N.E. With Additional Notes of his Life and Character, by Nehemiah Adams* (Boston: Pierce and Parker, 1832), p. 8. Subsequent references in parentheses in the texts.

9. This feature of the autobiography has been variously interpreted. See for example Shea, op. cit.; Sacvan Bercovitch, *The Puritan Origins of the American Self* (New Haven: Yale University Press, 1975) pp. 116–19; G. Thomas Couser, *American Autobiography: The Prophetic Mode* (Amherst: University of Massachusetts Press, 1979), pp. 13–17. The order of the chapters is arguably an editorial decision of 1832, but the editor's description of the bound manuscript book which is the source of his text, along with internal evidence of the text itself, suggest that it is Shepard's own, an assumption I have followed in this discussion.

10. *The Secret Diary of William Byrd of Westover, 1709–1712*, ed. Louis B. Wright and Marion Tenling (Richmond, VA: Dietz Press, 1941). In the words of the editors, 'Such diaries [as Byrd's], written only for the eyes of their authors, are, of all types of writing, the least self-conscious, the least embellished to make an impression on the reader.'

11. Luella M. Wright, *The Literary Life of the Early Friends, 1650–1725* (New York: Columbia University Press, 1932), refers to the more than twenty-five Quaker journals or personal accounts in print before 1725, but so far as I can determine all but one of these are British and published in London. The title of one collection of such narratives published in New York in 1700 is revealing: *A Brief Narration of the sufferings of the people called Quaker; who were put to death at Boston in New England. Also an account from their own hands, of their coming to Boston, and of their staying in their jurisdiction after banishment. With a precious epistle of Wm Robinson, to us his fellow-parishioners, and other epistles hereunto annexed.* The limitation of readership to 'us his fellow-parishioners' seems to be characteristic.

12. *The Apologia of Robert Keayne: A Puritan Case History*, ed. Bernard Bailyn, *Publications of the Colonial Society of Massachusetts*, Vol. XLII, 1952–56 (Boston: published by the Society, 1964), pp. 243–342. Subsequent references in parentheses in the text.

13. Richard Slotkin, *Regeneration Through Violence: The Mythology of the American Frontier 1600–1860* (Middletown, CT: Wesleyan University Press, 1973), p. 102.

14. 'A Narrative of the Captivity and Restoration of Mrs. Mary Rowlandson',

in Ronald Gottesman et al. (eds.), *The Norton Anthology of American Literature* (New York: W. W. Norton & Co., 1979), I. 59. Subsequent references in parentheses in the text. The full title says much about the author's ambivalent attitude towards the fact of publication and the assumption of a public readership: *The sovereignty and goodness of GOD, together with the faithfulness of his promises displayed; being a narrative of the captivity and restoration of Mrs. Mary Rowlandson, commended by her, to all that desires to know the Lord's doing to, and dealings with her. Especially to her dear children and relations. The second Addition Corrected and amended. Written by her own hand for her private use, and now made public at the earnest desire of some friends, and for the benefit of the afflicted. Deut. 32.39. See now that I, even I am he, and there is no god with me; I kill and I make alive, I wound and I heal, neither is there any can deliver out of my hand.*

15. Again we anticipate Hawthorne, whose facetious conclusion to 'The Custom House' contains a profound and chilling insight into the position of the writer in relation to that community which comprises both the human context of his active life and the readership of his Life: 'Keeping up the metaphor of the political guillotine, the whole may be considered as the POSTHUMOUS PAPERS OF A DECAPITATED SURVEYOR; and the sketch which I am now bringing to a close, if too autobiographical for a modest person to publish in his lifetime, will readily be excused in a gentleman who writes from beyond the grave. Peace be with all the world! My blessing on my friends! My forgiveness to my enemies! For I am in the realm of quiet!'

16. Bercovitch, op. cit.

2

Exemplary Selves: Jonathan Edwards and Benjamin Franklin

by DAVID SEED

1

The contrasts which cry out to be made between Jonathan
Edwards (1703–58) and Benjamin Franklin (1706–90) are no
less valid for being obvious. Conspicuously in these two writers
there can be seen the different developments which took place
in American Puritanism during the eighteenth century. We can,
too, apply the notion of Puritanism to their works if we
remember that they are both writing after the first wave of
religious energy has spent itself. Where the earlier Puritans
debated the finer points of Election Theology, Edwards
struggled to keep his faith alive and Franklin shifted whatever
faith he had into the background as an ultimate validation of
primarily secular activities. Put another way, Edwards pleaded
for and witnessed revivalism, while Franklin, under the influence
of his reading and later under the impetus of political affairs,
shifts his concern towards this world. The one stresses introspection, the other profitable action; the one is concerned
(initially) with the local community, the other with the formation
of the American republic; and where the one struggles to renew
Puritan beliefs, the other focuses on Puritan social style—on
frugality, thrift and plain dress. And so the list could continue.

Such contrasts need reasserting, but it also needs to be stressed that Edwards and Franklin held certain concerns in common. Both emphasized the notion of 'profit' in their writings and designed their autobiographies for use, taking themselves as exemplary (i.e. imitable) subjects. Since the term 'autobiography' does not come into use until 1809 (in Robert Southey's review of the Portuguese painter Francisco Vieira's memoirs of his life) there is an unavoidable anachronism in its application to Edwards's *Personal Narrative* (written in the 1730s) or to Franklin's *Memoirs* (written from 1771 to 1790) because irrelevant expectations can be aroused.[1] An anonymous contributor to the *Cornhill Magazine* in 1881 usefully took it upon himself to declare: 'The true autobiography is written by one who feels an irresistible longing for confidential expansion.'[2] For him it is axiomatic that an autobiography should be an intimate confession—hence he recalls Rousseau the 'prince of all autobiographers'—but confession in this sense is conspicuously lacking in both Edwards and Franklin. *The Autobiography of Benjamin Franklin* as the main standard title for Franklin's account of his life thus is a mid-nineteenth-century invention, first appearing in the 1840s.[3] For both of these eighteenth-century Americans the impulse to set their lives on record is inseparable from the impulse to instruct, and instruction can only take place if their biographies are harmonized with a general pattern of development from doubt to faith, or from poverty to prosperity. For both of them too, these developments involve a move from personal to the public spheres since, as Sacvan Bercovitch has pointed out, American autobiography is a 'mode of socialization'.[4] In what follows I shall divide the discussion between private and public issues, and also shall try to strike a balance between the relative contrasts and similarities which link Edwards and Franklin.

2

Edwards's *Personal Narrative* is by no means a simple conversion narrative. There is not so much a dramatic turning-point as a gradual process through stages, Edwards's purpose being to distinguish between the 'mixture of counterfeit religion with tone' which he saw as more of a threat than 'overt godlessness'.[5] In biographical terms Edwards repeatedly distinguishes between his youthful experiences and the authenticity gained from mature recollection. Like Franklin he sees his earlier life as a text (specifically his meditations and diary) which he is revising, identifying what Franklin calls 'errata'. Edwards describes an inner spiritual drama between the self and God where other characters are shadowy presences at best. For instance, while he was at Yale College (between 1716 and 1720) 'it pleased God to seize me with a pleurisy; in which he brought me nigh to the grave, and shook me over the pit of hell.'[6] God is an immediate and convincingly physical presence here (note the energy in 'seized' and 'shook'), although the illness is both internalized and moralized. The attack is not dated because Edwards is working to a different time-scheme, and place is rendered emblematically partly to keep absolutely clear the central relationship between the self and God. The Quaker John Woolman records a similar experience in his *Journal* (1774):

> But in this swift race it pleased God to visit me with sickness, so that I doubted of recovering. And then did darkness, horror and amazement with full force seize me.[7]

Woolman here uses the same formulaic phrases and follows the same pattern. For both writers illness becomes a spiritual crises, a divine means of subduing the profane self; illness is thus essentially a humbling experience, in Woolman's case leading him through struggles of resistance to an 'inward relief'. Both Woolman and Edwards organize what we would now see as a chance affliction into a divine act which can serve the reader as an *exemplum* of subduing pride. It should be remembered that Edwards saw fatal illness as a significant trigger to the revival of faith in Northampton and that Woolman explicitly describes a 1759 smallpox outbreak as a 'messenger sent from the Almighty to be an assistant in the cause of virtue'.[8]

Part of the terror in these attacks of illness grew out of the sufferer's ignorance of how God would act and Edwards builds this human limitation into the progression and even syntax of his *Personal Narrative*. He notes his early objections to the doctrine of God's sovereignty, for instance, and then continues: 'But I remember the time very well, when I seemed to be convinced, and fully satisfied.'[9] 'Seemed' is a key verb which Edwards uses throughout to stress how provisional are appearances or spiritual states. All is subject to revision and the *process* of that revision is signalled by terms of contrast: 'but', 'and yet', 'however', etc. The progression is thus antithetical. Edwards constantly relates a particular state to what has come before so that the key terms like 'new', 'alteration' or 'awakening' suggest stages in a spiritual series within which improvement is by no means steady. As each improvement takes place Edwards undermines its status with the inevitable 'but' and we move on. This rhetorical pattern implies that no state, not even after conversion or joining the ministry, is a final one since finality can only come in the future perfect tense when the soul merges with God.

Edwards analyses his earlier self with as harsh a rigour as possible partly to avoid the sin of pride (which is a liability built into the very idea of presenting one's self as an example) and partly to set an exemplary pattern of self-criticism which is directed polemically against spiritual complacency. He was particularly wary of having a superficial effect on the reader since a man

> may be affected with [the story of Christ] without believing it; as well as a man may be affected with what he reads in a romance, or sees acted in a stage-play.[10]

Edwards was as sensitive as Franklin to the consequences reading might have for behaviour—this is after all the premise of both autobiographies—but unlike his more secular counterpart he preferred to stay close to the prototypical text which has played such a decisive rôle in his own life—the Bible. Biblical allusions and quotations thus function for Edwards as reference-points, anchors to the particular spiritual issue he may be discussing at any particular stage in his narrative. He even incorporates psalmodic rhythms and balances into his prose:

> I have loved the doctrines of the gospel; they have been to my soul like green pastures. The gospel has seemed to me the richest treasure; the treasure that I have most desired.[11]

This passage skilfully conflates Old and New Testaments by combining allusions to Psalm 23 (and perhaps 135) with reference to the gospel. The Psalms and Song of Songs are given prominence by Edwards because they are specifically associated with joy.

At this point we need to stress that Edwards was aiming at the intellect as well as the feelings. Peaks of delight in his *Personal Narrative* are offset by passages of mature reflection. In this he anticipates Emerson who, as Erik Ingmar Thurin has argued, dispersed the autobiographical impulse throughout his whole oeuvre, in repeatedly withdrawing into the fields 'for secret converse with God'.[12] At the beginning of the first chapter of *Nature* (1836) Emerson similarly exhorts the reader to withdraw into a rural solitude which will facilitate spiritual realization, and both writers describe a vision of Nature as God's handiwork which leads to surges of delight. For the young Edwards, 'Gods excellency .. seemed to appear in everything; in the sun, moon and stars; in the clouds and blue sky.'[13] In short, all aspects of Nature become charged with God's presence.

Compare Emerson's rhapsodic account of sunrise from a hill top:

> From the earth, as a shore, I look out into the silent sea. I seem to partake its rapid transformations; the active enchantment reaches my dust, and I dilate and conspire with the morning wind.[14]

As with Edwards delight offers a means of spiritual access, in this case a delight concentrated heavily into the optical sense, and both writers exploit the imagery of radiance and brightness to convey spiritual presence. The glory of God, Edwards states, is fitly compared to 'an effulgence or emanation of light from a luminary'.[15] It is a ground condition of Edwards's writing that belief must be fervent and joyful and the adjective which he uses repeatedly to convey this quality is 'sweet', a term which he on the whole distinguishes from any particular sense. It refers to a 'principal of a new kind of perception or spiritual sensation, which is in its whole nature different from any former kinds of sensations of the mind', in other words to a sixth sense which conveys perceptual immediacy but shifts that immediacy to a higher level.[16] Here a particularly sharp contrast emerges between Edwards and Franklin. For Edwards God is a real and immediate presence whether he brings joy or terror; for Franklin God is a remote figure standing behind human actions who may audit man's accounts in the fullness of time.

Edwards's emphasis on the religious 'affections' looks forward to another autobiographer of the nineteenth century, Henry James, Senior.[17] Like Edwards James was reacting against a period of spiritual apathy (Albany in the 1810s and 1820s), retrospectively railing against a rigid Protestantism which had left his feelings disengaged, in fact positively stifled. His life is defined through conflict with repressive social applications of Puritan doctrine which hinder the 'sentiment of a life *within*' (James's emphasis) which James identifies with free self-realization.[18] His very parents become emblems of a split in society between commerce (father) and mindless faith (mother) which he attacks by moving spiritual vocabulary onto humanity itself. Unlike Edwards, James celebrates the individual and writes from a perspective outside any but the most idealized community whereas the former subdues individuality preparatory to focusing directly on the Christian community.

In an examination of Edwards's prose style J. F. Lynen has pointed out his use of repetition to give inevitability to his argument. 'The speaker becomes depersonalized', Lynen states, 'in that he is possessed and made the mouthpiece of an ineluctable logic.'[19] Thus, although the experiences described are of an intimate nature, Edwards's language constantly prevents them from being read as personal. The following passage is characteristic in that it grows out of a moment of spiritual realization but then employs repetition and grammatical permutation to rehearse God's qualities:

> I seemed to see them both in a *sweet* conjunction; majesty and meekness joined together; it was a *sweet*, and gentle, and holy majesty; and also majestic meekness; and awful *sweetness*; a high and great, and holy gentleness.[20] (emphasis added)

A passage like this could hardly be read in a biographical way because its rhetorical structure (grammatical variation reflecting the interdependence of divine characteristics) is geared to *what* is being perceived, to the local doctrinal issue. Just as the self is subdued to God, so the personal voice is subdued to logical or theological pattern, and ultimately to the community.

It has been argued by R. A. Banes that the latter is a specific characteristic of eighteenth-century American autobiography:

> the exemplary self emphasizes universal principle, while diminishing and individual importance. Although each autobiography records a unique history, the self-conception each author presents is a cultural model or ideal type, rather than a unique individuality.[21]

Although Banes does not discuss Edwards, his exploration of generalizing strategies and the identification with the community is directly relevant to the latter's *Personal Narrative*. Edwards's repeated presentation of his experiences as a series of spiritual 'cases' would confirm the first part of Banes's proposition and a shift in emphasis would confirm the second. There is a break in the *Personal Narrative* which coincides with Edwards's tutorship at Yale, marriage and ordination as a minister. From this point onwards he measures himself against other believers rather than against abstract qualities and explicitly readjusts his focus to the 'advancement of Christ's kingdom in the world'.[22] Once we have registered this shift, it becomes clear that an essential companion text to this account is Edwards's description of the Great Awakening, *A Faithful Narrative* (1737).

Covering the same period as the second half of his autobiography, Edwards's *Faithful Narrative* recounts the reaction to a 'time of extraordinary dullness in religion' and falls into four sections. Firstly, Edwards describes the revival of faith in Northampton, his own town; and then how the wave of enthusiasm sweeps through the surrounding communities. Thirdly, he examines the pattern of conversions and finally gives 'two particular instances' of the spirit at work. Essentially *A Faithful Narrative* deals with a collective conversion experience where the community itself is the protagonist. Edwards stresses family hierarchy to arrest the growing secularization of youth and because his concern is now communal. Conversion is symbolized by a change in social gathering from the tavern to the minister's house. Social life in general becomes transformed: 'Our public assemblies were then beautiful.'[23] Edwards has none of Woolman's sense of varied communities living together within America. Rather he sees the reborn Puritan community as a sign of a general change. The images of prophetic resurrection ('the noise amongst the dry bones waxed louder and louder') are transformed later into millenarian renewal. God's providence is now ideally harnessed to the historical course of America:

> This new world is probably now discovered, that the new and most glorious state of God's church on earth might commence there; that God might in it begin a new world in a spiritual respect, when he creates the new heavens and new earth.[24]

This kind of optimism is only implied in Edwards's *Personal Narrative*, and yet he is certainly beginning to present the community as exemplary. Only later would he place it firmly in the vanguard of a spiritual renewal.

3

When we move from Edwards's to Franklin's autobiography can any similarities in pattern be perceived? He, too, describes the drive towards improvement. The preoccupation with humility, the conversion of experience into exemplary parable, and the desire to affect the reader's behaviour are also common concerns. But the most obvious difference is that Franklin has attenuated the theoretical doctrine of Puritanism virtually out of existence while keeping the Puritan impulse towards improvement. When in 1790 the President of Yale asked Franklin what his beliefs were he was sent a brief creed in his reply. Franklin's fourth statement was 'that the most acceptable service we render to Him is doing good to His other children'.[25] More is involved, however, than just good works. At the beginning of his autobiography Franklin takes his bearing from the Puritans to show that he has inherited a dissenting sensibility and also a family inclination towards inventiveness (as witness his anecdote about his forefathers hiding their Bible from the spiritual authorities). There is a constant secular drag in Franklin's statements about religion which subjects religion to examination on the grounds of use. In a key passage Franklin sums up his attitude to Revelation:

> I entertained an opinion, that tho' certain actions might not be bad *because* they were forbidden by it, or good *because* it

commanded them; yet probably those actions might be forbidden *because* they were bad for us, or commanded *because* they were beneficial to us.[26] (Franklin's emphasis)

By this logical manoeuvre Franklin neatly transforms this world into a means of moral assessment. As G. Thomas Couser has put it, 'deism shifted the index of an individual's worth from his beliefs to his behaviour, from faith to works.'[27]

There are, then, two factors in Franklin's references to religion: a recognition of doubt, and an application of wordly systems. When he forms a prayer it will be in the form of a bargain; instead of planning a religious sect he devises a non-denominational party; and when a preacher complained that his services were poorly attended Franklin advises him to distribute rum immediately afterwards. These examples almost satirize religion but, more importantly, give a clear indication of Franklin's essentially practical temper. An example of the latter can be found in his description of an illness, coincidentally the same disease as that suffered at college by Edwards. At the time Franklin was working for a merchant who also fell ill. He writes:

> In the beginning of February, 1727, when I had just past my twenty-first year, we both were taken ill. My distemper was a pleurisy, which nearly carried me off. I suffered a good deal, gave up the point in my own mind, and was rather disappointed when I found myself recovering; regretting in some degree that I must now sometime or other have all that disagreeable work to go over again.[28]

Unlike Edwards or Woolman Franklin does not see illness in a spiritual or moral light and specifies exactly when and where it happened. Whereas both the former try to recreate the emotional drama of the seizure Franklin humorously distances himself from his youth and reveals an essentially business-like attitude to experience in describing a near-fatal illness as 'work'. Franklin never knew Edwards personally, although he took it upon himself to print *Distinguishing Marks of Work of the Spirit of God* in 1742; and he had only had a marginal contact with the Great Awakening, meeting the preacher George Whitefield on his visit to America in 1739. It is thus hardly surprising that contradictory applications of the term 'providence' appear in the autobiography.[29] Those different uses of the term are surely no more than token gestures towards religious orthodoxy. Any stress on providence would risk complicating the individual's freedom to act which is paramount in Franklin's ideology.

It is no contradiction for Franklin to quote from the Bible since the quotations come from the Book of Proverbs. Like Edwards, Franklin constantly strove to relate particular episodes in his life to general truths. His general pattern is to present the episode first, let the narrative or image do its work, and then explain or moralize. Principles are constantly emerging from his life-story such as the idea of 'industry as a means of obtaining wealth and distinction'.[30] These principles are often encapsulated in a proverb, maxim or epigram, in other words in easily remembered phrases such as those promised in *Poor Richard's Almanack* which Franklin started in 1732. Adopting the persona of an elderly, poor and selfless man ('I write Almanacks with no other view than that of the publick good'), Franklin packaged homespun wisdom which was calculated to instruct without appearing to do so.[31] Far more than Edwards Franklin adopts an epigrammatic style in his autobiography, partly as a means of throwing into prominence the general truths about experience which his life exemplifies. Edwards allows these truths to emerge from a gradual process of analysis.

Both writers were well aware of contemporary developments in science, Edwards being particularly influenced by Newton's *Optics*. Franklin, of course, includes famous examples of his scientific experiments within the autobiography and his writings on lightning brought on a disagreement with the French scientist Abbé Nollet. Franklin protested: 'my writings contained only a description of experiments which anyone might repeat and verify.'[32] This statement could stand as a gloss on his whole autobiography which breaks his life into component units, sometimes as short as a single paragraph but never longer than several pages, which are shaped and defined by a particular project. From Daniel Defoe Franklin took the notion of a project as an experimental undertaking in any field of life which might or might not succeed. Franklin's projects grow steadily in scale from building a wharf in his childhood to the ultimate task of creating the new republic but the basic pattern of projecting does not change.

The episodes of the autobiography are in that sense uniform, provisional and repeatable undertakings. R. J. Porter usefully describes this aspect of the autobiography as follows:

> Difficult moments in the life are smoothed over by the application of fact, generosity or in textual terms, euphemisms. Potential explosive episodes in the work which beg for exploration and analysis are passed by with a rhetorical equanimity and comic self-irony that belie the problem of self-evaluation they raise.[33]

Porter seems to be accusing Franklin of evasion here but the simplification of episodes surely explains one of the main pleasures in reading this autobiography: the sense of ease, the sense of how tractable circumstances are to the inventive intelligence. Porter also underestimates the reverses which Franklin suffers in his youth mainly because like Defoe's protagonists, Franklin's response to adversity is to roll up his sleeves and seek a practical solution. His curiosity and inventiveness together with his reluctance to formulate final doctrines leads at least one critic to declare that 'Franklin's greatest achievement in this book is that of characterizing himself repeatedly as a man of inquiry'.[34] It should also be added that Franklin's inventiveness often brings immediate and tangible rewards; when he outdoes his rival Keimer in speed and quality or printing there is a clear observable result in the increase of customers.

Edwards's *Personal Narrative* closes with him learning yet more about the gospel of Christ even though he is a minister and trained theologian, and by the same token Franklin too presents his life as an endless process of learning. This is particularly true of Franklin's youth when he was still comparatively ignorant of the way of the world. Thus when the governor of his province Sir William Keith condescends to notice him he is understandably flattered, particularly when Keith offers to set him up in business. The older and wiser Franklin comments: 'Yet unsolicited as he was by me, how could I think his generous offers insincere?'[35] This comment does not actually *state* Keith's insincerity so that the reader retraces the steps by which Franklin discovered the truth through his anxiety about missing letters of credit to the final revelation of Keith's character by a London stationers. The whole sequence becomes a parable about credit, an object lesson to the young Franklin not to be so swayed by rank. And sure enough one of the first sights which greets Franklin on his return to America is Keith walking the streets of Philadelphia this time as a 'common citizen'. The very notion of credit combines financial and moral issues of confidence, reputation, etc., which are crucial to Franklin's main ambition in Part I of his autobiography—to set himself up in business. At this stage the stationer joins the numerous minor characters who instruct the young Franklin. In Parts III and IV Franklin has gained enough wisdom to perform the advisory rôle himself.

Franklin's admiration for Defoe invites comparison between his autobiography and *Moll Flanders* or *Robinson Crusoe*. Relating Defoe's fiction to contemporary developments in British economic systems Ian Watt notes that the individual becomes the prime social unit and points out the importance of book-keeping and self-examination. For him 'Robinson Crusoe is a symbol of the processes associated with the rise of economic individualism'.[36] Similarly Franklin moves towards a position of individual self-reliance partly by rejecting his family who might have given him an inherited disposition towards industry but who also (especially his conservative father and suspicious brother) stand in the way of his progress. Characters are in fact grouped around Franklin as either helps or hindrances to his achievement of prosperity. His notorious scheme for moral improvement is an obvious case of the application of book-keeping principles to behaviour in a vain attempt to bring the self under firm control, and the humour of the episode grows out of the mature Franklin's wry admission of failure. Throughout the autobiography relationships are repeatedly reduced towards a mercenary level to suggest that they are as manageable as an economic problem.

Watt follows Max Weber in pointing out the hostility of economic individualism to sexuality or romance as forces likely to be unruly or unprofitable and similarly Franklin presents courtship as primarily a commercial undertaking. Mrs Godfrey, who is trying to arrange a match, emerges as a commercial opponent and the negotiations for the dowry prove to be inseparable from the reputation of the printing trade. When

Franklin breaks off negotiations this decision is presented as an example of financial prudence but Carl Van Doren shows in his life of Franklin that at this point a girl was pregnant by him which almost certainly affected his decision.[37] Franklin glosses over his sexual escapades as temporary aberrations ('that hard-to-be governed passion of youth had hurried me frequently into intrigues with low women') which he rectifies by finally marrying Deborah Read:

> I took her to wife, Sept. 1, 1730. None of the inconveniences happened that we had apprehended; she proved a good and faithful helpmate, assisted me much by attending the shop; we throve together and ever mutually endeavoured to make each other happy.[38]

The order of priorities is made clear. First his wife functions as an important aid to his prosperity and only secondly as a partner in feeling. This perfunctory summary of Franklin's married life suppresses the rôle of his wife because this would compromise his clear individual outline.

A turning-point in Franklin's life takes place in the 1730s when he begins to show interest in 'public affairs'. In textual terms the gap between Parts I and II of the autobiography is crucial. Initially Franklin adopted the fiction of addressing his son even though he had been brought up as a gentleman, had been a clerk of Assembly and at the time of writing was governor of New Jersey. This fiction enables Franklin to adopt the persona of a garrulous, digressive old man: 'The *persona* is part of the creation of a special relationship that will allow Franklin to be didactic and unreserved, to be a sage, though somewhat foolish and too human one.'[39] In 1782 and 1783 two friends wrote to Franklin urging him to take up his autobiography again for public reasons. According to Benjamin Vaughan (whose letter together with Abel James's are traditionally included in the text) the book would promote emigration to America and encourage a good opinion of the country. Thus Franklin is already being seen as the prototypical American, uniquely associated with its history. There is, however, a liability in the link. Even after we make allowance for the fact that Franklin wrote subsequent sections of the autobiography without having his papers to hand, it is striking that the biographical basis of his narrative lapses and, before the colonies' movement towards independence becomes clear, plot becomes replaced by a more or less fortuitous series of public projects. As the clear ironic gap between the old and young Franklin (between narrator and protagonist) disappears Franklin emerges in another rôle, that of self-effacing diplomat, manoeuvering altruistically for the realization of his schemes.

One such scheme demonstrates how history now becomes a major preoccupation in Franklin's narrative. In 1754 threats of an impending war with France impelled Franklin to try and raise a common militia among the colonies: 'I projected and drew up a plan for the union of all the Colonies under one government'. At first all goes smoothly but then the scheme is rejected by individual assemblies as too autocratic, and by the crown authorities as too democratic. Franklin subsequently moralizes on this failure, but only after setting this event in a chronological perspective:

> The Colonies so united would have been sufficiently strong to have defended themselves; there would then have been no need of troops from England; of course the subsequent pretence for taxing America and the bloody contest it occasioned, would have been avoided.[40]

Franklin now has identified himself with the nascent republic. Not only that, his narrative voice is now the voice of history, exploiting the reader's retrospective sense of events. Thomas Jefferson similarly merges his voice with the collective voice of the General Assembly in his autobiography, thus identifying himself with a general national purpose. For Franklin 1754 becomes an unsuccessful rehearsal for 1776. J. M. Cox has declared dramatically that 'Franklin's personal history *stands in place of the revolution*' (his emphasis) but he does not adequately explain how Franklin's concerns have moved from personal to public.[41]

Historical hindsight now underpins Franklin's sense of irony and even casts a retrospective political colouring over the earlier events of his life. Just as his family had fled to America to escape oppression so Franklin moves to Philadelphia to avoid family restrictions and then struggles to shake off his apprenticeship. In fact his early life could now be seen as a series of castings-off in his industrious progress towards independence, as a series of latently political acts whereby his individual destiny merges into the historical fate of the republic.[42] In an essay which Franklin wrote for would-be emigrants ('Information to those who would remove to America') he warns that birth and rank will carry no privileges but rather that 'every one will enjoy securely the profit of his industry'.[43] Speaking now on behalf of his new formed country Franklin makes explicit the ideology of his autobiography in presenting America as a place for individual producers. There is no hint of any tension between individual and national purposes; personal prosperity literally *is* the prosperity of the nation. The responsibility implied in Franklin's chosen slogan 'America is the land of labour' scarcely alters the basic opinion of his message. Sacvan Bercovitch has documented cases where Puritan biographers and autobiographers 'identify with the enterprise at large', identify sanctity with national prosperity, and Franklin continues in the same tradition by advertising the success of America as reflecting God's approval.[44]

Franklin's autobiography became steadily more and more popular throughout the nineteenth century. It was childhood reading for Jared Sparks who founded the Library of American Biography and wrote a continuation of Franklin's unfinished account. The autobiography went through numerous editions, promoting an ethic of individual enterprise long after the nineteenth-century concentrations of capital had rendered it anachronistic. One of the strangest editions to appear was a paraphrase of Part I published as *Franklin, The Apprentice Boy* in 1855. The sententious 'author' drags his youthful reader from one lesson to the next, making Franklin's moralism suffocatingly explicit. When Franklin tries to develop his powers of expression by converting stories into verse the anonymous instructor tells us: 'there is nothing more excellent that a spirited boy, who wishes to improve his mind, and increase his future power as a man, can do, than to practice composition in this manner.'[45] Franklin's warnings within the autobiography about the dangers of exhortation have obviously fallen on deaf ears!

Apart from such direct popularity Franklin's autobiography also influenced works such as Henry James's *The American* (1877) and Scott Fitzgerald's *The Great Gatsby* (1926), but in a significantly oblique way. Christopher Newman and Jay Gatsby are both presented as generic Americans: the one is repeatedly compared to Franklin, the other sets up for himself exercises in self-development following Franklin's model. And yet ironies surround both figures. The comparisons with Franklin lead us to expect that Newman might be as successful but the reverse is the case. The royalist aristocracy of Paris proves to be in-accessible to Newman's money. With Gatsby there is an even greater ambivalence. The national pattern of making one's own way to prosperity leads to crime and violent death, rendering totally ambiguous the 'great' of the novel's title. In a recent study Gary Lindberg has suggested that at some stage in the early nineteenth century, thanks partly to the careers of certain notorious tricksters and partly to radical changes in American society, the national archetype shifted from an embodiment of trust to one of deception.[46] He argues rightly that Franklin's autobiography is designed to stimulate confidence in the reader, to create a 'confidence man' in the literal sense.

But in the nineteenth century confidence-man became 'con-man' with all sorts of consequences for the national literature. One of the most relevant texts in this context is Herman Melville's *The Confidence Man* (1857) which uses the representa-tive passengers on a Mississippi steamboat to give a series of semi-parables on the theme advertised by the boat's placard—'NO TRUST'. Biography is no longer the means of instruction. Rather it has shrunk to a minor commodity to be hawked about the steamboat. Instead Melville uses a trickster figure, a kind of quick-change artist who appears in a number of different guises in scenes which constantly raise the issue of confidence. Hence the novel's sub-title 'masquerade'. In a letter written the same year that the novel was published Melville was casting about for a lecture subject and came up with the following: '*Daily progress of man towards a state of intellectual and moral perfection, as evidenced in history of 5th Avenue and 5 Points*', the latter being glossed by Melville's editors as a 'corrupt district in New York City'.[47] This ironic glance at one of Franklin's central faiths fits the temper of Melville's novel which creates uncertainty through the confidence-man's shifting rôles and which reveals mer-cenary distrust. Indeed the novel's anonymous reviewer in the *Literary Gazette* was so outraged by Melville's method that he wondered: 'Perhaps it is a hoax on the public—an emulation of Barnum.'[48]

We can see this same shift from didacticism to trickery and deception in the anonymous 'Autobiography of a Quack' which appeared in the *Atlantic Monthly* of 1867. This account reads like an inverted travesty of Franklin's autobiography. The narrator sets up in medical practice in Philadelphia but does not prosper until an opportunity is offered to him to forge a death-certificate. This is his moral turning-point and yet it leads directly to prosperity; it is in a sense his 'conversion'. Like Franklin he uses episodes as general examples, but of *negative* qualities—his beginnings are 'an illustration of how little value a man's intellect may be'. And he decides to include spiritualism in his activities because it 'had been very profitably turned to account in connection with medical practice'.[49] Where Franklin identifies moral with financial prosperity, the two are now forced apart. Profit here has become purely a matter of money and ethics an irritating obstacle. Where Franklin assumes an identity between individual and general prosperity, now the individual prospers at *the expense* of others. This economic imperative is used to justify trickery, deceit and smuggling. And yet ironically, although the underlying values have reversed, the literary procedures—even the vocabulary—remains similar to Franklin's. The narrator generalizes episodes, notes turning-points, shrugs off reverses and demonstrates versatility in his activities (to the extent of changing his name several times). His 'pleasant history' is written partly to pass the time as he lies in hospital and partly as an exemplary narrative to attack Franklin's cherished maxims. The narrator declares roundly at the beginning of his story that 'he never had much experience of virtue being its own reward'.[50] 'The Autobiography of a Quack' duplicitously nods towards conventional morality in its conclusion (corruption gets its just deserts) when in fact it demonstrates a more cynical ethic that prosperity depends on crime and deception. Similarly W. C. Spengemann and L. R. Lundquist have shown that P. T. Barnum professes to embody Franklin's cherished virtues by a simple process of renaming: avarice becomes thrift, guile becomes ingenuity, and so on.[51] Both cases demonstrate the increasing difficulties of maintaining Franklin's projected pattern of life in the nineteenth century as the social and economic circumstances of America became less and less congenial to a simple individual progression towards prosperity.

For all its technical agility Edwards's *Personal Narrative* has stayed bound to its own theological framework and thus has dated, while Franklin's *Autobiography* has become assimilated into American history. Where Edwards advocates stringent self-examination and the submission of the self to theological pattern, Franklin dramatizes the liberation of the self from prior allegiances—whether in the family or in religion. Franklin's do-it-yourself approach to experience induces a sense of possibility into his reader, a sense of applicability. The pattern, he implies can be repeated. As early as 1833 the reviewer of his newly published *Familiar Letters* grudgingly acknowledges the utility of his writings. 'The impression has always prevailed . . . that Franklin was a selfish man', the reviewer declares; but then continues: 'He gave practical rules for the government of life, he recommended a thriving minute attention to the details of business, a close regard to small gains.'[52] It is one of the achievements of his *Autobiography* that Franklin promotes individual prosperity while suggesting that, in pursuing this prosperity, the individual is at the same time participating in a national pattern.

NOTES

1. Robert Southey, 'Portuguese Literature', *Quarterly Review*, 1 (1809), 283.
2. 'Rambles among Books. No. II—Autobiography', *Cornhill Magazine*, 43 (1881), 410.
3. One of the earliest dated 'autobiographies' is that edited by the Rev. H. Hastings Weld (New York: Harper & Bros, 1848).
4. Sacvan Bercovitch, 'The Ritual of American Autobiography', *Revue Francaise d'Études Américaines*, 14 (1982), 148.
5. Jonathan Edwards, *Religious Affections*, ed. John E. Smith (New Haven: Yale University Press, 1959), p. 86. This standard edition of Edwards's works so far does not include *A Personal Narrative*.
6. Jonathan Edwards, *Basic Writings*, ed. Ola Elizabeth Winslow (New York: New American Library, 1966), p. 82. N. S. Garbo has argued that Edwards is using a cyclical time-scheme which divides into four seasons to which correspond four narrative segments ('Jonathan Edwards's *Personal Narrative*: Dynamic Stasis', *Literature in Wissenschaft und Unterricht*, 2 (1969), 143–45.

7. *The Journal and Major Essays of John Woolman*, ed. Philip P. Moulton (New York: Oxford University Press, 1971), p. 26.
8. *The Journal*, p. 102.
9. *Basic Writings*, p. 83.
10. 'A Divine and Supernatural Light', in *Basic Writings*, p. 127.
11. *Basic Writings*, p. 91.
12. E. I. Thurin, *The Universal Autobiography of Ralph Waldo Emerson* (Lund: C. W. K. Gleerup, 1974).
13. *Basic Writings*, p. 85.
14. *Nature*, Chapter 3.
15. 'Concerning the End which God created the World', *Basic Writings*, p. 236.
16. *Religious Affections*, pp. 205–6. Useful commentary on this spiritual sense is given by Paul Helm in his 'John Locke and Jonathan Edwards: A Reconsideration', *Journal of the History of Philosophy*, 7. i (1969) 55–6.
17. By 'affections' Edwards means a special exercise of the will or inclination which will carry beyond indifference. It shows the orientation of the self, the inclination of the soul towards God.
18. 'Autobiography' in *The James Family*, ed. F. O. Matthiesson (New York: Alfred A. Knopf, 1961), p. 33.
19. J. F. Lynen, *The Design of the Present* (New Haven: Yale University Press, 1969), p. 112.
20. *Basic Writings*, pp. 84–5.
21. R. A. Banes, 'The Exemplary Self: Autobiography in Eighteenth Century America', *Biography*, 5 (1982), 227.
22. *Basic Writings*, p. 94.
23. W. J. Scheick, 'Family, Conversion, and the Self in Jonathan Edwards's *A Faithful Narrative of the Surprising Work of God*', *Tennessee Studies in Literature*, 19 (1974), 81; *The Great Awakening*, ed. C. C. Greon (New Haven: Yale University Press, 1972), p. 151.
24. *The Great Awakening*, pp. 149, 354.
25. *Benjamin Franklin's Autobiographical Writings*, ed. Carl Van Doren (London: Cresset Press, 1946), p. 784.
26. *Benjamin Franklin's Autobiography*, ed. J. A. Leo Lemay and P. M. Zall (New York and London: W. W. Norton, 1986), p. 46.
27. G. Thomas Couser, *American Autobiography. The Prophetic Mode* (Amherst: University of Massachusetts Press, 1979), p. 43.
28. *The Autobiography*, p. 41.
29. Banes, 'The Exemplary Self', 236.
30. *The Autobiography*, p. 64.
31. *Poor Richard's Almanack* (London and New York: Paddington Press, 1976), p. 3.
32. *The Autobiography*, p. 132.
33. R. J. Porter, 'Unspeakable Practices, Writable Acts: Franklin's *Autobiography*', *Hudson Review*, 32 (1979–80), 230. I have explored Franklin's notion of project in 'Projecting the Self: An Approach to Franklin's *Autobiography*', *Études Anglaises*, 36. iv (1983) 385–400.
34. David Levin, 'The Autobiography of Benjamin Franklin: The Puritan

Experimenter in Life and Art', *Yale Review*, 53 (1963), 266.

35. *The Autobiography*, p. 27.
36. Ian Watt, *The Rise of the Novel* (Harmondsworth: Penguin Books, 1963), p. 66. G. A. Starr gives particularly valuable commentary in this context in his *Defoe and Spiritual Autobiography* (Princeton: Princeton University Press, 1966).
37. Carl Van Doren, *Benjamin Franklin* (New York: Viking Press, 1938), p. 93.
38. *The Autobiography*, p. 56.
39. J. A. L. Lemay, 'Franklin and the *Autobiography*: An Essay on Recent Scholarship', *Eighteenth Century Studies*, 1 (1967), 200.
40. *The Autobiography*, p. 110.
41. J. M. Cox, 'Autobiography and America', *Virginia Quarterly Review*, 47 (1971), 259.
42. Franklin's attitude to authority-figures is explored by Hugh J. Dawson, 'Fathers and Sons: Franklin's "Memoirs" as Myth and Metaphor', *Early American Literature*, 14 (1979–80), 269–92.
43. 'Information to Those Who Would Remove to America' in *Autobiography and Other Pieces*, ed. Denis Welland (Oxford: Oxford University Press, 1970), p. 172.
44. Sacvan Bercovitch, *The Puritan Origins of the American Self* (New Haven: Yale University Press, 1975), p. 120.
45. *Franklin, The Apprentice Boy* (New York: Harper, 1855), p. 27.
46. Gary Lindberg, *The Confidence Man in American Literature* (New York: Oxford University Press, 1982), pp. 3–7.
47. *The Letters of Herman Melville*, eds. M. R. Davis and W. H. Gilman (New Haven: Yale University Press, 1960), p. 189.
48. *Melville: The Critical Heritage*, ed. W. G. Branch (London: Routledge & Kegan Paul, 1974), p. 375.
49. 'The Autobiography of a Quack', *Atlantic Monthly*, 20 (1867), 470, 591.
50. 'The Autobiography of a Quack', 467.
51. W. C. Spengeman and L. R. Lundquist, 'Autobiography and the American Myth', *American Quarterly*, 17 (1965), 511.
52. *North American Review*, 37 (1833), 24.

3

Transcendentalism and Autobiography: Emerson, Whitman and Thoreau

by BRIAN HARDING

1

In 1827 Ralph Waldo Emerson noted in his journal that the age in which he lived was 'the age of the first person singular'.[1] Three years later he preached, for the first time, a sermon which he was to deliver nine times in the next nine years; its title was 'Self-Culture'. In it he argued that the spirit of Christianity diverts man's attention from the outer world and directs him to look inward. The introspective character of the age could, therefore, be understood as a result of the Christian Revelation.[2] In December 1830 Emerson first preached on the theme 'Trust Yourself'. In this sermon he stated that Scripture teaches us to value our own souls and to dare to be nonconformists. Religion, he claimed, produces greater self respect than is common among those without faith in God, because religion awakens man to a sense of the 'infinite spiritual estate' he possesses in his own soul.[3] In 'Self and Others', a sermon first preached in January 1831, Emerson reminded his listeners that the spirit of God dwells in man and that 'an Eternal Voice' speaks through the individual soul.[4]

Behind Emerson's belief that the Christian conception of the soul inspired self-concern and self-analysis lay, of course, a long foreground of Puritan preoccupation with the inner life. Behind his emphasis on the infinitude of the soul and the presence of God in man lay, more immediately, the liberal Christian concern with man's 'likeness to God'.[5] Yet, when Emerson resigned from the Unitarian ministry in 1832, his concern with self culture in no way lost its religious intensity. He had argued, in 'Self-Culture', that an unceasing effort to cultivate the self was a duty, for in calling on men to make themselves 'living sacrifices' St. Paul had implied nothing less than an obligation to develop the self to its full potential.[6] In 'The Individual', a lecture delivered at the Masonic Temple, Boston, early in 1837, Emerson spoke as the champion of the 'individual heart', the 'sanctuary and citadel of freedom and goodness'. To look steadily and deeply into one's own being, he stated, is to become aware of the immortality of the soul; to feel the 'perfection of the universal' within the 'imperfect private life'. In fact, the continuity in Emerson's thought concerning the self is such that many of his early lectures might well have been sermons, though the 'God' of the Unitarian minister was replaced by the 'infinite essence' of the lecturer on 'Being and Seeming' and by the 'universal mind' of the lecturer who introduced a series on Human Culture at Boston in the winter of 1837–38. In an address on education he gave in June 1837, Emerson justified self-exploration as the goal of human life by reference to the 'Universal Soul dwelling within the souls of all particular men'.[7]

As far as the young writers influenced by Emerson were concerned, the age was to be the age of the 'first person singular' quite literally. In the seven lines of the opening paragraph of *Walden* (1854), the first person pronoun occurs five times. In the first five lines of the first poem of *Leaves of Grass* (1855), the first person pronoun is used four times. Whitman's 'I celebrate myself' was to provide the more dramatic advertisement for the self, yet that 'I' was to remain anonymous until line 499 of the untitled poem that opened the first edition of *Leaves*. Only in what would become Section 24 of the poem did 'Walt Whitman' announce himself as 'One of the roughs, a kosmos'. Thoreau, in contrast, did put his name on the title page of *Walden*. He also devoted the second paragraph of that work to a spirited defence of his 'egotism', reminding his readers

that 'it is, after all, always the first person that is speaking.'
Recent commentary on the literary Transcendentalists has
called attention to the complexity of 'voice' and 'person' in their
writings. Lawrence Buell has argued persuasively that they
were concerned to convert the 'I' from a fallible personality into
an authoritative voice. Leonard Neufeldt has shown us what a
vital rôle the personae play in Emerson's later essays, and
has taught us not to identify the writer with the persona's
'rhetorical dance'.[8] Since the self is problematized in their
writings at the moment that it is most vigorously affirmed, it is
hardly surprising that their subjectivity did not lead them to the
creation of autobiography. On the contrary, their use of the first
person singular became a means of dissolving the solidity (or
continuity) of the self.

A glance at a recent scholarly definition of autobiography
may help to show why Emersonian devotion to self-culture
could not take the form of writing the book of his life. In his
'Conditions and Limits of Autobiography', Georges Gusdorf
argues that 'autobiography properly speaking assumes the task
of reconstructing the unity of a life across time.' In this view, the
author of an autobiography 'gives himself the job of narrating
his own history' and thus sets out 'to reassemble the scattered
elements of his individual life and to regroup them in a comprehensive sketch'. The *sine qua non* of autobiography, in this
theory, is that it 'recomposes and interprets a life in its totality'.
To Gusdorf, an autobiography necessarily imposes logical
coherence and rationalization on events and experiences that,
when lived, had no such clarity of definition. Consequently, it is
'condemned to substitute endlessly the completely formed for
that which is in the process of being formed'.[9] Since Emerson's
concern was to express in his writings the 'process of being
formed' rather than the 'completely formed' and since the unity
he valued was one that existed *ex tempore* rather than 'across
time', his project might well be considered the deconstruction of
autobiography.

Emerson's early journal comment on the introspective
character of his age and its use of the first person singular was
followed, after a very short interval, by lengthy reflections on
the theme of change, decay and death: on the theme of
mutability, in fact. 'We are the changing inhabitants of a

changing world', he wrote, and went on to say 'The ground we stand on is passing away under our feet.'[10] Self-consciousness often leads to intense awareness of the ephemerality of the self, in Emerson's thought, but his most daring and distinctive imaginative act was to transform 'mutability' into what he called 'metamorphosis'. The metamorphosis 'excites in the beholder an emotion of joy', as Emerson would argue in 'The Poet', because it liberates him from subjection to forms and allows him to participate in spiritual reality. The major statements of this idea would be published in his two volumes of *Essays* (1841 and 1844) but in 'The Protest', a lecture given in 1839, Emerson already made movement itself the attribute that distinguished the soul from the sensual or material life. 'Sense pauses: the soul pauses not' he wrote. 'In its world is incessant movement.' In the same lecture, he called for a spontaneity that was, he believed, only possible if men would free themselves from their memory and live 'extempore'. Here Emerson described 'the young soul' (and the source in the journals makes it clear that he was thinking of Henry Thoreau) as never satisfied and as seeking, determinedly, for 'the perfect, the illimitable'.[11] In rejecting the bonds of the finite, this exemplary young soul is, plainly, not to be satisfied with any state of the self.

Two years earlier, in 'The Present Age', Emerson had made one of the most emphatic statements of a major theme of his lectures, and of the essays that were to follow them: the need for incessant growth of the soul and the danger of spiritual death that would result from any sense of satisfaction with goals already achieved. The life of the spirit, he maintained, depends on continuous action (even conflict) within the self. Man's godlike quality is his capacity for endless growth, it cannot be found in any of his attainments. In the words of the lecture, 'man was made for conflict, not for rest. In action is his power. Not in his goals but in his transition man is great.' Since 'the truest state of mind rested in, becomes false',[12] there could be no achieved self, only the continuous process of becoming a self.

The thematic symbol of 'Circles' (1841) is in itself proof that Emerson could not have seriously engaged with an autobiographical project, for the 'self-evolving circle' rushing 'on all sides outwards to new and larger circles, and that without end' is incompatible with any attempt to construct a 'completely formed' life in letters. Believing that 'the only sin is limitation' and that a man ceases to be interesting the moment we discover his limitations, Emerson could not be interested in an auto-biography that was not open on the side of the future. In the concluding paragraph of the essay, the call for loss of 'our sempiternal memory' so that we can forget ourselves and 'do something without knowing how or why' leads to the statement that 'nothing great was ever achieved without enthusiasm', and this, in turn, leads to the claim that 'abandonment' is the 'way of life'. The symbolic meaning of the expanding circle in terms of the pursuit of truth applies—equally—to the pursuit of the self. The relentless unsettling of things by the 'endless seeker with no Past' at his back has disturbing implications for selfhood. 'Nothing is secure but life' we are told, but this can hardly reassure us since in this paradoxical affirmation 'life' is equated with 'transition, the energizing spirit'.[13]

'Abandonment' is the keynote of 'The Poet'—a major essay in *Second Series*. The intellectual man learns of a new energy beyond that of his 'possessed and conscious intellect' by an 'abandonment to the nature of things'. Only when the poet speaks 'somewhat wildly' can he speak adequately, and only then is the 'metamorphosis'[14] possible.

In the later lecture-essay 'Poetry and Imagination', Emerson again identifies the life of imagination with the perception of 'the incessant metamorphosis' and again attributes 'pure delight' to such awareness because it 'infuses a certain volatility and intoxication into all Nature'. Here, too, the value of poetry lies in its power to suggest 'the flux or fugaciousness of the poet'.[15]

Believing that power lay in transition and that the spiritual life was itself movement or change, Emerson could not interpret his own life 'in its totality', for his view of the self was, as G. Thomas Couser has said, 'prospective' rather than 'retro-spective'.[16] To Couser it seems that after Emerson auto-biography could become a tool in the process of self-creation, rather than a record of transcendence. This statement plainly implies a more flexible theory of autobiography than the one I have borrowed from Georges Gusdorf. It leads one, in fact, to James Olney's essay on 'The Ontology of Autobiography' where the meaning of the *bios* in autobiography is extended to include 'the course of a life seen as a process rather than a stable entity'. To Olney, even lyric poetry with its concentration of everything 'in passing moments of awareness' can be considered as a form of autobiography, if 'a legitimate definition of life— real life—can be 'consciousness' with its 'now and now and now immediacy'.[17]

No account of the ontology of autobiography could be better adapted to Transcendentalist writing than Olney's Heraclitean alternative to 'stable, unchanging, timeless reality'. Yet there are further reasons why Emerson's subjectivity threatens any autobiographical project with dissolution. To Emerson, the self whose culture was a religious duty was a self that not only contained God but was God. He had been able to preach self-trust without guilt because he believed that *true* reliance on the real *self* was a form of God-reliance. In his sermon 'Trust Yourself' (1830) he had stated—in prosaic terms—what would become part of the meaning of the great poetic essay 'Self Reliance' in *Essays* (1841). In the words of the sermon:

> Nor ... let it be thought that there is in this self-reliance anything of presumption, anything inconsistent with a spirit of dependence and piety toward God. In listening more intently to our own soul we are not becoming in the ordinary sense more selfish, but are departing farther from what is low and falling back upon truth and upon God. For the whole value of the soul depends upon the fact that it contains a divine principle, that it is a house of God, and the voice of the eternal inhabitant may always be heard within it.[18]

In 'Being and Seeming' and 'Holiness', two 1838 lectures that borrowed from earlier sermons, Emerson's insistence on the impersonality or universality of the essential self led him to deprecate the 'individual will' and to pay tribute to whatever destroyed it. Phrases for the essential self include 'infinite essence' and 'central fire' or 'germinating, ever-creating life'. The religious sentiment is, we are told in 'Holiness', an impersonal sentiment and God is defined as the light of the inner consciousness. Since mind is also defined as light, the distinction between mind, God and inner consciousness is obliterated or dissolved. In 'The Over-Soul' (1841), too, the self is merged with the greater Self and the individual is metaphorically dissolved into the water of the river that is the soul.

Not only was the Emersonian self a process rather than a state of being; it was also—at epiphanic moments of intense self-consciousness—a 'diffusion' of selfhood into the 'all-absorbing totality'. Expounding his paradoxical theory of the poetic self in 'The Poet', Emerson claimed that true artists, whether painters, composers, orators or poets, shared one desire, 'namely to express themselves symmetrically and abundantly, not dwarfishly and fragmentarily'. Dante, he claimed, was the poet who deserved admiration for his daring to write his autobiography 'in colossal cipher, or into universality'.[19]

2

There can be no doubt that Whitman wanted his *Leaves of Grass* to be a 'universal' autobiography of the sort Emerson had credited Dante with writing. In a letter to William O'Connor, written on 6 January 1865, he expressed himself satisfied that his book had achieved what he intended:

> namely, to express by sharp-cut self assertion, *One's-Self*, and also, or may be still more, to map out, to throw together for American use, a gigantic embryo or skeleton of Personality, fit for the West, for native models.[20]

'A Backward Glance O'er Travel'd Roads' reaffirmed Whitman's conception of his purpose. It was, he said, 'to articulate and faithfully express in literary or poetic form, and uncompromisingly, my own physical, emotional, moral, intellectual, and aesthetic Personality'[21] and to 'exploit' it for purposes beyond those of his individual life. The poet's Personality was to 'tally' the spirit of its age and of America. Whitman, it is clear, set out to write what has recently been called 'auto-American-biography'.[22]

'Song of Myself' can also be read as part of a 'prophetic autobiography' in which the distinction between literal and symbolic truth is dissolved. Certainly, as G. Thomas Couser points out, it is almost without verifiable facts of the individual life of the speaker.[23] It is, in fact, at the same time an intensely personal and a remarkably impersonal poem. The 'voice'—the

First Person Singular: Studies in American Autobiography

'valved voice'—that the speaker 'loves' is the voice of his own soul, or rather it *is* his soul when the self attains to a mystic union with God (in Section 5), but the voice of the 'Song' becomes the voice of the whole American people in the course of the poem. Paradoxically, in the very section where the speaker-singer identifies himself by announcing his own name (Section 24) he also claims that 'voices of the interminable generations of slaves' speak through him. The 'diversity' which the speaker says is his 'own' and which he cannot 'resist' (Section 16) makes him '*of* old and young, *of* the foolish as much as the wise' (emphasis added). It also makes a self of the vast and varied life 'voiced' in the poem's catalogues.

Having celebrated his physical being by worshipping his own body in words that blend the self with the natural world— "Mixed tussled hay of head and beard and brawn it shall be you,/ Trickling sap of maple, fibre of manly wheat, it shall be you'[24]—the speaker-singer in 'Song' returns, in a later section, to 'the puzzle of puzzles,/ And that we call Being' (Section 26). After all the affirmation the question comes again: 'To be in any form, what is that?' (Section 27). The answers are as diverse as the 'selves' of the poem. To be, for the speaker, is to be the culmination of all previous existence. Aeons have contributed towards him—towards the realization of his selfhood: 'All forces have been steadily employed to complete and delight me,/ Now I stand on this spot with my soul' (Section 44). Yet 'to be' in this poem is to be forever unwilling to accept the limitations of the self and to be forever dissatisfied with any 'being' attained:

> This day before dawn I ascended a hill and looked at the
>   crowded heaven,
> And I said to my spirit, When we become the enfolders of
>   those orbs and the pleasure and knowledge of every
>   thing in them, shall we be filled and satisfied then?
> And my spirit said No, we level that lift to pass and
>   continue beyond. (Section 46)

Tramping his perpetual journey, the 'endless seeker' of 'Song of Myself' acknowledges his 'fugaciousness' in the concluding sections of the poem. Departing 'as air', he is uncertain that future readers will know 'who I am or what I mean'. Thus,

64

'Song of Myself' does not fit the archetypal myth of the American autobiography, as described by W. C. Spengemann and L. R. Lundquist.[25] It does not take us on a pilgrimage with the speaker from imperfection to perfection, or from alienation to union with nature. It does give us moments of ecstatic union with God and moments of intense celebration of the self, but it enacts one of Whitman's intensest beliefs as recorded in his notes: 'If I have any principle & lesson', he wrote, 'it is that . . . of continual development, of arriving at any one result or degree only to start on further results and degrees.'[26] In another prose statement, Whitman argues that the greatness of humanity is 'that it never at any time or under any circumstances arrives at its finality—never is able to say: "Now I stand fixed forever." ' The insistence on incessant movement here—'Always changing, advancing, retreating, enlarging, condensing'[27]—is unmistakably Emersonian, as is Whitman's programmatic subordination of the singer to the song.

The revisions to 'Song of Myself' after the first edition are—generally speaking—in the direction of impersonality. The 'egotism' and 'omnivorous words' of the 1855 version are given a new resonance when, in a new line in Section 13, the singer explains that he is 'Absorbing all to myself and for this song'. Following the vast catalogue in Section 15, a new line states 'And of these one and all I weave the song of myself.' Other additions to the *Leaves* in later editions were, of course, frankly more personal, and in particular the whole 'Calamus' section of the 1860 edition marks a shift away from the rôle of the public poet. Yet the 1860 *Leaves* concluded with a new poem called 'So long!' and this contained a stanza, dropped in the 1867 *Leaves*, that indicates how seriously Whitman took the Emersonian theory of the poet's fugaciousness:

> Yet not me, after all—let none be content with me,
> I myself seek a man better than I am, or a woman
>   better than I am,
> I invite defiance, and to make myself superseded.
> All I have done, I would cheerfully give to be trod
>   under foot, if it might only be the soil of superior poems.

The stanza may have been dropped because, as Gay Wilson Allen suggests, 'in 1867 Walt Whitman no longer regards his poems either as failures or as tentative experiments for which he must apologize.'[28] It is true that, by 1867, Whitman had embarked on the vicarious creation of an 'autobiography', collaborating with O'Connor and Burroughs to build a myth of the poet's idealized life, yet he did not drop from the 1867 *Leaves*—or later versions of 'Song of Myself'—other lines on the poet's ephemerality:

> I am the teacher of athletes,
> He that by me spreads a wider breast than my own proves
>   the width of my own,
> He most honors my style who learns under it to destroy the
>   teacher. (Section 47)

Equally, the final section of 'Song of Myself' retains—through all editions of *Leaves of Grass*—the poet's bequest of himself 'to the dirt' and his invitation to future readers to look for him 'under your bootsoles'. Perhaps, then, the stanza was dropped from 'So long!' because Whitman realized that it was redundant after a careful reading of 'Song of Myself'.

Whitman's *Blue Book* revisions of the 1860 'Proto-Leaf' show him building his 'myth' of himself and continuing to construct a symbolic or 'universal' autobiography. The grandiloquent opening of the 1860 version of the poem—'Free, fresh, savage,/ Fluent, luxuriant, self-content . . ./ Fond of fish-shape Paumanok, where I was born'—is emended to a more 'personal' reference that belongs to the developing myth of the 'Good Gray Poet': 'Starting from fish-shape Paumanok, where I was born,/ Well-begotten and raised by a perfect mother'. Yet the 'I' of these opening lines is not an individual only. He breathes Californian, Texan, or Cuban air in the 1860 version, and Nebraskan air in the *Blue Book* revision, where his home is changed from the 'Kanuck Woods' to 'Dakotah's Woods'. The poem that became 'Starting from Paumanok' remains less impressive than 'Song of Myself', not because it is limited by its reference to a particular self but because it lacks the tension between the intensely realized moments of self-consciousness and the diffusion of the self into the 'universal'.

3

Compared to Whitman's ambitious project for his own 'Personality' in *Leaves of Grass*, Thoreau's 'egotism' in *Walden* seems modest in scope. The 'I' of Thoreau's narrative does not 'incorporate gneiss and coal and long-threaded moss' nor are his words 'omnivorous'. The speaker in *Walden* does not 'become' John Field, John Farmer, Therien, or any of the people he encounters or describes. On the contrary, the speaker maintains an unambiguous and unblurred individuality. The 'Life in the Woods' of the book's subtitle is a particular life lived in a particular woods; it is not generalized. Time and place are specified. On 4 July 1845, the narrator 'took up [his] abode . . . by the shore of a small pond, about a mile and a half south of the village of Concord'.[29] His personal past—even his infancy— is relevant to his narrative, it seems, for he considers it appropriate to mention that he was brought 'through these very woods and this field, to the pond' when he was 4 years old (p. 155). Consequently, we are told, Walden Pond is 'one of the oldest scenes' stamped on his memory. Later memories are also mentioned by the speaker, who recalls hours spent drifting on the pond in his boat when he was younger (p. 191). Personal experience also helps to explain the particular attraction of the Hollowell Farm, for recollections from his earliest voyages up the river Concord are adduced when the narrator tells of his imaginative experiment in buying a farm (p. 83).

Walden, then, invites discussion as an autobiography, for it tells the story of part, at least, of one man's life. Moreover it appears to conform more closely to Gusdorf's conception of autobiography than any other Transcendentalist work, for it clearly does 'regroup' elements of the writer's individual life in a 'comprehensive sketch' and plainly does construct a 'completely formed' narrative out of the processes of living. The structuring that condenses two years' residence and almost nine years' experience into a narrative with a seasonal rhythm gives to the work a clarity of definition appropriate to autobiography. Yet, for all its insistent use of the first person pronoun, and for all its dependence on the writer's personal experience—'Where *I* Lived and What *I* Lived For'—*Walden* is obviously much more than the record and interpretation of an individual's life. The 'exemplary' quality of the life lived at the pond and the 'exemplary'[30] nature of the egotism displayed by the narrator is implicit even in the brashest advertisement for the self. On the title page, beneath the picture of the house in the woods, words from the second chapter of the book are given as epigraph: 'I do not propose to write an ode to dejection, but to brag as lustily as chanticleer in the morning, standing on his roost, if only to wake my neighbours up' (p. 84). In the 'Economy' chapter, the speaker tells us that if he seems to boast when he explains how little money he spent on his house, his excuse is that he brags 'for humanity' rather than for himself (p. 49). He has merely demonstrated what can be done if there is the will to do it and the self-reliance necessary to break with conventional notions (of house-building, of indispensable comfort, or of propriety). Chanticleer is only one of the speaker's changes of garments, for he later sees himself ranging the woods as a half-starved hound (p. 210). In almost buying the Hollowell Farm he almost becomes Atlas, bearing the world on his shoulders (p. 83). In 'The Bean-Field' he does become a Greek hero as he levels a 'lusty crest-waving Hector' of a weed to the dust (p. 172). In 'The Village' he becomes Orpheus, drowning the voices of the sirens who would lure him onto the domestic rocks (p. 169). In 'Brute Neighbours' he appears in the form of the 'Hermit' and engages in repartee with the 'Poet'. So Protean a self cannot, evidently, he equated with the actual Henry David Thoreau who lived at the pond. Obviously, as many have noticed, the 'self' of *Walden* is a 'deliberately created verbal personality'.[31]

In 'Where I Lived and What I Lived For', the speaker makes it plain that his life at the pond is to be understood as an 'experiment' in finding an actual site for a house that conforms to the needs of his imagination. Having bought various farms, or considered buying them, in his imagination, he has now taken possession of a particular spot and has decided to make that the scene of an experiment in living. Beginning with a critique of the lives that his contemporary New Englanders 'are said' to live, the narrator adopts the rôle of the *Eiron* to disturb the complacency of the believer in common-sense notions of business and enterprise and adopts the rôle of the hero who acts out the possibilities of a nobler life. That life climaxes in the revelation of the 'Spring' chapter, when the metamorphosis of the thawing sand and clay into organic forms convinces the narrator that there is nothing inorganic in creation, that the earth is living poetry (pp. 308–9).

Yet the revelation does not bring the book to an end, nor does it provide the final fulfilment of the self, for, having vividly evoked the renewal of life in the spring and having perceived the thawing of the pond as a Christ-like resurrection ('Walden was dead and is alive again'), the narrator tells us that he left the woods finally on 6 September 1847. The apparently baffling statement (in 'Conclusion')—'I left the woods for as good a reason as I went there' (p. 323)—must be taken as an assertion of self-reliance. The speaker's reasons have to do with intuition rather than common sense. Having 'several more lives to live', he clearly cannot allow himself to remain within even the magic circle of Walden. Appropriately, the 'Spring' chapter is followed by a 'Conclusion' whose theme is breaking out of bounds or limits and exploring unknown realms of the self. The 'village life' that would stagnate 'if it were not for the unexplored forests and meadows which surround it' represents all life that is content to stand still. The wildness needed as a 'tonic' for our lives causes us to 'transgress' the limits of our known selves.

The story of *Walden* can be read as the story of the narrator's recognition of the true nature of the soul. In the Hindu fable recounted in the second chapter of the book, the soul mistakes its identity and assumes an unworthy character until a holy teacher reveals its higher nature 'and then it knows itself to be *Brahme*' (p. 96). The narrator in *Walden*, like the singer in 'Song of Myself', is both a 'holy teacher' and the one who learns. To learn that the soul is *Brahme* is to become aware of its unity—to realize that the essential or real self is, in the words of V. K. Chari, who interprets Whitman (and Thoreau) in the light of Vedantic mysticism, not a process, but 'the protagonist of a ceaseless action'.[32] Acknowledging the preponderance of kinetic images in Whitman's poems, and their emphasis on the self as becoming, Chari insists on the 'still point' at the centre of the movement. Going to the Emersonian source, Chari quotes from 'Circles' words which acknowledge 'some principle of fixture or stability in the soul' in contrast to the 'incessant movement and progression which all things partake'. Certainly, the Transcendentalists' conception of the self was posited upon the belief

69

in a changeless 'real self' beneath or beyond the ever-changing forms of selfhood, but—as Emerson went on to say in 'Circles'—the 'central life' with which that fixture or stability is equated is unable 'to create a life and thought as large and excellent as itself' in the world. Instead, it 'forever labors' to do so, and any story of the self must be the account of those labours rather than of the stability.

NOTES

1. *The Journals and Miscellaneous Notebooks of Ralph Waldo Emerson*, ed. William H. Gilman et al. (Cambridge, Mass., 1960–), III, p. 70. Hereafter referred to as JMN.
2. *Young Emerson Speaks: Unpublished Discourses on Many Subjects*, ed. Arthur C. McGiffert, Jr. (Boston, 1938), p. 100. Hereafter referred to as *Y.E.S.*
3. *Y.E.S.*, p. 105.
4. *Y.E.S.*, p. 136.
5. On the Puritan tradition see Daniel B. Shea, Jr., *Spiritual Autobiography in Early America* (Princeton, 1968). William Ellery Channing's sermon 'Likeness to God' was given in 1828. His 'Address on Self-Culture' was given in 1838.
6. *Y.E.S.*, p. 101.
7. *The Early Lectures of Ralph Waldo Emerson*, eds. Stephen E. Whicher, Robert E. Spiller et al. (Cambridge, Mass., 1959–72), II, pp. 186; 188; 309; 220; 198. Hereafter referred to as EL.
8. Lawrence Buell, *Literary Transcendentalism: Style and Vision in the American Renaissance* (Ithaca and London, 1973), p. 283. Leonard Neufeldt, *The House of Emerson* (Lincoln, Nebraska and London, 1984), p. 230.
9. Georges Gusdorf, 'Conditions and Limits of Autobiography', in James Olney (ed.), *Autobiography: Essays Theoretical and Critical* (Princeton, 1980), pp. 28–48.
10. JMN, II, pp. 72–3.
11. EL, III, pp. 89; 95.
12. EL, II, p. 158.
13. *The Complete Works of Ralph Waldo Emerson*, eds. Edward Waldo Emerson and Waldo Emerson Forbes (Boston, 1909–14), II, pp. 301–22. Hereafter referred to as W.
14. W, III, pp. 26–30.
15. W, VIII, pp. 18–21.
16. Thomas G. Couser, *American Autobiography: the Prophetic Mode* (Amhurst, Mass., 1979), p. 65.
17. 'Some Versions of Memory/Some Versions of *Bios*: The Ontology of Autobiography', in James Olney (ed.) *Autobiography: Essays Theoretical and Critical*, pp. 238–42.

18. *Y.E.S.*, p. 110.
19. W, III, pp. 37–9.
20. *Walt Whitman: The Correspondence. Volume I: 1842–1867*, ed. Haviland Miller (New York, 1961), p. 247.
21. *Prose Works, 1892. Volume II, Collect and Other Prose*, ed. Floyd Stovall (New York, 1964), p. 714.
22. Sacvan Bercovitch, 'Emerson the Prophet: Romanticism, Puritanism, and Auto-American-Biography', in David Levin (ed.), *Emerson: Prophecy, Metamorphosis, and Influence* (New York and London, 1975), pp. 1–27.
23. *American Autobiography: the Prophetic Mode*, p. 83.
24. All quotations from 'Song of Myself' follow the text of the 1855 edition of *Leaves of Grass*.
25. 'Autobiography and the American Myth', *American Quarterly*, 17, No. 3 (1965), 501–19.
26. *Walt Whitman's Workshop. A Collection of Unpublished Manuscripts*, ed. Clifton J. Furness (Cambridge, Mass., 1928), p. 53.
27. *Notes and Fragments*, ed. Richard Maurice Bucke (London, Ontario, 1899), p. 85.
28. *The New Walt Whitman Handbook* (New York, 1975), p. 128.
29. *Walden*, ed. J. Lyndon Shanley (Princeton, 1971), pp. 84, 86. All references to *Walden* will be to this edition and will be included in parenthesis in my text.
30. For a helpful discussion of Thoreau's propensity to 'universalize' his personal experience, see Buell, *Literary Transcendentalism*, Ch. 11. Buell, however, denies the term 'exemplary' to the 'I' of *Walden*.
31. Joseph J. Moldenhauer, 'Paradox in Walden', in *Twentieth Century Interpretations of 'Walden'*, ed. Richard Ruland (Englewood Cliffs, N.J., 1963), p. 77. My comments on the narrator's rôle as *Eiron* are derived from this article.
32. V. J. Chari, *Whitman in the Light of Vedantic Mysticism* (Lincoln, Nebraska, 1964), p. 119.

4

The Ever-receding Dream: Henry Adams and Mark Twain as Autobiographers

by WARREN L. CHERNAIK

1

At first glance, no two American writers would appear to have less in common than Mark Twain and Henry Adams. One was the quintessential redskin, the other the quintessential paleface: the robust Westerner, upholder of democratic values, defiantly provincial and anti-intellectual, and the reserved, fastidious Easterner, an aristocrat by birth and instinct, girded round with irony and weighed down by the burden of tradition. One cherished and sought to retain the innocent eye of childhood even into old age; the other seemed to have been born middle-aged, complaining of being 'tired of this life', 'beaten back everywhere' at 24, and rapidly subsided into valetudinarianism:

> One goes on by habit, playing more or less clumsily that one is alive. It is ludicrous and at times humiliating, but there is a certain style in it which youth has not.[1]

Where Twain for most of his career could be confident of reaching a large and receptive audience, with whom he actively identified, giving their unspoken thoughts and aspirations voice, Adams in contrast gloomily saw his words as dropping into a void, and, like his friend and fellow cosmopolite Henry

James, sought to encourage an aristocracy of taste, a finer tone of feeling, as moral and aesthetic ideal:

> Among the two or three hundreds of millions of people about us in Europe and America, our public could hardly be five hundred. For my own practical life, the number certainly never exceeded a score. Anything which has helped bring that score into closer understanding and sympathy, has been worth doing.[2]

The two men, contemporaries and equally long-lived, can be seen as enacting a symbolic Jamesian confrontation of 'Europe' and 'America', representing alternative paths for the American artist in the late nineteenth century. Their characteristic prose styles reflect the incompatible aims of frontiersman and connoisseur: the energy and spontaneity of the vernacular, as against the elaborate, rounded periods of the habitual ironist and sceptic, holding experience at a distance. And yet, when one looks more closely at the two figures, the neat contrasts tend to break down. Adams was uncomfortable with his New England Puritan heritage and his friends tended to be Westerners, less constrained in their manners and assumptions. John Hay, whose intimate friendship and spiritual affinity with Adams are celebrated in the *Education*, began his career as a writer of colloquial Western ballads, similar in manner to the early writings of Twain, with whom he remained close throughout his life. Though Adams spent a great deal of time in England and on the continent as a young man, he was far from a Gilbert Osmond; indeed, Henry James, who drew on Adams and his wife in several works of fiction, saw them as 'a pair of patriots' (the phrase comes from Alice James's diary, but there are many parallels in letters to and about the Adamses by both William and Henry James), staunch in their preference for American modernity over the 'old pageants and ceremonies' of Europe:

> I go in an hour to bid farewell to my friends the Henry Adamses, who after a year of London life are returning to their beloved Washington. One sees so many 'cultivated Americans' who prefer living abroad that it is a great refreshment to encounter two specimens of this class who find the charms of their native land so much greater than those of Europe. In England they appear to have suffered more than enjoyed, and their experience

is not unedifying, for they have seen and known a good deal of English life. But they are rather too critical and invidious. I shall miss them much though—we have had such inveterate discussions and comparing of notes. They have been much liked here. Mrs. Adams in comparison with the usual British female is a perfect Voltaire in petticoats.[3]

Clover Adams, whose entire absence from the *Education* is the most striking of that book's many omissions and silences, served a similar symbolic function to Henry James and her husband. To both, she was the representative American, the embodiment of an independence of spirit and freshness of response which they saw as 'Western' rather than 'Eastern'. Her fondness for the writings of Mark Twain—she referred to her visit to Europe as 'the second half of the *Innocents Abroad*' and praised Twain as the best author to read 'in moments of depression'—fit in with the rôle she characteristically played in friendly debate with James:

> He had better not hang around Europe much longer. . . . [It was] high time Harry James was ordered home by his family—he is too good a fellow to be spoiled by injudicious old ladies in London. . . . he had better go to Cheyenne and run a hog ranch.[4]

On at least two occasions, James wrote of Clover as 'the incarnation of my native land' (Clover, with wry irony, considered this 'a most equivocal compliment'), the 'genius of my beloved country'. In a letter written before her marriage, he linked her with his cousin Minnie Temple as a prototypical Jamesian heroine, characterized by an eagerness to embrace experience, an avoidance of 'the cut and dried' which he contrasted favourably with the conventionality of the English women he knew: 'I revolt from their dreary deathly want of—what shall I call it?—Clover Hooper has it—intellectual grace—Minnie Temple has it—moral spontaneity.'[5] Adams's own comments about his fiancée in letters to friends again stress her quick intuitive intelligence, her individuality, her responsiveness, her promise. One is irresistibly reminded of Isabel Archer, for whom Clover served as partial model.

> My young female has a very active and quick mind and has run over many things, but she really knows nothing well, and laughs at the idea of being thought a blue. . . . I think you will like her,

not for beauty, for she is certainly not beautiful, and her features
are much too prominent, but for intelligence and sympathy,
which are what hold me.

From having had no mother to take responsibility off her
shoulders, she has grown up to look after herself and has a
certain vein of personality which approaches eccentricity. This is
very attractive to me, but then I am absurdly in love, and I won't
guaranty your liking it.

She is certainly not handsome: nor would she quite be called
plain, I think. She is twenty-eight years old. She knows her own
mind uncommon well. She does not talk *very* American. Her
manners are quiet. She reads German—also Latin—also, I fear,
a little Greek, but very little. She talks garrulously, but on the
whole pretty sensibly. She is very open to instruction. *We* shall
improve her. She dresses badly. She decidedly has humor and
will appreciate *our* wit. She has enough money to be quite
independent. She rules me as only American women rule men,
and I cower before her. Lord! How she would lash me if she read
the above description of her![6]

The recurrent contrast in these passages, as in James's many
treatments of the 'European' theme, is innocence as against
experience, the free flow of impulse as against settled and
established forms. For Adams, Clover represented a vitality
which he felt he lacked; if the irony is to some extent patronizing
and defensive, reflecting fear or unease at the prospect of
Clover's youthful energy, each of the passages quoted is
primarily a tribute to the life-force, rather than an attempt to
exert masculine control. Though Clover is not mentioned in the
Education, her death by suicide haunts the work, provides the
figure in the carpet for its overwhelming sense of loss, failure,
illusions shattered. One powerful passage on the death of his
sister may be read as a displacement of his feelings on the death
of his wife; or perhaps it expresses a profound insight that what
matters is the experience of loss and disillusionment and not its
particular occasion:

The last lesson—the sum and term of education,—began then.
He had passed through thirty years of rather varied experience
without having once felt the shell of custom broken. He had
never seen nature,—only her surface,—the sugar-coating that
she shows to youth. Flung suddenly in his face, with the harsh
brutality of chance, the terror of the blow stayed by him

thenceforth for life, until repetition made it more than the will could struggle with; more than he could call on himself to bear. . . . For the first time, the stage-scenery of the senses collapsed; the human mind felt itself stripped naked, vibrating in a void of shapeless energies, with resistless mass, colliding, crushing, wasting and destroying what these same energies had created and labored from eternity to perfect.[7]

A similar metaphor of dream and awakening, departed innocence brought into collision with an intolerable, shaming reality, lies at the heart of all Adams's major works, *Mont Saint Michel and Chartres* and the *History* as well the *Education*. The passage just quoted characteristically shows Adams universalizing the personal; he has other aims in mind than to document his own loss of faith, or even to make the reader participate in his journey to awareness (though phrases like 'flung suddenly in his face' encourage the reader's emotional involvement). What the passage seeks to do is to demonstrate the impossibility of faith, except for those fortunate enough to retain their childhood or to die young. Though the balance of hope and despair differs in *Mont Saint Michel and Chartres*, the central contrast is the same:

> It was very childlike, very foolish, very beautiful, and very true,—as art, at least:—so true that everything else shades off into vulgarity. . . . We have done with Chartres. For seven hundred years Chartres has seen pilgrims, coming and going more or less like us; and will perhaps see them for another seven hundred years, but we shall see it no more, and can safely leave the Virgin in her Majesty, with her three great prophets on either hand, as calm and confident in their own strength and in God's providence as they were when Saint Louis was born, but looking down from a deserted heaven, into an empty church, on a dead faith. (Ch. X, p. 522)

What the later Adams and the later Twain had in common was a persistent consciousness of loss and emptiness, in part personal in origin, but invested by each of them with historical, political, and metaphysical significance. For Twain, the autobiographical impetus behind his later writings appears to have been a series of deaths—that of his wife, his daughter Jean, and especially his daughter Susy—which he invests with symbolic import. Once again the contrast is between self-deluding dream and intolerable reality, the expanding vistas of youth and the unrelieved bleakness of age. There is no middle term, no possibility of gaining wisdom through experience, or weighing up gains against losses; either, against all odds, the vivid, uncompromising childhood vision can be retained infinitely, inviolate within the stronghold of the imagination, or, brutally, it can be blotted out. Twain's *Autobiography* is structured round a series of contrasts between past and present, which are persistently identified with life and death, hope and despair, natural abundance and the monotonous void.

> Would I bring her to life again if I could do it? I would not. If a word could do it, I would beg for strength to withhold the word. And I would have the strength: I am sure of it. In her loss I am almost bankrupt, and my life is a bitterness, but I am content: for she has been enriched with the most precious of all gifts—that gift which makes all other gifts mean and poor—death.[8]

Though, as we shall see, there is no stable final text of Twain's *Autobiography*, which has to be recovered and pieced together from several fragmentary versions, he clearly expressed his intention that his account of the death of his daughter Jean should be the final chapter of any published edition; the end of the journey is thus seen as desolation, the reluctant awakening from a 'fair dream' of comradeship and harmony.[9] This mood of angry and bitter disillusionment is common to Twain's writings in his last period—his philosophical testament *What is Man?*, the fragmentary dream and voyage narratives, *The Mysterious Stranger*—and characteristically finds expression in passages setting forth a programmatic pessimism and determinism. As with Adams, the harsh, unwelcome truths of scientific materialism are contrasted with the pleasing consolatory fictions of faith. If in each of these works by Twain, as in the *Education*, the irony is poised uneasily between compassion and contempt, the reason may partly be the author's ambivalence toward the new universe of indifferent colliding forces of 'resistless mass', partly his perceived shame that the folly he is anatomizing is his own.

I shall argue later that the persistent tendency in both Twain and Adams to universalize personal experience has specific historical roots in late nineteenth-century America. Both men saw the fading of the dream in political terms, reacting to changes they perceived in American society between the 1830s, when both were born, and the first decade of the twentieth century. Old men looking backward tend to idealize their youth and find little to recommend about the present. But what is particularly striking in passages of cosmic pessimism in Twain's later writing is the bitterness they express at being cheated, a smouldering resentment, half personal and half political, which differentiates such passages in tone from contemporaneous expressions of atheist determinism, doctrinally similar, in the writings of Thomas Hardy or Stephen Crane:

> A myriad of men are born; they labor and sweat and struggle for bread; they squabble and scold and fight; they scramble for little mean advantages over each other. Age creeps upon them; infirmities follow; shames and humiliations bring down their prides and their vanities. Those they love are taken from them and the joy of life is turned to aching grief. The burden of pain, care, misery, grows heavier year by year. At length ambition is dead; pride is dead; vanity is dead; longing for release is in their place. It comes at last—the only unpoisoned gift earth ever had for them—and they vanish from a world where they were of no consequence; where they achieved nothing; where they were a mistake and a failure and a foolishness; where they have left no sign that they existed—a world which will lament them a day and forget them forever. (Paine, II, 37–8)

The statement could hardly be phrased in more universal terms, allowing no exceptions, and as a Satire against Mankind it builds up cumulative force effectively; both in its rhetorical devices and in its view of human folly, it resembles passages in *The Mysterious Stranger*. But when we look at the passage in its original context in the *Autobiography*, we find that it serves to introduce an extended treatment of the life and death of Susy Clemens, in which all the anecdotes of her youth and promise are coloured by the knowledge that she died young, with that promise unfulfilled.[10] The lines I have just quoted are framed by passages extolling Susy in which the author's stylistic control seems to have deserted him; it is as though Mark Twain had turned his pen over to Emmeline Grangerford:

> As a little child aged seven she was oppressed and perplexed by the maddening repetition of the stock incidents of our race's fleeting sojourn here, just as the same thing has oppressed and perplexed maturer minds from the beginning of time. . . .

'Mamma, what is it all for?' asked Susy, preliminarily stating the above details in her own halting language, after long brooding over them alone in the privacy of the nursery.

(Paine, II, 37, 38)

What has gone wrong here is a blurring of perspective, which allows the author, violating probability, to attribute his own *Weltschmerz* to the prescient child and, coincidentally, to indulge himself in the kind of sentimental cliché he satirized in others. The paradox Twain is facing, with some discomfort, in this passage is central to the *Autobiography*: the child who asks questions and the man who knows the answers are irrevocably cut off from one another by reason of that very knowledge, the cold touch of death, and yet the two are linked, and insofar as the child the man once was lives within him, and the child the old man sees serves to rekindle memories of that earlier child, they are one.

Twain's *Autobiography*, then, like the *Education*, enacts a dialogue between innocence and experience, past and present, child and man. The pessimism of some passages in the *Autobiography* is balanced by others which powerfully evoke a life in nature which is ever-renewing. Such passages, closer in tone and style to *The Adventures of Huckleberry Finn* and *Life on the Mississippi* than to the corrosive irony of *The Mysterious Stranger*, assert the possibility that the direct, truthful vision of childhood can endure into later life:

> I can see the farm yet, with perfect clearness. I can see all its belongings, all its details: the family room of the house, with a 'trundle' bed in one corner and a spinning wheel in another—a wheel whose rising and falling wail, heard from a distance, was the mournfullest of all sounds to me, and made me homesick and low spirited, and filled my atmosphere with the wandering spirits of the dead; the vast fireplace, piled high, on winter nights, with flaming hickory logs from whose end a sugary sap bubbled out, but did not go to waste, for we scraped it off and ate it; the lazy cat spread out on the rough hearthstones; the drowsy dogs braced against the jambs and blinking; my aunt in one chimney corner, knitting; my uncle in the other, smoking his corn-cob pipe; the slick and carpetless oak floor fainly mirroring the dancing flame tongues and freckled with black indentations where fire coals had popped out and died a leisurely death; half a dozen children

79

romping in the background twilight; 'split'-bottomed chairs here and there, some with rockers; a cradle—out of service, but waiting, with confidence; in the early cold mornings a snuggle of children, in shirts and chemises, occupying the hearthstone and procrastinating—they could not bear to leave that comfortable place and go out on the wind-swept floor space between the kitchen where the general tin basin stood, and wash. (Paine, I, 102–3)

The keynote is stated in the first words: as in the famous account of the raft idyll in Chapter XIX of *Huck Finn*, with its similar hypnotic rhythms and sharply etched details, Twain's verbal art is deployed in order to make the reader *see*, feel, participate. If the passage has the ring of authenticity, it is partly its inclusiveness that convinces. The wind-swept floor space, the dents on the carpetless floor, the mournful sound of the wheel have some of the same functions as the dead fish and trading-scows of *Huck Finn* in making the passage seem honest rather than edited or softened, unmediated rather than refracted through the shopworn vocabulary of painterly conventions or sentimental fiction (no 'long brooding', halting language, or 'fleeting sojourn' here).[11] Twain is adept at what rhetoricians call the 'ethical proof', making us trust his narrator. The touches of humour in the passage provide a certain distancing, in making us aware of a reflective observer who is both inside and outside the room; all this, we half-realize in reading, is being consciously recreated, conjured up in words. But the central assumption of the passage is the romantic doctrine that the act of remembering and the act of writing are one and the same, that the eye of the artist is the eye of the child.

This sense of imaginative participation in bringing the past to life is even more explicit in a passage a few pages later:

I can call back the solemn twilight and mystery of the deep woods, the earthy smells, the faint odors of the wild flowers, the sheen of rain-washed foliage, the rattling clatter of drops when the wind shook the trees, the far-off hammering of woodpeckers and the muffled drumming of wood pheasants in the remoteness of the forest, the snapshot glimpses of disturbed wild creatures scurrying through the forest—I can call it all back and make it as real as it ever was, and as blessed. (Paine, I, 110)

What is striking here is the emotional investment in the repeated 'I can call back', or later in the passage 'I can see', 'I remember',

'I know'. The magical, incantatory quality of the passage is pronounced, and the appeal to all the senses (sight, sound, and smell here, touch and taste a moment later) once again seeks to involve the reader. It shares with the earlier passage the concreteness and immediacy of Twain's best writing, but it is far more intense, pitched at a higher key, and it is possible to attribute the emotional power of the passage to a fear of loss. There is no room here for the relaxed humour of the cradle 'waiting, with confidence', none of the tolerant acceptance of the darkness outside; this passage is a propitiatory offering on the altar of nature, as Twain seeks by an act of will to obliterate the distinction between past and present:

> I can see the blue clusters of wild grapes hanging among the foliage of the saplings, and I remember the taste of them and the smell. I know how the wild blackberries looked, and how they tasted, and the same with the pawpaws, the hazelnuts, and the persimmons; and I can feel the thumping rain, upon my head, of hickory nuts and walnuts when we were out in the frosty dawn to scramble for them with the pigs, and the gusts of wind loosed them and sent them down. . . . (Ibid.)

The appeal here is to common experience, involving a solidarity of author and reader. What can be tasted, smelt, felt along the pulses is real, and the only knowledge that matters. Authenticity is attested by being 'there'. The gorgeous, mouth-watering sentence on the watermelon triumphantly affirms the continuing life in nature, as it seeks to break down the customary barriers between author and reader, child and man, perceived and perceiver. Yet what is celebrated here can equally be said to be the artistic imagination, which brings the dead world to life on the page before us:

> I know how a prize watermelon looks when it is sunning its fat rotundity among pumpkin vines and 'simblins'. I know how to tell when it is ripe without 'plugging' it; I know how inviting it looks when it is cooling itself in a tub of water under the bed, waiting; I know how it looks when it lies on the table in the sheltered great floor space between house and kitchen, and the children gathered for the sacrifice and their mouths watering; I know the crackling sound it makes when the carving knife enters its end, and I can see the split fly along in front of the blade as the knife cleaves its way to the other end; I can see its halves fall

81

apart and display the rich red meat and the black seeds, and the heart standing up, a luxury fit for the elect; I know how a boy looks behind a yard-long slice of that melon, and I know how it feels; for I have been there. (Paine, I, 111)

2

Adams and Twain had widely differing conceptions of the form of autobiography. Adams was committed to an austere ideal of selectivity, 'erasure', impersonality; the conscious artist, in such a view, expresses himself by unremitting control over his medium, seeking 'annihilation of self':

> I believe silence now to be the only sensible form of expression. I have deliberately and systematically effaced myself, even in my own history. . . . The ego may pass in a letter or a diary, but not in a serious book. . . . Further, if my own opinion has any value, you will find it only in my general rule of correction: to strike out remorselessly every superfluous word, syllable and letter. Every omission improves.[12]

'Silence' is seen here as both a moral and aesthetic strategy; in other letters, Adams presents silence and withdrawal as explicitly self-protective, a visceral reaction to a debased outer world which nauseates:

> All that remains is to hold one's tongue, and vomit gracefully, until the time comes when no man needs to be sea-sick more. Therefore it is that this year I have withdrawn deeper than ever into the obscurity of my cave, and the fear that I shall say something, if I speak at all, has made me shut my mouth into a sort of lockjaw.
>
> (*Letters*, II, 122–23)

Adams differs from both James and Twain in the doubts he casts on the stability of the ego and the effectiveness of its defences. For Adams, the forces of hostile reality are always on the verge of overwhelming the fortress, and the passage above, with its characteristic self-effacing irony, presents the individual sensibility as a carrier of disease rather than a source of possible renewal. The stance of helpless victim, pervasive in the *Education* as in Adams's letters after the death of his wife, sharply differentiates his version of aesthetic detachment from that of

James, who in tracing in his own autobiography his development as one who lived through the 'imaginative faculty' rather than through 'direct participation', stressed the element of conscious choice as well as native predisposition.[13] Though, as we have seen, there are elements of determinism in the later Twain, both he and James in their autobiographical writings as well as their fiction saw man as an active moral agent. Insofar as Adams in the *Education* expresses a passivity before experience, insofar as his systematic irony devalues the possibility of 'education' as anything but growing awareness of one's own folly, then his attitude toward experience and that of James are incompatible. Roy Pascal suggests that one passage in James's autobiography is a 'direct challenge' to Adams, in the continuing dialogue between the two men: 'No education avails for the intelligence that doesn't stir in it some subjective passions, and on the other hand almost anything that does so act is largely educative.'[14]

Adams's habitual self-distrust and pessimism intensified after his wife's death and, like Twain's pessimism, had its specifically political aspects: both men predicted apocalypse as a revenge against a world that had rejected all political idealism and mocked innocence. Yet as early as 1882, in a letter to his friend and fellow author Hay, Adams expresses radical doubts about the vocation of the artist. Not only is it ignominious to court 'popularity', but to write at all is a sign of weakness, and appearance in print occasions profound 'disgust' and 'shame'. Where James and Twain, in their different ways, celebrate the endurance of the child's apprehension of nature in the artist, 'on whom nothing is lost',[15] Adams sardonically urges infanticide:

> My John Randolph is just coming into the world. Do you know, a book to me always seems a part of myself, a kind of intellectual brat or segment, and I never bring one into the world without a sense of shame. They are naked, helpless and beggarly, yet the poor wretches must live forever and curse their father for their silent tomb. This particular brat is the first I ever detested. He is the only one I never wish to see again; but I know he will live to dance, in the obituaries, over my cold grave. Don't read him, should you by any chance meet him. Kick him gently, and let him go. (*Letters*, I, 341, 342)

83

Adams's comments on the *Education* in letters to friends are rarely this overt in their self-hatred and fear of exposure (or, indeed, in their masochistic identification with the father whose rejection he feared and anticipated). Though these letters again and again proclaim the inevitability of failure, they do so less out of diffidence than out of the conviction that any literary 'experiment' is an assault on the unattainable. Indeed, it is arguable that all the predictions of failure with which he hedged round the *Education* are testimony not to his modesty, but to his vaulting ambition. Modest men do not write monumental, definitive nine-volume histories of their native land, or see their own lives as symbolic of the recent and future course of American history: to have a President for a grandfather and an Ambassador for a father may lead to deep-seated feelings of inadequacy and uncertainty about how to compete with those who have already won all the available prizes, but it is more likely to promote a redirection of goals than a scaling down of ambitions. Adams's choice of an artistic vocation was partly, as with James, a matter of temperament, partly an attempt to find a sphere of activity where none of the previous Adamses had excelled.

In letters to and about James, Adams frequently remarks on the spiritual and artistic affinity between the two. His comment on *The Sacred Fount* is 'I recognised at once that Harry and I had the same disease', and on James's biographical memoir *William Wetmore Story and his Friends* he writes 'verily I believe I wrote it . . . You have written not Story's life, but your own and mine,—pure autobiography,—the more keen for what is beneath, implied, intelligible only to me, and half a dozen other people still living' (*Letters*, II, 333, 414). Thus his statement in a letter to William James that the *Education* resembles a Jamesian novel in its approach to form provides valuable clues to his intentions:

> As for the volume [*Education*], it interests me chiefly as a literary experiment, hitherto, as far as I know, never tried or never successful. Your brother Harry tries such experiments in literary art daily, and would know instantly what I mean; but I doubt whether a dozen people in America—except architects or decorators—would know or care. (*Letters*, II, 490)

The comparison of literature to the visual arts here is typical: consistently Adams stresses *composition*, the concatenation of individual elements into an artistic whole. For James and Adams, the eye of the literary artist is not, as in Twain and romanticism, that of the celebrant, picking out the single animating detail that encapsulates the beauty of the moment, but the practised eye of the professional, who sees the plan in his mind before he begins to work:

> Between artists, or people trying to be artists, the sole interest is that of form. Whether one builds a house, or paints a picture, or tells a story, our point of vision regards only the form—not the matter— . . . The arrangement, the construction, the composition, the art of climax are our only serious study. Now that I have the stuff before me—in clay—I can see where the form fails, but I cannot see how to correct the failures.[16]

All this, of course, is familiar to us from the critical writings of James—what matters is the treatment, not the subject; the artist must be granted his donnée; the choice of a particular 'point of vision' determines what will be seen. The *Education*, like a Jamesian narrative, is controlled by a rigorous principle of unity and seeks to be faithful to a particular point of view, whose limitations it scrupulously respects, while treating them with ironic detachment:

> This is the story of an education, and the person or persons who figure in it are supposed to have values only as educators or educated. The surroundings concern it only so far as they affect education. Sumner, Dana, Palfrey, had values of their own . . . which any one may study in their works; here all appear only as influences on the mind of a boy very nearly the average of most boys in physical and mental stature. (*Education*, Ch. II, p. 753)

Yet, as the above passage indicates, Adams's comparison of his own narrative methods with those of James is profoundly misleading. In the obtrusiveness of the authorial voice, the addresses to the reader, and the persistent drive to generalize experience, seeing the particular events as instances of universal truths, passages like this one resemble the authorial digressions in the novels of Fielding or George Eliot, far more than anything in James. There is relatively little suspense in the *Education*, little opportunity for the reader to share in the errors and confusions of the protagonist, and Adams rarely seeks to render the pressure of immediate experience on the perceiving sensibility,

as both James and Twain do. Everything is reflective, everything is retrospective. Most effective autobiographies, as Roy
Pascal points out, present life as a 'process', an unfolding: 'not
simply the narrative of the voyage, but also the voyage itself'.
The *Education*, though one of the greatest of autobiographies,
deliberately suppresses the 'sense of discovery', in the interests
of thematic unity and 'didactic purpose'.[17] The end is known to
the author and reader from the beginning, and this knowledge
colours all the details: the *Education* is not so much the narrative
presentation of a life as a commentary on it.

> Of all the conditions of his youth which afterwards puzzled the
> grown up man, this disappearance of religion puzzled him most.
> The boy went to church twice every Sunday; he was taught to
> read his Bible, and he learned religious poetry by heart; he
> believed in a mild Deism; he prayed; he went through all the
> forms; but to neither him nor his brothers was religion real. Even
> the mild discipline of the Unitarian church was so irksome that
> they all threw it off at the first possible moment, and never
> afterwards entered a church. The religious instinct had vanished,
> and could not be revived, though one made in later life many
> efforts to recover it. (*Education*, Ch. II, p. 751)

The first thing to say about the passage is that it is a marvellous
piece of controlled, effective prose, exquisitely balanced in its
rhythms, syntax, and choice and placement of words. Like so
much of the *Education*, it is based on the contrast of the boy
and the grown-up man; one feels that the emphasis on being
'puzzled' is not mere ironic pretence, since the summarizing
narrative expresses pattern and emptiness at once, a pattern
which could only be apparent to the older man looking back,
but which reflects a larger historical pattern which the older
man can recognize without being able to explain. The only
offered explanation suggests a return to the magical, inexplicable
world of early childhood, where things appear and vanish at
will. Adams skilfully and unobtrusively moves from the initial
tantalizing generalization to the particular instance and then
back to historical generalization, presenting the boy successively,
in widening circles, as a discrete individual, part of a family,
and a member of a generation. Though the irony, the historian's
stance, and the overriding moral intent—to explore not only his
own lived experience, but that of his generation and that of his

nation—require him to see the boy's encounters with religion as entirely representative (here, too, the boy is 'very nearly the average'), he also seeks to be true to that early experience, as he remembers it, and to recapture it in words.

On several occasions, Adams identified St. Augustine as his model in the *Education*. To some extent the relationship between the *Confessions* and the *Education* is one of ironic inversion: not the narrative of a conversion, progressing from darkness to light, but the discovery of a void. As Yvor Winters has said, Adams's temper was in some ways that of a Puritan allegorist deprived of the certainty of faith: 'instead of seeing God's meaning in every event, he saw the meaninglessness of a godless universe, but with a Calvinistic intensity of vision'.[18] But the main lesson St. Augustine taught Adams was aesthetic:

> Did you ever read the Confessions of St. Augustine, or of Cardinal de Retz, or of Rousseau, or of Benvenuto Cellini, or even of my dear Gibbon? Of them all, I think St. Augustine alone has an idea of literary form,—a notion of writing a story with an end and object, not for the sake of the object, but for the form, like a romance. (*Letters*, II, 490)

Form in the *Education* and the *Confessions* means, above all else, exclusion; anything which does not bear directly on the main theme, fit into the simple determining pattern—in both cases, a journey toward self-knowledge and the discovery of that informing pattern—must be ruthlessly excised, however interesting it may be in its own right. Yet one could argue that the overtness, the drumming insistence, of the pattern in the *Education* is that work's chief aesthetic flaw. In his bitter, fanatical determinism, Adams allows the reader no freedom, as each event narrated conforms to expectations in illustrating the same repetitive moral:

> All that a historian won was a vehement wish to escape. He saw his education complete, and was sorry he ever began it. As a matter of taste, he greatly preferred his eighteenth-century education when God was a father and nature a mother, and all was for the best in a scientific universe. He repudiated all share in the world as it was to be, and yet he could not detect the point where his responsibility began or ended. (*Education*, Ch. XXXI, p. 1138)

As this passage illustrates, the emotional range of the *Education* is narrow, and this stance of studied neutrality, of helpless, weary submission before the inevitable ('he had submitted to force all his life', ibid., p. 1140), seems somehow an abdication on the author's part.

The hiatus of twenty years which gives the book (rather like Twain's *Life on the Mississippi*) a clearly defined two-part structure is, like the choice of third-person narration, a conscious aesthetic strategy by an author concerned to give coherence to his material. But we are entitled to ask, in a book which so consistently interprets events, rather than presenting them and allowing us to draw conclusions, whether experience is being edited, falsified or selectively distorted to fit the pre-existing model. The test is not comparison with historical fact (as attested by some unimaginably unimpeachable source), but verisimilitude, psychological penetration, fidelity to remembered experience, which the artist seeks to render in all its contours. The account of the stealing of the pears in the *Confessions* is no less retrospective and no less analytical, but St. Augustine, unlike Adams, uses the contrast of present enlightenment and earlier darkness to present in powerful and immediate terms the wanderings and confusions of his former self:

> What then did wretched I so love in thee, thou theft of mine, thou deed of darkness, in that sixteenth year of my age? . . . Fair were those pears, but not them did my wretched soul desire; for I had store of better, and those I gathered, only that I might steal. For, when gathered, I flung them away, my only feast therein being my own sin, which I was pleased to enjoy. For if aught of those pears came in my mouth, what sweetened it was the sin. . . . What is, in truth? Who can teach me, save He that enlighteneth my heart, and discovereth its dark corners? What is it which hath come in my mind to enquire, and discuss, and consider? For had I loved the pears I stole, and wished to enjoy them, I might have done it alone, had the bare commission of the theft sufficed to attain my pleasure; nor needed I have inflamed the itching of my desires, by the excitement of accomplices. But since my pleasure was not in those pears, it was in the offence itself, which the company of fellow-sinners occasioned. . . . Behold my God, before Thee, the vivid remembrance of my soul; alone, I had never committed that theft, wherein what I stole pleased me not, but that I stole; not had it alone liked me to do it, nor had I done it.[19]

Here the passionate desire to understand, the attempt to relive the experience by putting it into words, thus encouraging the reader's participation, and the analytical journey into the heart of the experience, are one, and the lyrical, brooding style further reinforces the inseparability of 'remembrance' and enlightenment. Adams recognizes his own inability to unite the 'narrative' and 'didactic' in a long and interesting letter comparing his own autobiography to those of St. Augustine and Rousseau:

> Our failures are not really due to ourselves alone. . . . When I read St. Augustine's *Confessions*, or Rousseau's, I feel certain that their faults, as literary artists, are worse than mine. We have all three undertaken to do what cannot be successfully done—mix narrative and didactic purpose and style. The charm of the effort is not in winning the game but playing it. We all enjoy the failure. St. Augustine's narrative subsides at last into the dry sands of metaphysical theology. Rousseau's narrative fails wholly in didactic result; it subsides into still less artistic egoism. And I found that a narrative style was so incompatible with a didactic or scientific style, that I had to write a long supplementary chapter to explain in scientific terms what I could not put into narration without ruining the narrative. . . .
>
> My conclusion is that we need far more art than ever to accomplish a much smaller artistic effect. That is to say, we are unduly handicapped. We are forced to write science because our purpose is scientific, and cannot be rendered by narrative. (Cater, p. 646)

The perceived conflict of 'narrative' and 'didactic' causes problems in the *Education* not only in the undigested lumps of 'scientific' exposition in Chapters XXXIII-IV, but in the extent to which the didactic aims invade, distort, and impoverish the narrative. If an artist is convinced that his 'purpose' cannot be rendered by narrative, then he is defeated before he begins.

Twain was equally haunted during the composition of his *Autobiography* by the feeling that the task he had undertaken was a hopeless one, beset with internal contradictions, but for different reasons:

> The more I think of this, the more nearly impossible the project seems. The difficulties grow upon me all the time. For instance, the idea of blocking out a consecutive series of events which have happened to me, or which I imagine have happened to me—I

can see that is impossible for me. The only thing possible for me is to talk about the thing that something suggests at the moment— something in the middle of my life, perhaps, or something that happened only a few months ago. (Paine, I, 269)

Adams was convinced that the task of the artist was to strike away the 'mass of stuff' which obscured what really mattered, to reveal the statue imprisoned in the inert stone:

> A man is generally artistic in proportion as he sees what is wrong, and most work is good in proportion not so much to what one leaves in it as to what one strikes out. Hardly anyone who has any faculty of perception can write a volume without saying something worth keeping, but generally he swamps it in a mass of stuff that prevents the reader from noticing it. (Cater, p. 541)

Twain, on the other hand, felt that the act of selection necessarily distorted, that a writer of autobiography who carefully arranged, highlighted, and shaped his material in accordance with a pre-determined end was likely to be deceiving both himself and his reader. In some ways, his attitude toward autobiography resembled that of both Johnson and Boswell toward biography: what matters is not the author's general conclusion, but the authenticating and enlivening detail, not the destination but the journey, not pattern but life. Nothing is too little for so little a creature as man[20]:

> That is what human life consists of—little incidents and big incidents, and they are all the same size if we let them alone. An autobiography that leaves out the little things and enumerates only the big ones is no proper picture of the man's life at all; his life consists of his feelings and his interests, with here and there an incident apparently big or little to hang the feelings on. (Paine, I, 288)

Twain's distrust of the hierarchical and predictable went beyond a conviction that all incidents were equally revelatory, and that a false emphasis on the 'showy episodes' of a life, rather than 'the common experiences which go to make up the life of the average human being' (Paine, II, 245) may simply reflect an author's vanity. His guiding assumption in the *Autobiography* is that truth can be unearthed only in the process of re-living it in the act of writing; present and past are a single continuum, linked in unexpected ways.

After several false starts at composing an autobiographical memoir, at the age of 70 Twain, with great feelings of excitement and release ('When I passed the seventieth mile-stone . . . I instantly realized that I had entered a new country and a new atmosphere'[21]), announced his discovery of an 'apparently systemless system' (Paine, II, 246) ideally suited for autobiography:

> Finally in Florence, in 1904, I hit upon the right way to do an Autobiography: start it at no particular time of your life; wander at your free will all over your life; talk only about the thing that interests you for the moment; drop it the moment its interest threatens to pale, and turn your talk upon the new and more interesting thing that intruded itself into your mind meantime. . . .
> In this way you have the vivid things of the present to make a contrast with memories of like things in the past, and these contrasts have a charm which is all their own. (Paine, I, 193)

One advantage of this method of seemingly random mixture of 'diary and history' is that it 'brings together widely separated things that are in a manner related to each other' (Paine, I, 328); its appeal to both reader and author is that it comprises 'a form and method whereby the past and the present are constantly brought face to face, resulting in contrasts which newly fire up the interest all along like contact of flint with steel' (*ibid.*, II, 245). The metaphors in this last passage are revealing— confrontation, renewal, bringing dying embers to life. Memory, as Twain conceives of it, is not only potentially restorative, but a natural force of unimaginable power, which like the great river in *Life on the Mississippi*, rejoices in its own lawlessness, resisting any attempt to 'curb it or confine it'.[22]

Much of the excitement that Twain derived from his new method in autobiography came from a conviction that he had found a way to tap the springs of the unconscious. He had started on a preliminary version in 1897, after the shock of Susy's death and his wife's consequent severe depression, as a kind of therapy, working on four projected books at once and turning from one to another as the inspiration ran dry: 'I have mapped out four books this morning, and will begin an emancipated life this afternoon.'[23] Twain's discovery of the method of free association inaugurated a second concentrated period of creativity immediately following his wife's death, to which he seems to have reacted with characteristic ambivalence, alternating feelings of deep unworthiness and unassuageable loss with a sense of release amounting to elation. If we can accept Van Wyck Brooks's identification of Livy Clemens with the forces of civilization and respectability as they were internalized in Twain himself—Aunt Polly rather than Miss Watson—then an additional dimension becomes apparent in a long, amusing satirical fantasia on men's clothing included among 'Chapters from my Autobiography' in the *North American Review*:

> The men, dressed in dismal black, are scattered here and there and everywhere over the Garden, like so many charred stumps, and they damage the effect, but cannot annihilate it. . . . I would like to dress in a loose and flowing costume made all of silks and velvets, resplendent with all the stunning dyes of the rainbow, and so would any man I have ever known; but none of us dares to venture it. . . . It is the way human beings are made; they are always keeping their true feelings shut up inside, and publicly exploiting their fictitious ones.
>
> Next after fine colours, I like plain white. One of my sorrows, when the summer ends, is that I must put off my cheery and comfortable white clothes and enter for the winter into the depressing captivity of the shapeless and depressing black mass. . . .
>
> I am nearly seventy-one, and I recognize that my age has given me a good many privileges; valuable privileges; privileges which are not granted to younger persons. Little by little I hope to get together courage enough to wear white clothes all through the winter, in New York. It will be a great satisfaction for me to show off in this way; and perhaps the largest of all the satisfactions will be the knowledge that every scoffer, of my sex, will secretly envy me and wish he had dared to follow my lead.[24]

In old age, Twain suggests, one can return to the freedom of childhood, identified here with the unconscious desires and energies whose expression men come to fear. The reason men willingly enter a 'captivity' they know to be 'degrading' is that repression is intrinsic to civilization and to such of its bastions as marriage, the home, professional advancement—the 'family conscience' (Paine, II, 25) to which most people, as Twain tells us in another passage, sacrifice their moral independence. Moral cowardice is one of the main charges Twain levels at man in his later satiric writings, and in the *Autobiography* he does not exempt himself from the charges:

> Every man is in his own person the whole human race, with not a detail lacking. I am the whole human race without a detail lacking. I have studied the human race with diligence and strong interest all these years in my own person; in myself I find in big or little proportion every quality and every defect that is findable in the mass of the race. . . . What a coward man is! and how surely he will find it out if he will just let other people alone and sit down and examine himself. The human race is a race of cowards; and I am not only marching in that procession but carrying a banner. (*MTE*, xxix)

It is striking how Twain, at the very beginning of the *Autobiography*, sees man's 'real life', and hence the material of autobiography, in terms of unconscious forces. The secret life of the mind is presented here in powerfully physical terms; Twain's metaphors evoke a fearsome subterranean force which must for reasons of psychic equilibrium or propriety remain hidden, but which *will* be expressed, one way or another:

> What a wee little part of a person's life are his acts and words! His real life is led in his head, and is known to none but himself. All day long, and every day, the mill of his brain is grinding, and his thoughts, not those other things, are his history. His acts and his words are merely the visible, thin crust of his world, with its scattered snow summits and its vacant wastes of water—and they are so trifling a part of his bulk! a mere skin enveloping it. The mass of him is hidden—it and its volcanic fires that toss and boil, and never rest, night nor day. (Paine, I, 2)

From this basic perception about the nature of human existence, Twain draws two different conclusions: first, that no autobiography could ever do justice to 'the storm of thoughts that is forever blowing through one's head', so that the writer of autobiography is engaged in an impossible task; second, that the only way to write an autobiography with any pretensions of truth is to submit oneself to the flow. In a passage of serio-comic fantasy reminiscent of *Tristram Shandy*, he imagines a monstrous autobiography coterminous with a man's life, endlessly increasing in bulk as the days pass:

> Fifteen stenographers hard at work couldn't keep up. Therefore a full autobiography has never been written, and it never will be. It

would consist of 365 double-size volumes per year—and so if I had been doing my whole autobiographical duty ever since my youth, all the library buildings on the earth could not contain the result. (Paine, I, 283)

Yet elsewhere he sees the random and protean not as threats, but as the artist's guide and inspiration, suggesting to him ways of distinguishing the 'real' from the 'artificial', pleasure from 'work'.[25] Like the Freudian method of free association it so resembles, Twain's 'wandering' is a way of reaching the truth by unexpected paths, finding access to the volcanic fires which underlie the quotidian:

> *The thing uppermost in a person's mind* is the thing to talk about or write about. The thing of new and immediate interest is the pleasantest text he can have. . . . That text, when I am done with it—if I ever get done with it, and I don't seem to get done with any text—but it doesn't matter, I am not interested in getting done with anything. I am only interested in talking along and wandering around as much as I want to, regardless of results. . . . As soon as I wander from the present text—the thought of today—that digression takes me far and wide over an uncharted sea of recollection. (Paine, I, 327)

Like his fellow satirist Swift, Twain held consistently to the view that the artist's primary responsibility was to speak the truth, while recognizing the strength of the defences by which both society and the psyche keep the truth at bay: 'There were things which he stretched, but mainly he told the truth. That is nothing. I never seen anybody but lied, one time or another.'[26] In *Huck Finn* (rather as with Synge on the Aran Islands), Twain sought truth through the vernacular, submerging his own personality in that of his uneducated speaker. A similar dislike of the evasions and formal constraints of 'literary' language is evident in his comments on the *Autobiography* as well as a similar conviction that the heart not the mind is the seat of truth, so that the artist must work backwards, stripping away the encrustations of civilization as he approaches the source. As De Voto has remarked, Twain's 'artistic creativeness . . . was rooted in his boyhood', and he reworked the rich Hannibal vein over and over again (*MTE*, p. xvii). But in a letter to Howells about the *Autobiography*, his emphasis is somewhat different; here it is not the artist who unearths the hidden truth, but the reader who is enabled to find the writer out despite all the writer's equivocations and distortions. An author may not understand his own experience and may be self-serving in his motivation; nevertheless, the words he commits to paper provide clues which may be deciphered, telling the truth he was unable to see for himself:

> An Autobiography is the truest of all books; for while it inevitably consists mainly of extinctions of the truth, skirtings of the truth, partial revealments of the truth, with hardly an instance of plain straight truth, the remorseless truth *is* there, between the lines, where the author-cat is raking dust upon it which hides from the disinterested spectator neither it nor its smell. The result being that the reader knows the author in spite of his wily diligences. (*Mark Twain-Howells Letters*, II, 782)

In arguing the advantages of the vernacular style as against the rigid confinement of the 'decorous', carefully considered prose society expects of its authors—'too literary, too prim, too nice'—Twain characteristically associates colloquial language both with nature and with impulse (Paine, I, 237). Words should flow like a brook or like the wind of inspiration; the artist acts as a kind of Æolian harp, or invokes the deity by imitating it in his sentence structure:

> And you will be astonished (and charmed) to see how like *talk* it is, and how real it sounds, and how well and compactly and sequentially it constructs itself, and what a dewy and breezy and woodsy freshness it has, and what a darling and worshipful absence of the signs of starch, and flatiron, and labor and fuss and the other artificialities. . . . There are little slips here and there, little inexactnesses . . . but these are not blemishes, they are merits, their removal would take away the naturalness of the flow and banish the very thing—the nameless something—which differentiates real narrative from artificial and makes the one so vastly better than the other. (*Mark Twain-Howells Letters*, II, 778)

Twain is recommending a particular technical innovation to his fellow writer Howells, the experiment of dictating a literary wish rather than slowly labouring over the materials with a pen (Howells declined the advice, and said he would go on writing his works by hand). But the real interest in the passage lies in its making explicit the moral and aesthetic principle which underlies both the *Autobiography* and Twain's other major writings, the impulse toward communion. Nature knows no barriers, and the artist must strive after the same inclusiveness, the same spontaneity, in his endless search to discover and express elusive truth:

> With the pen in one's hand, narrative is a difficult art; narrative should flow as flows the brook down through the hills and the leafy woodlands, its course changed by every boulder it comes across and by every grass-clad gravelly spur that projects into its path; its surface broken, but its course not stayed by rock and gravel on the bottom in the shoal places; a brook that never goes straight for a minute, but *goes*, and goes briskly, sometimes ungrammatically, and sometimes fetching a horseshoe three-quarters of a mile around, and at the end of the circuit flowing within a yard of the path it traversed an hour before; but always *going*, and always following at least one law, always loyal to that law, the law of *narrative*, which *has no law*. Nothing to do but make the trip; the how of it is not important, so that the trip is made. (Paine, I, 237)

3

What then makes these two strange books—one of them published in a tiny edition of 100 copies and circulated, almost in a clandestine way, to a small group of friends, and one of them never yet fully published, existing only in scattered fragments difficult of access, the idea of a book still not come to fruition—so compelling? What justifies us in seeing these two works, labelled by their authors as failures, as among the greatest works of their age? Part of the answer lies in the unrelenting honesty of each author, in the dedicated search for truth that each book embodies. That honesty is in no sense sexual, or even emotional; each book is the work of a deeply reticent man who never relaxes his defences even in a work intended to strip away the veils of conventionality. Though Twain (who characterizes himself as 'born *reserved* as to endearments of speech, and caresses') talks about sexual frankness at several points in the *Autobiography*, he never exhibits it. An unrepressed state ('don't be ashamed; don't be afraid') in which men and women are no longer 'servants of convention' is presented as unattainable ideal, and his account of the 'daring frankness' with which he and the young writer Elinor Glyn conversed is quite extraordinarily coy and euphemistic:

> Take it all around, it was a very pleasant conversation, and glaringly unprintable, particularly those considerable parts of it to which I haven't had the courage to more than vaguely hint at in this account of our talk.[27]

The stance of uncompromising honesty in both books, then, is directed outward as much as inward, and both authors see themselves as instances of persistent self-deception even in the would-be truth seeker. The one great, shaming folly from which both authors present themselves as free is the fear of death. Standing on the edge of the grave, with the conviction that there is nothing left to lose, Adams and Twain can leave a testament to later times. Adams, who ends his autobiography with an 'assent to dismissal' on hearing of Hay's death, begins it by stating his intention 'as teacher' to present his own life as 'working model' or guide 'to avoid, or to follow' (pp. 721, 1181); Twain, too, sees his *Autobiography* as a message left behind for posterity, written by one 'who shall be dead when this book issues from the press':

> I speak from the grave rather than with my living tongue, for a good reason: I can speak thence freely. When a man is writing a book dealing with the privacies of his life—a book which is to be read while he is still alive—he shrinks from speaking his whole frank mind; all his attempts to do it fail, he recognizes that he is trying to do a thing which is impossible to a human being. . . . It has seemed to me that I could be as frank and free and un-embarrassed as a love letter if I knew that what I was writing would be exposed to no eye until I was dead, and unaware, and indifferent. (Paine, I, xv-xvi)

The peculiar mixture of secrecy and openness here reflects Twain's awareness of the status of his book as subversive scripture. His legacy, like that of Adams in the *Education*, is intended to disturb, as it re-tells the ruling myth of American promise as a testament of loss of faith. One thing that unites the *Education* and the *Autobiography* is that both books are meditations on history, in which the individual life is seen as representative or paradigmatic, a node of energy on which historical forces can be shown to operate: 'The object of study is the garment, not the figure' (*Education*, Preface, p. 722). Like Twain, Adams was fond of using the language of contemporary science to demonstrate human impotence, and the scorn he directed at those who would exalt the dignity of man suggests, as with Twain, that the cynic was a disappointed idealist:

> The sum of force attracts; the feeble atom or molecule called man is attracted; he suffers education or growth; he is the sum of the forces that attract him; his body and his thought are alike their product; the movement of the forces controls the progress of his mind, since he can know nothing but the motions which impinge on his senses, whose sum makes education.
>
> (*Education*, Ch. XXXIII, p. 1153)

The failure which both Adams and Twain wrote obsessively about was the failure of America, as they preceived it, the ever-receding dream of youth and hope. Adams's *History of the United States* and his *Education* enact the same story, a decline from innocent virtue to tainted knowledge. Adams's historical necessitarianism, as George Hochfield has pointed out, reinforces his conviction that idealism in men and nations 'must have been doomed from the start by the very nature of history. . . . Failure induces resignation to the forces that make failure inevitable'.[28] This suggests a certain ambivalence toward innocence in both Adams and Twain, who present the catastrophic journey from 'unity' to 'multiplicity' in the individual life and the American nation as though it were an unalterable law; one cannot learn from experience, but only decline, enacting a predetermined rôle. And yet the very existence of the *Education* and *Autobiography*, each in its own way a tribute to the innocent eye and the hunger for experience, serves to refute the strong strain of pessimism running through both works. The composition of a book is in itself an act of faith, and each reader is a potential disciple. Both Adams and Twain, somewhat unexpectedly, present women as intrinsically 'superior' to men, embodying energies which are potentially creative rather than destructive, even though they may be unable to find satisfactory outlets for these vital energies.[29] Thus we can say of the aristocrat Adams as of the democrat Twain that seventy years of exposure to nineteenth-century American society led them to the same conclusion: not an abandonment of hope, but its redirection. As Adams wrote in 1910:

> My idea is that the world outside—the so-called modern world—can only pervert and degrade the conceptions of the primitive instinct of art and feeling, and that our only chance is to accept the limited number of survivors . . . and to intensify the energy of feeling within that radiant centre. (*Letters*, II, 546)[30]

What may not be immediately apparent is that both the *Education* and *Autobiography* are profoundly political in their concerns. Each work is an essay in de-mythologizing, which mounts a coherent critique of the capitalist ethos as it had developed in America in the later nineteenth century. Though Twain in particular seeks to provide a counter-myth to the prevailing ideology of the day, neither holds out any real hope of reversing the course of history, however much they may deplore its manifestations. In a letter to Hay of 1910, Adams, defining his position in terms which would apply equally well to Twain, speaks of himself as 'one who belongs wholly to the past, and whose traditional sympathies are with all the forces that resist concentration, and love what used to be called liberty, but has now become anarchy, or resistance to civilization' (*Letters*, II, 290). As in so many of the comments of both men on political issues of the day, the tone of this letter oddly mixes nostalgia and apocalypticism. Both Twain and Adams were fascinated and repelled by power ('I gravitate to a capital by a primary law of nature,' Adams wrote in 1877: 'here too I can fancy that we are of use in the world'), and both were particularly offended by the concentration of economic power which led to wholesale bribery and corruption and the naked worship of the dollar.[31] The political education of both men began in the 1870s, with the ascendancy of the charismatic, dishonest James G. Blaine, memorably portrayed in Adams's novel *Democracy*, and culminated with the Presidency of Theodore Roosevelt, whom both men knew and extravagantly loathed as the embodiment of a kind of monstrous parody of innocence, the small boy turned bully. Twain, revealingly, called Roosevelt 'the Tom Sawyer of the political world of the twentieth century' in a strong attack on his imperialist policies (*MTE*, p. 49). This association of his *bête noire* with his own creation (a character based, as the

Autobiography makes clear, not simply on Twain's early Hannibal experience, but on the young Samuel Clemens) might suggest a partial explanation for the bitterness and feelings of impotence so pervasive in the *Autobiography*; like Adams, scourging the naïveté of the younger self seeking an education in the world, he blames himself for the failure of the dream. Yet even when predicting the imminent demise of American democracy, the satirist and novelist in Twain suggests a possible cure in the terms of the diagnosis:

> Human nature being what it is, I suppose we must drift into monarchy by and by. It is a saddening thought but we cannot change our nature—we are all alike, we human beings; and in our blood and bone, and ineradicably, we carry the seeds out of which monarchies and aristocracies are grown: worship of gauds, titles, distinctions, power. We have to worship these things and their possessors, we are all born so and we cannot help it. (*MTE*, p. 64)

If a passage like this, or the many comparable passages in the *Education*, seems to us the reverse of dispiriting, it is partly because any work of art, even one of 'unmitigated blackness', is what James in a letter to Adams called 'an act of life'. Though James is arguing against Adams in presenting art as antidote to despair, the terms he uses are applicable to Adams's own writings, and indeed James makes this connection explicitly ('you perform them still yourself . . . it's a blessing that you understand'). The artist builds an ark out of the materials of despair, and in the midst of death affirms continuing life:

> *Of course* we are lone survivors, of course the past that was our lives is at the bottom of an abyss—if the abyss *has* any bottom; of course, too, there's no use talking unless one particularly *wants* to. But the purpose, almost, of my printed divagations was to show you that one *can*, strange to say, still want to. . . . I still find my consciousness interesting. . . . *Why* mine yields an interest I don't know that I can tell you, but I don't challenge or quarrel with it. . . . It's, I suppose, because I am that queer monster, the artist, an obstinate finality, an inexhaustible sensibility. . . . It all takes doing, and I *do*. I believe I shall do yet again—it is still an act of life.[32]

100

NOTES

1. J. C. Levenson, *The Mind and Art of Henry Adams* (Boston, 1957), p. 15; *Letters of Henry Adams*, ed. Worthington Chauncey Ford, 2 vols. (Boston, 1930–38), II, p. 251.
2. *Letters*, II, p. 450.
3. Eugenia Kaledin, *The Education of Mrs. Henry Adams* (Philadelphia, 1981), pp. 165–66; Henry James, *Letters*, ed. Leon Edel (London, 1974–   ), II, p. 307; Elizabeth Stevenson, *Henry Adams: A Biography* (New York, 1956), p. 141. For an account of the relationship between Adams and James, see Robert F. Sayre, *The Examined Self: Benjamin Franklin, Henry Adams, Henry James* (Princeton, 1964), pp. 44–89; on James's use of the Adamses in fiction, see ibid., pp. 55–8, 62–5.
4. Kaledin, pp. 161–62.
5. Kaledin, pp. 77, 181; James, *Letters*, I, p. 208.
6. *Letters*, I, pp. 223, 227, 229.
7. *The Education of Henry Adams*, in *Henry Adams* (New York: Library of America, 1983), pp. 982–83; all subsequent references to the *Education* and to *Mont Saint Michel and Chartres* will be to this standard edition.
8. *The Autobiography of Mark Twain*, ed. Charles Neider (New York, 1975), p. 408; subsequent references to Neider.
9. Neider, pp. 403, 413. There is no adequate modern edition of the *Autobiography*. Passages from the *Autobiography* appear in four printed sources: Neider; *Mark Twain's Autobiography*, ed. Albert Bigelow Paine, 2 vols. (New York and London, 1924); *Mark Twain in Eruption*, ed. Bernard de Voto (New York, 1940); and, in twenty-five instalments, in *North American Review*, Vols. 183–84 (September 1906–December 1907). Subsequent references will be to Paine, *MTE*, and *NAR*. Passages quoted from Neider normally appear only there; where a passage occurs in both Neider and Paine, Paine usually provides a superior text, since Neider's text is 'arranged' and reorganized, as well as being cut severely. A complete typescript of the *Autobiography*, except for those passages published in Paine and *NAR*, is preserved among the Mark Twain Papers, University of California; presumably, a complete edition will eventually appear as part of the California edition of *The Works of Mark Twain*.
10. In Paine's edition, which follows Twain's original dictation, this section of the *Autobiography* begins with an account of Susy's final illness and death. The passage quoted, in a paragraph beginning with the words 'The summer season of Susy's childhood', thus alludes not only to Susy's early death but to the blighting of the father's hopes of renewal through his daughter. Neider's edition lessens the effect of the passage considerably by rearranging the material chronologically, destroying any unity of conception by placing the account of Susy's death in a chapter by itself on pp. 373–75, inserting before the passage quoted a paragraph and several sentences taken from other sections of the Autobiography, and inventing an entirely new context for the passage, which appears on p. 209 of his edition.

11. See Leo Marx, 'The Pilot and the Passenger: Landscape Conventions and the Style of *Huckleberry Finn*', in *Mark Twain: A Collection of Critical Essays*, ed. Henry Nash Smith (Englewood Cliffs, N.J., 1963), pp. 47–63; and Tony Tanner, *The Reign of Wonder* (Cambridge, 1977), pp. 127–83.

12. *Letters*, I, p. 132; II, pp. 70–1; John Pilling, *Autobiography and Imagination* (London, 1981), p. 9.

13. Henry James, *Autobiography*, ed. Frederick W. Dupee (New York, 1956), pp. 112, 454–55. See the discussions of James's autobiographical writings in Roy Pascal, *Design and Truth in Autobiography* (London, 1960), pp. 140–42; and in F. W. Dupee, *Henry James* (London, 1951), pp. 27–35.

14. Pascal, p. 142; Leon Edel, *The Life of Henry James*, 2 vols. (Harmondsworth, 1977), I, pp. 99–100.

15. Henry James, 'The Art of Fiction', in *The Future of the Novel*, ed. Leon Edel (New York, 1956), p. 13.

16. *Henry Adams and his Friends*, ed. Harold Dean Cater (Boston, 1947), pp. 614–15; Pilling, p. 15. Subsequent references will be to Cater. For further parallels between Adams and James, see R. P. Blackmur, 'The Expense of Greatness', in *The Lion and the Honeycomb* (New York, 1955), pp. 79–96.

17. Pascal, p. 182; Cater, p. 645.

18. Yvor Winters, *In Defense of Reason* (Denver, 1947), p. 405; quoted in George Hochfield, *Henry Adams* (New York, 1962), p. 116.

19. *The Confessions of St. Augustine*, tr. E. B. Pusey (London, 1953), Book II, par. 12, 16, 17, pp. 27–31; cf. Sayre, *The Examined Self*, pp. 7–12.

20. *Boswell's London Journal, 1763–1763*, ed. Frederick A. Pottle (London, 1950), p. 305. For parallels, see *Rambler*, No. 60; *Idler*, No. 84; and James Boswell, *Life of Johnson*, ed. R. W. Chapman (London, 1953), pp. 22–6.

21. *NAR*, 184 (1907), p. 677.

22. *Life on the Mississippi*, ed. James M. Cox (Harmondsworth: Penguin Books, 1984), Ch. XXVIII, p. 205.

23. Letter to Wayne MacVeigh, 22 August 1897, in William Macnaughton, *Mark Twain's Last Years as a Writer* (Columbia, Missouri, and London, 1979), p. 27. He told Howells of his need to work incessantly because of 'the deadness which invaded me when Susy died'; see *Mark Twain-Howells Letters*, ed. Henry Nash Smith and William M. Gibson, 2 vols. (Cambridge, Mass., 1960), II, p. 670; Philip S. Foner, *Mark Twain Social Critic* (New York, 1972), p. 44; and Bernard De Voto, 'The Symbols of Despair', in *Mark Twain*, ed. Smith, pp. 143–44.

24. *NAR*, 184 (1907), pp. 676–77. The passage is not printed in Paine, Neider, or *MTE*. See Van Wyck Brooks, *The Ordeal of Mark Twain* (London, 1934), esp. pp. 130–62, 219–30.

25. *Mark Twain-Howells Letters*, II, p. 778; Paine, I, p. 327.

26. Mark Twain, *The Adventures of Huckleberry Finn*, ed. Peter Coveney (Harmondsworth, 1966), Chapter I, p. 49.

27. Paine, II, p. 27; *MTE*, pp. 209, 316, 318–19.

28. Hochfield, *Henry Adams*, p. 71.

29. *Education*, Chapters XXV, XXX, pp. 1070–72, 1123–128; cf. Paine, II, pp. 26–8, 48–51.

30. Tony Tanner, in his interesting essay 'The Lost America—The Despair of Henry Adams and Mark Twain', in *Mark Twain*, ed. Smith, pp. 159–74, sees no element of hope in either Adams or the later Twain. Tanner does not discuss the *Autobiography*.
31. *Letters*, I, p. 302. On the unaffiliated reformist 'mugwump' allegiances of the two men, see Paine, II, pp. 15, 160–61; *Education*, Chapters XVIII–XIX; and Adams, *Letters*, I, p. 184. On the rôle of Blaine's candidacy in the development of Twain's political and moral views, see Paine, II, pp. 6–26.
32. *Selected Letters of Henry James*, ed. Leon Edel (London, 1956), pp. 204–5; cf. Levenson, *The Mind and Art of Henry Adams*, pp. 382–85.

5

Henry James's Autobiography: The Education of a Novelist

by DAVID ELLIS

1

From time to time a casual literary allusion provides a useful indication of the relativity of taste. Trying to convince his brother Edmund that play-acting would not be wholly out of place in Mansfield Park, Tom Bertram reminds him how as boys they 'mourned over the dead body of Julius Caesar, and "to be'd" and "not to be'd", in this very room, for his amusement! And I am sure', he adds, ' "my name was Norval", every evening of my life through one Christmas holidays.'[1] The playwright with the honour of being cheek by jowl with Shakespeare here is John Home whose *Douglas* (1757) held a prominent place in the repertory for over a hundred years. But who now reads *Douglas* or can be heard claiming that his name is Norval? To realize how easily the minor classics of one age can find themselves in the literary dustbin of the next guards against the instinctive illusion that the taste of our own time is the culminating point in some evolutionary process.

Works which, outside specialist circles, are so relatively under-valued as the three volumes of James's 'Autobiography'[2]— *A Small Boy and Others* (1913), *Notes of a Son and Brother* (1914) and the unfinished *The Middle Years* (1917)—can only benefit from a reminder that standards, or at least reading habits, are not fixed for ever. He himself provides another such reminder when, close to the beginning of *A Small Boy and Others*, he alludes to a work of similar vintage and style as Home's *Douglas*. The occasion is his recollection of holidays spent with his family at a hotel on 'the south Long Island shore'. It was there, he says, that he quite 'succumbed to the charm of the world seen in a larger way':

> For there, incomparably, was the chance to dawdle and gape; there were human appearances in endless variety and on the exhibition-stage of a piazza that my gape measured almost as by miles; it was even as if I had become positively conscious that the social scene so peopled would pretty well always say more to me than anything else. What it did say I of course but scantly understood; but I none the less knew it spoke, and I listened to its voice, I seem to recall, very much as 'young Edwin', in Dr. Beattie's poem, listened to the roar of tempests and torrents from the nobler eminence of beetling crags and in exposure to still deeper abysses. (20)

Whether or not 'Dr. Beattie's poem' held its place longer in America than in its country of origin, it must now be a long time since it had any other existence on either side of the Atlantic beyond that of putative forerunner to Wordsworth's *Prelude*. Between the present currency of *Douglas* and of Beattie's *The Minstrel: or, The Progress of Genius* there would not be much to choose. *The Minstrel*'s appearance here is a datum for the history of American taste, but it also significantly re-enforces the distinction James is anxious to make. Although his Autobiography began as a tribute to his brother and retained throughout many features of the family memoir, it is also and perhaps predominantly a portrait of the artist. With rather more justification than Wordsworth could James have said towards the end of his 'long labour' that Imagination had been its 'moving soul'.[3] Like *The Prelude*, James's Autobiography traces the growth of a mind, but the mind of a novelist rather than a minstrel or poet. The chief agency of development—of education, is not therefore 'Nature', as it is for 'young Edwin' or, rather more memorably, for the young Wordsworth, but 'human appearances in endless variety . . . the social scene'. James's Autobiography is the record of someone not totally insensible to the natural world but inclined nevertheless to treat it as incidental: a setting for human action or for art. Shortly after installing himself in Lamb House, his thoughts turned to improving his garden. At that time, Leon Edel records, 'he barely knew a dahlia from a mignonette.'[4]

The contrast between novelists and poets, and the training appropriate to each, runs throughout James's three volumes which in one sense are just as much a pondering on an experiment in education as the autobiography of J. S. Mill. Announced here at the beginning of the autobiographical enterprise, it receives its longest and most explicit development in the wonderfully elaborated description of visits to two leading literary celebrities just before *The Middle Years* breaks off. That both of these initially belong (like Beattie) to the history of literature in Britain can be offered as a mnemonic for how many of the influences James describes as determining his life can be adduced to lessen the scandal of an approach to the Autobiography from an English point of view—especially when enumeration of those influences is joined with the recollection of where and who James was when he wrote it. (The most difficult truth to keep in mind when reading autobiographies is that they are always descriptions of present as well as past selves.) One of the celebrities James describes meeting is Tennyson, generally regarded at the time—the 1870s—as conforming more closely than anyone else to the ideal of the poet, particularly the poet in his more traditional, Romantic guise of minstrel or bard ('the Bard' is what James persistently calls him). After an important account of a preliminary meeting, James tells how he was taken by his friend Mrs. Greville to Tennyson's country house at Aldworth and there had confirmed his previous impression of a startling contrast between the coarse humour and rough cordiality of his host and the qualities one might have attributed to him from reading his poems. (As an essay on a literary enthusiast's disappointed expectations, the whole episode bears comparison with Proust's classic treatment of Marcel and Bergotte.)[5] That Tennyson is not 'pale and penetrating and emphasizing in every aspect that he was fastidious' (586) is corroborated when Mrs. Greville happens to mention that she has a French relative called Laure de Sade. The Poet Laureate is stirred by this allusion into talking at great length about the

Marquis de Sade and his various books. What was most remarkable about the occasion, James comments, is that it left

> none of us save myself, by my impression, in the least embarrassed or bewildered; largely, I think, because of the failure—a failure the most charmingly flat—of all measure on the part of the auditors and speaker alike of what might be intended or understood, of what, in fine, the latter was talking about.

And as if that were not enough, he says in a devastating addendum,

> [Tennyson] struck me in truth as neither knowing nor communicating knowledge, and I recall how I felt this note in his own case to belong to that general intimation with which the whole air was charged of the want of proportion between the great spaces and reaches and echoes commanded, the great eminence attained, and the quantity and variety of experience supposable. (591)

This revelation prepares the ground for what comes later, after James has 'made bold to suggest that [Tennyson] should spout' (something—the general implication is—he was always perhaps slightly too willing to do); and after he has requested 'Locksley Hall' as his favourite amongst all the works of the poet he has 'earliest known and best loved'. Sitting in the Bard's study, looking out into a wet and dull English countryside, James has to ask himself why he fails 'to swoon away under the heaviest pressure I had doubtless ever known the romantic situation bring to bear'. He has to pinch himself, not at all to keep from swooning

> but much rather to set up some rush of sensibility. It was all interesting, it was at least all odd; but why in the name of poetic justice had one anciently heaved and flushed with one's own recital of the splendid stuff if one was now only to sigh in secret, 'Oh dear, oh dear'?

The answer is not merely that, in the arresting, summarizing phrase most frequently recalled from this episode, Tennyson did not turn out to be Tennysonian.

> What the case came to for me, I take it—and by the case I mean the intellectual, the artistic—was that it lacked the intelligence, the play of discrimination, I should have taken for granted in it. . . .

107

This disappointment does not make Tennyson any less of a poet for James, or at least any less of a poet of a certain type.

> My critical reaction hadn't in the least invalidated our great man's being a Bard—it had in fact made him and left him more of a Bard than ever: it had only settled to my perception as not before what a Bard might and mightn't be. (592–93).

Coming as it does at almost the end of *The Middle Years*, this conveniently explicit summing-up of the Bardic character can be seen as triumphantly justifying what might be called a 'life-choice': a direction which James is conscious of having taken as early as those family holidays on the south Long Island shore. Analogous moments are very common in auto-biographies, help to structure them and can of course *be* common because the point of view is always retrospective. The meeting with Tennyson does have a self-justifying effect, but to associate it too closely with any specific category of auto-biographical event would be to risk making it appear simpler than anything in late James could ever be. Notoriously, simplicity is not exactly the most striking feature of his Autobiography which, if it recounts the growth of a novelist's rather than poet's mind, does nevertheless have one charac-teristic conventionally attributed to poetry in being scarcely paraphraseable. To give an account of incidents in it which is manageably brief, and free from gross distortion, is very difficult, as I think can be demonstrated by examining closely Leon Edel's inevitable reliance on the Autobiography in his life of James.[6] Certainly it would be distorting here not to make clear that James's description of his visit to Tennyson and his reflections on the Bardic character are in the context of one he recalls having made the day before to the house of Witley in Surrey where George Eliot and G. H. Lewes lived. His companion on this occasion was the same Mrs. Greville who provided such a guarantee of warm welcome at Aldworth. That she could not quite do the same at Witley is evident from James catching once again as he writes,

> the impression of no occurrence of anything at all appreciable but their liking us to have come, with our terribly trivial con-tribution, mainly from a prevision of how they should more devoutly like it when we departed. (582–83)

108

The 'chill desert' of the room where James and Mrs. Greville are received seemed to contain, he recalls, 'rather the minimum of the paraphernalia of reading and writing, not to speak of that of tea, a conceivable feature of the hour, but which was not provided for' (593). Lewes makes clear that their visit is not much appreciated by becoming sociable and animated only as they are about to leave. It is then that, with Mrs. Greville already in the carriage (and as everyone who has ever read *The Middle Years* remembers), Lewes thrusts into James's hand a pair of blue-bound volumes with the desperate cry, 'Ah those books—take them away, please, away, away!' Only when he is in the carriage is James able to confirm that the two volumes are indeed his own latest work (*The Europeans*), passed on to the Leweses by Mrs. Greville—a loan

> dropped with the best conscience in the world into the Witley abyss out of which it had jumped with violence, under the touch of accident, straight up again into my own exposed face. (583)

The immediate point of this rather painful incident lies in its contrast with Tennyson's treatment of James as a fellow-writer. In talking of his preliminary meetings with the great poet, before the visit to Aldworth, James records his stupefaction at discovering that Tennyson had actually read one of his stories; and had not only read it but been willing to tell James it was excellent and 'more to his taste than no matter what other like attempt'. 'My alarmed sense of the Bard's restriction to giving what he had as a bard only', he writes, 'became under a single turn of his hand a vision of quite general munificence' (589). The hint here of self-mockery is taken up when, in a remark which can nevertheless be taken seriously and as a sign of good nature, James adds that this approval of the author of *In Memoriam* for his own twenty pages meant that he would like Tennyson for ever. It may well be that it is this confession which encourages Edel to say in his biography, as he attempts with self-imposed and perhaps inevitable economy to convey the significance of the two meetings, that praise from the Poet Laureate was 'some kind of compensation for the rebuff at the Leweses'.[7] But although it is true that in writing of his drive out to Aldworth, James recalls comparing Tennyson's recent compliments with the even more recent behaviour of Lewes, and drawing from the comparison the comforting feeling that he and Mrs. Greville were likely to be better received at Aldworth than they had been at Witley, that emphasis is surely very misleading. It must be when what happens at Aldworth exemplifies the sad, familiar truth that there is usually far more praise around from those not qualified to give it than from those who are. Human, or perhaps in this case Jamesian, nature being what it is, Tennyson's lack of qualifications does not prevent James from responding to his approval; but that he could ever have wanted his readers to see it in the light of 'compensation' is made improbable by the trouble he takes to describe the benefit he derived from what Edel calls Lewes's 'rebuff'. He does not deny that the incident inflicted 'a bruise', even though in returning Mrs. Greville's loan of the books and thus James's own 'unattended plea', Lewes was clearly ignorant of the identity of their author; but he considers in retrospect that this bruise, 'this particular wrong—inflicted all unawares, which exactly made it sublime—was the only rightness of our visit.' 'I quite recall my grasp of the *interest* of our distinguished friends' inaccessibility to the unattended plea, with the light it seemed to throw on what it was really to *be* attended' (584). Explaining that for his plea to be attended in this instance would have meant presumptions on his part far other than any then 'hanging about' him, James goes on to claim that the line of thought started here led to a 'finally just qualified beatitude'— qualified because, although he feels he has profited from Lewes's behaviour and 'even positively enjoyed in my own person adorning such a tale', he is sorry for any pain Mrs. Greville might have suffered. That aside,

> there was positively a fine high thrill in thinking of persons—or at least of a person, for any fact about Lewes was but derivative— engaged in my own pursuit and yet detached, by what I conceived, detached by a pitch of intellectual life, from all that made it actual to myself. *There* was the lift of contemplation, there the inspiring image and big supporting truth; . . . (584)

The parenthesis which concerns Lewes suggests that even James cannot wholly free himself from the resentment to which any humiliating experience gives rise; but it does not destroy the general impression of humiliation sufficiently mastered for there to be no need to seek compensation elsewhere. On the contrary, James makes it clear that there was more interest, value and even perhaps as much genuine pleasure for him in being ignored by a great novelist, because of the pitch of intellectual life at which she lived, than there was in being praised by a Bard who seemed to be someone 'neither knowing nor communicating knowledge'.

Although James appears to have abandoned *The Middle Years* in 1914, there is no certainty that he might not one day have come back to it, and no way of telling therefore whether or not it is not only the unhappy accident of his illness and death which makes these two meetings the climax of his life story. They serve it well in that capacity, whatever the reasons for his breaking off. The great writers concerned are seen from too great a distance for their portraits to have much historical or critical value, but they figure effectively in a moral fable that shows (to what one can suppose is James's own satisfaction at least) how right he was to turn to the 'social scene' of the novelist rather than the beetling crags and abysses of young Edwin. Not that this 'life-choice', as I have called it, could ever have involved much real choosing. If James had not always been so ready to confess it himself, there would still be one or two early reviews to indicate that poetry was never a real option for him.[8] A long tradition in religious thought has it that no option is ever real. James recalls its less gloomy aspects by demonstrating so vividly and with such humour in these episodes that the choice he was, as it were, pre-destined to make was very much the right one. He is faithful in doing so to the general scheme of his Autobiography which adds to its more explicit filial pieties the tribute of being dominated by his father's optimistic and providential view. With only one or two exceptions, everything in it that happens to Henry James, Jnr. happens for the best—the best in this case being the emergence of someone who can look back on an extraordinarily productive and distinguished career as a novelist. But since this way of putting it might suggest complacency on James's part, it becomes important to note that George Eliot and Tennyson are not simply illustrations of how much more intelligent a great novelist is likely to be than a Bard. What they also allow James to show, through his own dramatized responses to both, is how much more arduous than a Bard's a novelist's training is likely to be.

It is difficult to clarify this final observation without saying a word about Mrs. Greville who is no more a mere supernumerary in these events than is Mrs. Wix in *What Maisie Knew*. A combination of 'exquisite good nature' and 'innocent fatuity' the speciality of Mrs. Greville, as James presents her, is to drift round upper middle-class English drawing-rooms 'saying' things. She has a fondness, that is, for reciting 'choice morceaux, whether French or English, with a marked oddity of manner, of "attack", a general incongruity of drawing-room art' (579). What amazes James is the capacity of English society for tolerating having things 'said' to it in this way: for putting up with this absurd if kind lady. The phenomenon strikes him as further proof of the truth that 'nowhere so much as in England was it fortunate to *be* fortunate' in those days, since that condition was one against which 'a number of the sharp truths one might privately apprehend beat themselves beautifully in vain' (580). Insofar as this refers to Mrs. Greville, the 'one' in question is James himself, since the truth about her is that it was doubtful 'whether in the whole course of her career she had ever once been brought up, as it were, against a revealed reality' (579). There is obvious dramatic point therefore in her being James's companion when he demonstrates at Whitley how prepared *he* is to accept a sharp truth and recognize reality; and a not much less obvious one, it seems to me, in her reception there being so much less warm and enthusiastic than at Aldworth. It is not of course that James presents Tennyson as in any way absurd, as Mrs. Greville certainly is; yet the impression he nevertheless gives is of someone who shares with her, at his infinitely higher level, a comfortable absence of awareness—being alert. He is not a man who suggests that he has reached his present eminence after a long struggle with sharp truths and realities. On the contrary, to fall back on one of James's favourite and most habitual metaphors, he illustrates rather how it is possible to become a great poet 'on the cheap'. The impression he tended to give, James himself says, is 'that of the poetic character more worn than paid for' (592). What James is conveying in his account of his two meetings, on the other hand, is the day-to-day cost of aspiring to assume the character of a novelist, and the ability to profit intelligently and courageously from experience, even or perhaps especially when it is painful, which that aspiration involves. The abysses to which Dr. Beattie's 'Young Edwin' was exposed may have been deeper than the Witley abyss, but at least he could have dropped things into them on the reasonable expectation that they would not jump violently back into his own exposed face.

2

This inevitably lengthy reading of the Autobiography's near final episodes seems to me in broad agreement with James's deliberate design, even though he can never have meant their position to have quite such organizing force. I have read the episodes as I believe James wanted them to be read (a 'first stage' in autobiographical interpretation which his leisurely subtleties make so demanding that it is hard to find room for any other); but the result could well seem strange to anyone recalling the details in his account of his education. The first impression they give is hardly of an apprenticeship in any way arduous so that the complaint might be that, although it is possible to imagine a prospective Bard having had (according to the criteria James establishes) an easier time, it is difficult to think who else could have been so lucky. The initial sense of relatively effortless profit comes chiefly from James attributing to himself an ability to live very happily on 'impressions' in what were often distinctly unpromising situations—from the more conventionally educational point of view but also from that of his own emotional comfort. It is the memory of this ability which allows him to avoid any too obvious criticism of his father for having sent his children to such a bewilderingly haphazard number of educational institutions at home and abroad. He may in doing so have been pursuing an educational experiment, but it was one which proved, James recalls, 'no plotted thing at all but only an accident of accidents' (127); there was an 'incorrigible vagueness of current in our educational drift' (239). William James appears to have felt more resentment at the consequences than his younger brother. On several occasions in the Autobiography he is shown criticizing their schooling, and he was later to declare much of it a waste of time. (Some of that feeling must still have been with him when he wrote the chapters on 'Habit' and 'Attention' in *The Principles of Psychology*.) Henry, on the other hand, could feel that he had avoided waste by an instinctive policy of systematic indirection. He describes himself as remembering vividly how his teachers looked, who else they taught, the rooms in which they did their teaching and above all the towns or cities—Albany, New York, London, Geneva, Boulogne . . .—in which those rooms could be found. But he appears to recall next-to-nothing of what they managed to impart. Of course, everyone is inclined to insult the teaching profession by forgetting when and how various skills or items of knowledge were first acquired; and to the extent that the educational views of James's father were dominated by 'that New York fetish or our young time, an "acquisition of the languages" ' (112), James himself not only shows himself more inclined to this insult than most, but also rather scandalously unappreciative of how *directly* he was indebted to his father's views for his future career. (A James without his extraordinary fluency in French would be inconceivable.) The profit he does appreciate is all indirect. His account is of a series of educational expedients which were almost uniformly ill-conceived or inappropriate, but which are justifiable nevertheless as the occasion for impressions which helped to make him a novelist, and a novelist of a quality illustrated by the way the impressions are recorded in the Autobiography. This means that, although the idiom would have been very foreign to him, he could nevertheless have endorsed on his own behalf the providential optimism of his father when he wrote,

> whatever befalls my dear boys in this world, they and you and I are all alike, and after all absolute creatures of God, vivified every moment by Him, cared for every moment by Him, guided every moment by an infallible wisdom and an irreproachable tenderness.[9]

In those circumstances, what did it matter which schools the boys went to or how many bad habits of inattention (or attention to the wrong things) they picked up?

The beautiful daguerreotype which Dupee reproduces at the beginning of *A Small Boy and Others* shows a seated Henry James, Snr. resting his hands on the walking-stick between his legs. Beside him stands the 11-year-old Henry, his right hand on his father's left shoulder in a gesture which seems, in the light of the subsequent text, both protective and proprietorial. On several occasions in *A Small Boy and Others*, James marvels at the affection and patience which must have prompted his father to take his very young second son with him on all kinds of professional and social visits; and in *Notes of a Son and Brother* he deliberately falsified the record (of a brief return to Newport) in order, he said, that the reader should not attribute to his father too much 'aimless vacillation'.[10] As a filial tribute, James's Autobiography is far more unambiguously the genuine article than Mill's. Yet if it did not matter at all which schools James went to, the large part of it which concerns his father's philosophy of education would fall rather flat; and there would be other, equally serious implications of insisting too exclusively on the proposition that James was so fitted to profit from experience that what the experience was mattered very little. With an aphoristic point common in the Autobiography, despite its length and elaboration, he writes of his early days in New York: 'For the wonder was the experience, and that was everywhere, even if I didn't as much find it as take it with me, to be sure of not falling short' (54). But if James's capacity for wonder could illuminate any scene, why, in looking back, does he endorse with such comparative unreserve his early feeling that he would have to live abroad? Why could he not have become an artist—as he implies in the Autobiography Hawthorne became one—'just by being American *enough*' (480)?

Both these issues would be worth pursuing, but they are less relevant in this context than the question of 'cost' raised by the meetings with Tennyson and George Eliot. James's account is of an education where the usual price one has to pay, because of emulation (for example) or the discomfort of serious application to subjects for which one has no natural taste, appears to have been reduced to a minimum. He describes a privately developed and self-sustaining pedagogic method which is parasitic on the official one, using it as the occasion for 'impressions'. For the young James (as of course the older one recalls him), incidentals become central and what is supposedly central becomes incidental. 'There was interest always, certainly', he writes, '—but it strikes me today as interest in everything that wasn't supposedly or prescriptively of the question at all and in nothing that *was* so respectably involved and accredited' (111). Practised as systematically as James gives the impression of having practised it, this method might do as much as any avant-garde educational psychology to lessen the immemorial association between learning and pain. But there are several sequences in the Autobiography which suggest that it was not completely painless for James, and not therefore in such complete contradiction with the significance one can attach to his meeting with Lewes and George Eliot. The one where he is most conveniently explicit about the price he sometimes had to pay for impressions—his novelist's education—involves taking this last word in its widest sense since it is a sequence which postdates his formal schooling. The occasion is his first return to Europe as a young man in 1869, and the good fortune, as he sees it, of being invited to the breakfasts of a well-connected fellow-lodger along with Englishmen from the Temple, The Home Office, The Foreign Office, the House of Commons and 'goodness knew what other scarce discernible Olympian altitudes' (560). Here was a magnificent opportunity for impressions, the only drawback being that if he treated his 'fellow-breakfasters' as specimen material, so did they him, wanting to know, for example, what James, as a representative American, thought of General Grant's first cabinet and thereby forcing him, since politics were hardly his *forte*, into 'rather an abject acceptance of the air of imbecility' (559). All of which leads James to speculate that,

> the authenticity of whatever one was going to learn in the world would probably always have for its sign that one got it at some personal cost. To this generalisation mightn't one even add that in proportion as the cost was great, or became fairly excruciating, the lesson, the value acquired would probably be a thing to treasure? I remember really going so far as to wonder if any act of acquisition of the life-loving, life-searching sort that most appealed to me wouldn't mostly be fallacious if unaccompanied by that tag of the price paid in personal discomfort, in some self-exposure and some none too impossible consequent discomfiture, for the sake of it. (560)

In relatively close proximity to James's account of his encounter with Lewes, these sentences are the best possible clue to its interpretation.

On the whole, and as everyone knows, James's strategy in life was to be the *spectator ab extra*. But it is difficult to remain an observer without being observed. (If the Marcel to whom one can suppose Proust attributed his own temperamental leanings achieves this feat, it is at the expense of being transformed from observer into *voyeur*.[11]) To observe at all one usually needs to be present and it does not take much reading between the lines to recognize that presence at school was frequently for James something of an ordeal. So much was this the case at the Institution Vergnès in New York, where he spent a winter early in his life, that in recalling the experience with something very like 'unmitigated horror' James simultaneously suggests how closely allied with his early development of an observer stance may have been that 'aestheticising' of threatening realities which can be so disconcerting in his work, especially in his treatment of death. The 'pastors and masters at the Institution Vergnès', he says, 'and especially all fellow-occupants of benches and desks, all elbowing and kicking presences within touch or view' became for him

> so many monsters and horrors, so many wonders and splendours and mysteries, but never, so far as I can recollect, realities of relation, dispensers either of knowledge or of fate, playmates, intimates, mere coevals and coequals. (112)

But neither this tactic, nor the allied one which consisted in finding interest everywhere except where it was officially supposed to be, could work all the time so that in looking back carefully over his schooling, the reader can see without too much difficulty how far James was from being able to make everything serve his purpose (of gathering the impressions which would help to make him a novelist) with complete impunity. His time at Geneva, for instance, must have brought valuable grist to his mill, but it was not without the dismay of being called to the blackboard to tackle mathematical problems he found quite defeating, and of therefore feeling all his efforts in that direction 'mere darkness, waste and anguish' (240).

More obviously illustrative of experience having occasionally to be paid for is James's period at the Harvard Law School. Whether he went to Harvard to give himself the appearance of activity when so many of his contemporaries were enlisting, or to pursue his literary ambitions in secret, what certainly does not seem to have taken him there is any serious interest in the Law. The advantages of his presence proved to be the characteristically private ones of free time, interesting acquaintances and the general (in this case, Cambridge) 'scene'. But since he inevitably mixed with more conventionally serious students than himself, the Law, which even as a pretext he found so boring, could not be avoided entirely. 'I have kept to this hour', he writes,

> a black little memory of my having attempted to argue one afternoon, by way of exercise and under what seemed to me a perfect glare of publicity, the fierce light of a 'moot-court', some case proposed to me by a fellow-student—who can only have been one of the most benign of men unless he was darkly the designingest, and to whom I was at any rate to owe it that I figured my shame for years much in the image of my having stood forth before an audience with a fiddle and bow and trusted myself to rub them together desperately enough (after the fashion of Rousseau in a passage of the Confessions), to make some appearance of music. My music, I recall, before the look on the faces around me, quavered away into mere collapse and cessation, a void now engulfing memory itself, so that I liken it all to a merciful fall of the curtain on some actor stricken and stammering. (438)

Although there is no episode in the *Confessions* where Rousseau attempts to play the violin in public,[12] the reference here to the founding-father of the treatment of self-consciousness in modern autobiographical writing and to one of literature's leading specialists on self-exposure (in all its aspects) is very apt. It suggests how vulnerable James could be when not able to pursue his quietly observant way, and also how right Edel probably is to attribute such crucial, biographical importance to the fiasco on the first night of *Guy Domville*.[13] Even more incidentally, it also suggests how very different an effect the same institution can have on different people. Almost the only positive benefit Henry Adams is willing to attribute to his 'education' at Harvard (much longer and more regular of course than that of James) was 'self-possession', the ability to 'stand up before any audience in America or Europe with nerves rather steadier for the excitement'.[14] It is clear that for James on the other hand standing up in this way was an experience to which he only partially and very gradually became accustomed. He appears to have expressed his apprehension of it in a light, epigrammatic remark which provides a useful complement to the speculations about learning and cost associated with his memory of being interrogated on the subject of Grant's first cabinet. They stress that valuable experiences would have to be paid for but, in that case, at what point would the cost become too high: when would the discomfiture consequent on self-exposure become 'too impossible'? In 1904, James must have intimated to W. D. Howells that he would after all be prepared to give public lectures in order to help finance his impression-seeking return to America; but not 'if the personal exposure is out of proportion to the tip'.[15]

In *the Middle Years*, James concedes that the conclusions he draws from the memory of his embarrassment at knowing nothing about American politics must seem 'a great ado about the long since so bedimmed Half-Moon Street breakfasts' (561); and certainly there is a characteristic smallness of scale about all the incidents in the Autobiography which, by showing he often had to 'pay' for experience, support that idea of the strenuous nature of a novelist's education implicit in his account of meeting Tennyson and George Eliot. What 'scale' might mean here can be established by noting that, although James says that at the time he envied his young brothers' experiences of the Civil War and the 'wondrous opportunity of vision' (460) it provided, he must surely have been aware in doing so that his own involvement would have cost too much (even if it did not cost everything). The Autobiography conveys a sense, which can be corroborated from elsewhere, of someone extraordinarily receptive to impressions and with such a capacity—as regards 'experience'—for making a little go a long way that it suggests vulnerability to being overwhelmed by a lot. James describes how as a boy he felt sandwiched between the intellectual brilliance of the elder William and the social gifts of his younger brother Wilky. Wilky's personality made him realize that

> one way of taking life was to go in for everything and everyone, which kept you abundantly occupied, and the other way was to be as occupied, quite as occupied, just with the sense and the image of it all, and on only a fifth of the actual immersion. (164)

It was perhaps an early, unconscious understanding of the relatively small amount of experience with which he himself would be able to deal comfortably ('a fifth of the actual immersion') which made him able to say so memorably of Ruskin that he had been 'scared back by the grim face of reality into the world of unreason and illusion'.[16]

There is of course a critical commonplace in sight here which is hard to avoid because of its indirect bearing on any satisfactory, general description of James's Autobiography. If it is not to degenerate into mere reminiscence, what any autobiography requires from its author is a strong, controlling sense of comparative value. There must be principles of selection to which the memories which crowd into an autobiographer's mind can be instinctively referred: principles not of course necessarily similar to the readers' own but appreciable by them as corresponding to a possible, enlivening sense of what most matters. It is clear that once James turned to the past, memories crowded in with a peculiar abundance and insistence. It is not always immediately evident that his feeling for priorities was capable of managing them, so that the impression the Autobiography often gives is of formlessness or at least of magnificent passages—passages that ought to have classic status, such as his account of how his father's optimism could co-exist with sharp awareness of day-to-day realities—and others tainted with self-indulgence, where the remembering is, as it were, for remembering's sake. On first reading especially, the narrative movement can often seem inordinantly sluggish. This is a judgement which has to be qualified immediately by remembering that the text in question is family memoir as well as autobiography strictly defined, and that James's evident attitude to the latter precludes the dramas of urgent self-discovery or intimate revelation. He is not at all in the supposedly frank, truth-telling tradition established by Rousseau and no subscriber to the view Rousseau's example did so much to propagate that any autobiography without an account of sexual life must be incomplete. Too intelligent not to realize that the autobiographical form is always and inevitably betraying, he often has the air of deliberately limiting his account to areas where self-betrayal would not much matter. That of course is an impossibility, so that it is disconcerting, it seems to me, to find him implicitly comparing the convalescent soldiers he visited at Portsmouth Grove in 1863 to specimens in 'some school of natural history' (425), or making the chief burden of his complaint against Lincoln's successor that he was so deplorably vulgar in appearance, unphotogenic (491). In both cases, the importance of the topic make James's 'aesthetic' response seem trivial. More disconcerting, however, are the much-discussed obscurities in James's description of how he first acquired what thousands of people all over the world would be inclined to identify sympathetically—could they only understand the language being used—as a 'bad back' (415). James's account of his 'obscure hurt' is confused in ways which appear to betray, at the very least, an unresolved guilt over his failure to enlist. In the Autobiography as a whole, he extends our notion of what it is to be intelligent by showing how widely and significantly the most apparently unimportant incident in a life can resonate. But this characteristically 'modernist' power of enriching life by both privileging and celebrating its briefest moments only seems fully available to him when the moment concerned is one he can look back on with perfect equanimity.

The critical commonplace I mentioned accuses James of inexperience in certain of the vital matters with which any novelist is expected to deal. There is an obvious difficulty in deciding how far it is confirmed by evidence from the Autobiography when that work, even in so far as it is properly autobiographical, is so deliberately and self-consciously reticent in its method. If the dramatic episodes which structure and give momentum to so many other autobiographies—conflict with parents, for example, or falling in love—are absent, who can say *for certain* that it is because they never occurred, or even that the air of detachment which surrounds the young James is not something foisted on him by the older man after the events? To the extent that it is limited to the published works, the charge of inexperience must therefore continue to rely very largely on the contrast in his fiction between a customary sureness and refinement of treatment and either occasional lurches into melodrama or a suspiciously melodramatic quality in the situations being treated. It is as if in certain areas, many of which are what are now considered vital subsections of that 'love' traditionally resorted to by novelists for most of their material, melodrama—

to use that conveniently blanket term—had for James to be a substitute for first-hand knowledge. The reticence of his Autobiography means that it has little to say on why this should be so, yet it is at least very revealing about James's addiction to melodrama (in the form, for example, of second- or third-rate theatre) as a child and adolescent. And in a way which has its relevance for this topic of a writer's need to know what he is talking about ('We must know', James wrote to Hugh Walpole in 1913, 'as much as possible, in our beautiful art, yours and mine, what we are talking about—and the only way to know it is to have lived and loved and cursed and floundered and enjoyed and suffered'[17]), the Autobiography also helps to show why *What Maisie Knew* could be the triumph it is. By choosing to adopt in *Maisie* the child's point of view, James of course legitimizes his depiction as melodramatically comic and grotesque those supposedly vital sub-sections just mentioned. But as many commentators point out, only a writer who remembered so vividly his own experiences as a sharply observant but not entirely comprehending child could have adopted it so successfully. There is an obvious and suggestive relation between many parts of *Maisie* and the passage in *A Small Boy and Others* where James describes very early morning walks with older female cousins in the area of the Palais Royal. Together with a French maid or governess, they would stare into jewellers' windows, James records, whilst he himself wondered what the 'anything' he felt they would do for this or that stone might be (216).

In singing the praises of *What Maisie Knew*, one is sometimes asked where then in James one *could* find adult sexual relations treated seriously. The challenge is likely to come from readers inclined also to ask—not without some justification—whether James was ever in a position to treat Tennyson's reflections on de Sade so dismissively. It does not seem to me as easy to meet as one kind of admirer of *The Golden Bowl* or *The Ambassadors* (and there is no point in discussion with whoever does not admire these two works) would claim—as it is not easy to meet in the comparable case of Jane Austen. Since generations of English examiners have obliged her to shoulder the additional burden of not having taken proper account of the Napoleonic wars, it is a wonder that she was able to put pen to paper at all. There are certain judgements about great writers, which, though they may accurately define their limits, are in one sense so obvious and in another so unimaginatively narrow and prescriptive about the necessary ingredients of fiction that they open the door to platitude if not impertinence. I began with a quotation from *Mansfield Park* in order to prepare the way for a reading of a classic of American autobiography from an English point of view. 'Pray Miss Price', says the distinctly obtuse Mr. Rushworth in that novel 'are you such a great admirer of this Mr. Crawford as some people are? For my part, I can see nothing in him.' And he adds a little later, with the air of a man settling Crawford's hash for ever, 'He is not five foot nine. I should not wonder if he was not more than five foot eight.'[18]

NOTES

1. Jane Austen, *Mansfield Park*, ed. R. W. Chapman (Oxford University Press, 1934), pp. 126–27.
2. It is F. W. Dupee, in his eminently serviceable edition of James's autobiographical writings (Criterion Books, 1956) who entitles them an 'Autobiography'. I am happy to follow this critical lead. The page numbers which follow quotations from the writings in my text are to Dupee's edition.
3. See the recent Norton edition of *The Prelude* (New York, 1979), XIII, p. 172 (p. 468).
4. *Henry James: The Master 1901–1916* (London, 1972), p. 28.
5. Compare especially vol. I of *A La Recherche du Temps Perdu* in the Pléiade edition, pp. 547–73.
6. For an illustration of how difficult the Autobiography is to use as a source, one could compare Edel's account of James's feelings for his mother in *The Untried Years* (London, 1953), pp. 50–1 with p. 344 of *Notes of a Son and Brother*. There is a less excusable example of distortion in the present writer's *Wordsworth, Freud and the Spots of Time* (Cambridge University Press, 1985), p. 62 (a reference to James's memory of being driven through the Place Vendôme in his second year).
7. *The Conquest of London 1870–1883* (London, 1962), p. 374. It could be of course that Edel is here attempting to describe how James felt at the time of his encounter with Lewes, rather than interpreting his later account of the incident in *The Middle Years*. But there is no indication in Edel's text that this is the case. The only source which, apart from *The Middle Years*, he cites in his notes is a letter to Norton dated 17 Nov. [1878]. (See Vol. II in Edel's own edition of the *Letters* (London, 1975), pp. 194–98.) Apart from mentioning that the Leweses asked after Norton, James says nothing

about what happened at their house, although he does say that his visit there took place the day before (not after) he and Mrs. Greville lunched with Tennyson. In beginning the paragraph which ends with his talk of 'rebuff'—'It was on the day after Henry's visit in the downpour to George Eliot and Lewes . . .'—and going on to talk of the lunch with Tennyson, Edel declares an obvious preference for the retrospective rather than contemporary record.

8. I am thinking of his reviews of Whitman and Baudelaire, but if the evidence they provide were disputed one could fall back on James's avowal in the Autobiography that his 'muse was of course the muse of prose fiction—never for the briefest hour in my case, the presumable, not to say the premusing, the much-taking-for-granted muse of rhyme; with whom I had never had, even in thought, the faintest flirtation. . . .' (439).

9. Quoted by Edel in *The Untried Years*, p. 136.

10. The phrase is from an unpublished record of a conversation with James left by his nephew. See *The Untried Years*, p. 141.

11. There are several episodes in *A la Recherche* where Marcel is able to observe the intimate doings of others without being seen himself. Compare especially the description of the sexual predelictions of Charlus in the scene in Jupien's brothel (Vol. III, p. 815).

12. The closest appears to be the episode in Book IV when Rousseau conducts his own first and wholly incompetent composition for small orchestra at the house of M. de Treytorens in Lausanne. See Vol. 1 of Rousseau's *Oeuvres Complètes* in the Pléiade edition (Paris, 1959), p. 149. The likely connections between James's remarks, this episode in Rousseau and the first night of *Guy Domville* have been very well discussed by Carol Holly in 'A Drama of Intention in Henry James' Autobiography'. See a Henry James issue of *Modern Language Studies* (Fall 1983), XIII:4, 22–9.

13. See Leon Edel, *Henry James: The Treacherous Years 1895–1901* (London, 1969), pp. 66–74.

14. Ernest Samuels (ed.), *The Education of Henry Adams* (Riverside edition, 1973), p. 69.

15. Leon Edel, *Henry James: The Master*, p. 236.

16. See James's letter to his mother on 20 March 1869 in Vol. I of Edel's edition of the *Letters* (London, 1974), p. 103.

17. Leon Edel, *The Letters of Henry James*, Vol. IV (London, 1984), p. 680. This whole letter provides an interesting contrast with James's description, much earlier in his career, of the English novelist who was able to convey the spirit of French Protestant youth after a single glimpse of some young French Protestants at table. See 'The Art of Fiction' in *Selected Literary Criticism of Henry James*, ed. Morris Shapira (London, 1963), p. 56.

18. *Mansfield Park*, p. 102.

6

Enclosure/Disclosure: A Tradition of American Autobiography by Women

by FAITH PULLIN

1

That is really the trouble with an autobiography you do not of course you do not really believe yourself why should you, you know so well so very well that it is not yourself, it could not be yourself, it could not be yourself because you cannot remember right and if you do remember right it does not sound right and of course it does not sound right because it is not right. You are of course never yourself.[1]

—Gertrude Stein

. . . in the early diaries I spoke of my feelings that I was playing all the rôles demanded of woman, which I had been programmed to play. But I knew also that there was a part of myself that stood apart from that and wanted some other kind of life, some other kind of authenticity.[2]

—Anaïs Nin

Of necessity Autobiography concerns itself with the problem of identity: a problem particularly complex for women writers for whom the very concept of 'self' has long been strikingly elusive. When considered, too, in the context of *American* literary auto- biography the problem raises yet further ramifications: where in

125

the broadest sense has 'self'—identity—been more avidly pursued and argued over than in the New World? To take Gertrude Stein as a major point-of-departure, thus, serves several ends at once. She offers an instance of her own kind of sexual autonomy. She in certain ways could not have been more American. And in *The Autobiography of Alice B. Toklas* (1933), she offers a landmark twentieth-century instance of the way in which an autobiography must establish its own characteristic vision.

For in *The Autobiography of Alice B. Toklas* Gertrude Stein performs an act which verges on a species of ventriloquism. She, as it were, re-enacts Alice Toklas's own style to render a comic portrait of herself, viewing herself from the outside as if an artefact, a moving object in space—in all a stunning mimetic coup. It is a book whose shocking charm derives from the matter-of-fact description of a totally extraordinary life and experience. In this, the contrast with Stein's earlier meditations on personality could not be greater. In *The Making of Americans* (1925), for instance, she had eschewed examination of the individual in favour of 'an exact description of inner and outer reality', an attempt to link the non-individualized self with the outside world. *The Making of Americans* (a none too disguised portrait-gallery of her own family) presents characters as separate units, having little connection with each other, except in terms of their family relationships and as examples of specific classifications; they are defined purely in terms of their modes of being in the universe, whether they attack or resist, are independent or dependent. Paradoxically, although projected as the history of 'everyone who ever was or is or will be living', Stein actually presents a uniquely individualized account of the interior life of a human being.

In *The Autobiography of Alice B. Toklas*, Stein, in the *persona* of Alice, gives a pedantic account of her own narrative method:

> Gertrude Stein, in her work, has always been possessed by the intellectual passion for exactitude in the description of inner and outer reality. She has produced a simplification by this concentration, and as a result the destruction of associational emotion in poetry and prose.[3]

Not only does Stein here reject emotion but she rejects the fictional as well; in fact, her aim is to collapse into one another

126

the categories of fiction and nonfiction: 'There is no real reality
to a really imagined life any more. . . . What is the difference
between remembering what has been happening and remembering what has been as dreaming. None.'[4] Again: 'an autobiography is not a novel no indeed it is not a novel.' Autobiography, then, validates non-fiction as the dominant genre.
The intense difficulty in distinguishing fiction from non-fiction
has exercised many autobiographers, involving, as it does,
considerations of literal truth (fact) and symbolic truth. Mary
McCarthy, almost thirty years later, makes an identical point in
her Introduction to *Memories of a Catholic Girlhood* (1957):

> Many a time, in the course of doing these memoirs, I have
> wished that I *were* writing fiction. The temptation to invent has
> been very strong, particularly where recollection is hazy and I
> remember the substance of an event but not the details. . . . Then
> there are cases where I am not sure myself whether I am making
> something up. I *think* I remember but I am not positive.[5]

Stein's controlling image for expressing experience in *Toklas* is
that of the kaleidoscope; there is no hierarchy of importance in the
memories she describes any more than there is any form of moral
assessment, or attempt to define temporality. For McCarthy to
some degree, what has been thought to have happened *has*
happened; for Stein, in all cases, the present is superimposed on
the past so that the current pattern is the definitive one. *The
Autobiography of Alice B. Toklas* is meta-fictional in that it is a
narrative that discusses itself and its own self-reflexivity as well as
the identity of its writer. In the final words of the book Stein
merges herself as narrator with herself as personality, redefining
the categories of autobiographer, novelist and reporter:

> About six weeks ago Gertrude Stein said, it does not look to me
> as if you were ever going to write that autobiography. You know
> what I am going to do. I am going to write it for you. I am going
> to write it as simply as Defoe did the autobiography of Robinson
> Crusoe. And she has and this is it.[6]

The same position with regard to contemporaneity is arrived
at at the close of *Everybody's Autobiography* (1936) in Stein's
concluding statement about the nature of identity: 'perhaps I
am not I even if my little dog knows me but any way I like what
I have and now it is today.'[7] During the course of *Everybody's*

Autobiography, Stein makes many retrospective comments on the nature of her achievement in *Toklas*. She now regards the previous work as, in some respects, illegitimate since it was 'a description and a creation of something that having happened was in a way happening not again'. In other words, it was 'history', 'newspaper', 'illustration', but not autobiography. Although Stein claims in the Preface to *Everybody's Autobiography* that 'anything is an autobiography' and 'autobiography is easy', she had, in fact, refused, consistently, to write her own, rejecting the requests of publishers, and it was a profound, traumatic shock for her to find that the 'easy' work *Toklas* was so much more successful and more highly valued than the 'difficult', innovative *Making of Americans*. Even so, *Toklas* is a more overtly sophisticated performance than the later book; Stein recreates Alice's personality as the teller of the tale and at the same time presents a self which is more grandiose and more authoritative than the deliberately naïve and friendly protagonist who traverses and rediscovers America in *Everybody's Autobiography*. It seems that the very success of *Toklas* allowed the relaxation and lack of pretension that characterize Stein's encounters and travels as a celebrity, a celebrity who, paradoxically, is identified with her audience rather than marked out by her superiority as self-proclaimed genius. Her impact as a lecturer comes from the fact that, like the students, Stein does not know the answer: 'I do not even know whether there is a question let alone having an answer for a question.'[8]

Stein attempts to avoid the essential disjunction between self as object and subject, the internal and the external by the calculatedly ambiguous use of the word autobiography itself. *Everybody's Autobiography* refers both to the book and the life, the fiction and the facts of her actual journey and its events. However, contained within the book's linear structure are meditations on the impact on her life and her vision of her 'self' caused by sudden fame, late in life, after a career of strenuous disappointment. Large areas of *Everybody's Autobiography* are simple picaresque; it is inevitable that Stein's intention of collapsing her audience and herself into one total entity that will be the subject-matter of the autobiography can only be minimally successful. In point of fact, all Stein's writings aspire to the condition of the literary essay since only in this form can she escape the conflicts of character-creation.

The Stein character as represented in *Everybody's Autobiography* is dedicated to the word: 'I like anything that a word can do. And words do do all they do and then they can do what they never do do.'[9] Stylistically, the abstracted but intimate mode of the Stein autobiography can be contrasted with the imaginative gloss on real events provided by H.D.'s imagistic method in the roman-à-clef *Bid me to Live* (1927). This has been described by Perdita Schaffner, H.D.'s daughter, as 'straight autobiography, a word-for-word transcript'. Nevertheless, as with Stein, the word remains paramount; the three central characters of *Bid me to Live* are writers and H.D.'s struggle is to define and control her own text, her life. In *Her* (also written in 1927), the protagonist evolves an autobiographical myth, wakening into selfhood and creativity and discovering that 'love is writing'. Hermione must reject the image imposed on her by George Lowndes (Ezra Pound) both as a woman and as a writer:

> 'Well I'm ballyhoo damned if I'm going to help you with your bally writing.' . . .
> Pages fluttered in the hands of George Lowndes. His hands fluttered white pages. What George holds in his hands is my life's beginning. What George flutters is my life's ending.[10]

Fayne Rabb, rather than George Lowndes, represents the way forward for Her Gart. Fayne indicates that writing is the means to avoid unreality:

> Your writing is the thin flute holding you to eternity. Take away your flute and you remain, lost in a world of unreality. . . . It is all—*all* unreal. You accept false, superimposed standards . . . all these people.[11]

Association with society through marriage can only alienate Her totally from herself, destroying her essence, her spirit. She resists practising the cultural schizophrenia experienced by other women writers, in which truth (told in diaries and journals) is denied and repressed in the rôle-playing of 'real' life. Such a situation can result in the development of strategies of invisibility, referred to, notably, by Joyce Carol Oates in a *Paris Review* interview:

> Being a woman allows me a certain invisibility. Like *Invisible Man*. (My long journal, which must be several hundred pages by

now, has the title *Invisible Woman.* Because a woman, being so mechanically judged by her appearance, has the advantage of hiding within it—of being absolutely whatever she knows herself to be, in contrast with what others imagine her to be. . . .)[12]

Her doesn't learn and mature through contact with society but by a tactical retreat from it, by a plunge into the depth of her own being. To become herself, Her must not function as a mirror for the man, reflecting his image, or his distorted image of her; confirmation and authenticity come from identification with another woman. If this path is not followed, life becomes a charade, a crude and melodramatic fiction:

> George sitting there looked Polish or something, the count of something out of a shocking novel. They were out of a shocking novel. . . . They were out of a bad play or a bad novel for it was evident there was no reality.[13]

Her has to develop the strength to create and identify her own myth, rather than submit to that imposed by George:

> He wanted Her, but he wanted a Her that he called decorative. . . . George saw Her at best as some Florentine page or some Florentine girl dressed for a pageant as the Queen Diana. To George, Her was Dian or Diana, never Artemis. To George, she was the Queen of Love, never white Aphrodite. People are in things. I am in Her. George never understood me.[14]

'Her' has to insist on her self-identification and in pursuit of that necessity, insistently names herself, using her name as a talismanic invocation ('I am the word AUM, I am Her. I am Her). Words are magic and must be used precisely; the words of other people degrade reality ('normal, unwholesome, their vocabulary gets more meagre'). Her must preserve herself for herself: 'Her for Her, Her for Fayne exactly.'

Her has to find and learn her own kind of writing, her own form of discourse. Again, as George Lowndes represents conventional sexuality so, too, he defines and limits the possibilities of literature:

> Writing was an achievement like playing the violin or singing like Tetrazzini. . . . Writing had somehow got connected up with George Lowndes who even in his advanced progress could make no dynamic statement that would assure her mind that writing had to do with the underside of a peony petal that covered the

whole of a house like a nutshell housing woodgnats. . . . George Lowndes, the high-water mark of the intelligentsia of the period, proffered Shaw, Maeterlinck, Bertrand de Born and, half-apologetic, the unexpurgated *Morte d'Arthur*. Writing had no mere relationship with trees on trees and octopus arms that reached out with eyes, too all over-seeing.[15]

Her's central experience is in the recognition of a female culture, intrinsically different from that manifested in the life and work of George Lowndes ('I was not what George wanted. . . . It was to disguise himself that George would so disguise me'). George has defined Her as 'essentially feminine', but the task she undertakes in *Her* is the discovery of what it means to be a creative woman, not a decorative adjunct to the male. This is a procedure both daunting and painful. Developing a language expressive of one's own 'real' experience is problematic, a process also enunciated by Virginia Woolf in *A Writer's Diary*:

> I'm fundamentally, I think, an outsider. I do my best work and feel most braced with my back to the wall. It's an odd feeling though, writing against the current; difficult entirely to disregard the current. Yet of course I shall.

'Writing against the current', elaborating her individualistic method, H.D. was, nevertheless, referring back to the myth-making capacities of all women. In *The Gift*, written in 1941 and 1943 and so after *Her* and *Bid me to Live*, H.D. begins with a death: 'There was a girl who was burnt to death at the seminary, as they called the old school where our grandfather was principal'[16]—a death that in itself symbolizes the creative deaths of all women who have been silenced under patriarchy. Again, discovery is the motif of this autobiography of H.D.'s childhood. The discovery is of the gift of creativity and of the child's links with her mother and with all the sisters who have gone before her:

> I would be like Mama; in a sense, I would be Mama, I would have important sisters, and brothers only as seemly ballast. Why was it always a girl who had died? Why did Alice die and not Alfred? Why did Edith die and not Gilbert? I did not cry because Fanny died, but I had inherited Fanny. Mama cried (although I had seldom seen her cry) because Fanny died, so Mama had cried. I did not cry. The crying was frozen in me, but it was my own, it was my own crying.[17]

In *The Gift*, the masculine world is made peripheral, not central; yet much of the material that forms the basis of *The Gift* was brought back into H.D.'s conscious mind from analytic discussions with Freud, discussions which were especially fruitful because they allowed H.D. to know and repossess her mother. 'Mythology is actuality'; H.D.'s dream of the old man who singled her out because she was a girl and promised to send his sleigh 'whenever the girl wanted it' is proved to have had no existence in the everyday world, only in the world of the imagination. Like fairy tales, like myth itself, the dream goes on happening, 'it did not stop.' The shape of *The Gift* is circular, but, at the end, the protagonist is enabled, through experience and meditation, to appreciate the meaning of her life. Initially, in the final chapter, *Morning Star*, H.D., on 17 January 1943, recalls during the London bombing, her mother's prediction that the papers would be burnt or she would be burnt. 'She' can refer to mother or daughter or the girl burnt to death at the memoir's beginning. H.D. experiences a collapse of consciousness in which the potential bomb in London is identified with a shooting star in her childhood that was 'going to fall on the house and burn us all up and burn us all to death'. This, in turn, leads back to the Indian past of North America, 'burning and poisonous arrows' and the memories of H.D.'s grandmother when 'the unbaptized King of the Shawanese gave his beloved and only wife to the Brotherhood'. *The Gift* ends in reconciliation; H.D. accepts her own beginnings and the beginnings of the life of her people in America:

> I had gone down under the wave and I was still alive, I was breathing. I was not drowning though in a sense, I had drowned: I had gone down, been submerged by the wave of memories and terrors repressed since the age of ten and long before, but with the terrors, I had found the joys, too.[18]

H.D. shares Gertrude Stein's sense of the poetry of the commonplace, the magical properties of naming and stating. *The Gift* shows H.D. in retrospect recognizing herself as the gifted child. *Her* presents a picture of a girl learning to resist both stereotypical forms of male/female relationships and the rejection of the female, myth-making imagination; the process of self-defining continues in *Bid me to Live* in which the protagonist engages in debate about sexuality, and writing with a group of fellow writers in London in 1917. As in *Her*, where H.D. creates herself in opposition to the values embodied in the George Lowndes character, here Julia's vital, female mode of living and writing is born out of conflict with Frederico (D. H. Lawrence) and denial of his methods and ideas. If Lawrence's subject is the proper relationship between the sexes, H.D.'s contribution is the female view of sexuality and work. In *Bid me to Live*, the woman with no pretensions other than that of a vital sex life is caricatured in the figure of Bella (Dorothy Yorke), mistress of Julia's husband Rafe (Richard Aldington). Although, on the surface, the dominant character in this roman-à-clef is Frederico, the emotional logic of the book reveals that it is a lyrical meditation on loss, waste and death. As Helen McNeil notes in her fine introduction to the Virago edition of *Bid me to Live*,

> H.D. was badly war-wounded. Between 1915 and 1919, H.D., an expatriate without family contact, had a stillborn child: Aldington began an affair under the same roof, and as the marriage broke up H.D. had a brief affair with Cecil Gray whom she didn't see after their child, Perdita, was born. Her brother was killed at the front and her father died; she had a breakdown.[19]

Nevertheless, the overt intention of the text is the subversion of female stereotypes and the denial of categorization:

> But Bella was not a harlot. Julia was not a saint, When Rafe Ashton said to Julia, 'I would give her a mind, I would give you a body,' he was biting off, extravagantly, much more than even he could chew.[20]

Julia assures herself of her own value and significance by refusing the escape from London offered by friends and by the ritual incantation of phrases such as 'I myself, I myself, I myself. This is my room.' Her sardonic references to her marital status indicate a profound unease:

> Mrs. Rafe Ashton. That is my name. It was a blithe arrangement. They might have made a signal success of their experiment. They made a signal success of it, but in the tradition not so much of Robert Browning and Elizabeth Barrett as of Punch and Judy.[21]

Julia resists the dogmatic formulations of Rico as much as the sexual games-playing of Rafe—both are manifestations of the need to control ('I love you, I desire l'autre'):

What did any of that matter? What did Rico matter with his blood-stream, his sex-fixations, his man-is-man, woman-is-woman? . . . This man-, this woman-theory of Rico's was false, it creaked in the joints. Rico could write elaborately on the woman mood, describe women to their marrow in his writing but if she turned round, wrote the Orpheus part of her Orpheus-Eurydice sequence, he snapped back. 'Stick to the woman-consciousness, it is the intuitive woman-mood that matters'. . . . But if he could enter, so diabolically, into the feelings of women, why should not she enter into the feelings of men?[22]

Rico's overtly stated charge is that Julia is entangled in her own dream, whereas he would have preferred that she be entangled in his. The potential relationship between the two of them is extremely intense but it is cerebral and spiritual—the essence of their communication is in their writing:

I am not this person, . . . there was all of me in the manuscript which you didn't even trouble to write me about. . . .
Here I am, but really I am tied up in the rough copy of the poems hidden behind the *Mercure de France* volumes . . that is me. This isn't.[23]

Rico needs the security of his relationship with Elsa. Life is a dangerous game

unless you are tethered to your own dynamic centre as Rico was tethered (so far, no further) to the totem-pole of Rule Germania. Rico able to dart out, make his frantic little excursions into any unknown dimension, because there, firm as a rock, was Elsa.[24]

Bid me to Live presents a variety of different kinds of rôle that women can assume. Bella's mother, Mrs. Carter, is a 'modern' woman:

'I believe in women doing what they like. I believe in the modern woman'. In 1913, the 'modern woman' had no special place on the map, and to be 'modern' in Mrs. Carter's sense, after 1914, required some very special handling. 'I believe in intelligent women having experience' was then a very, very thin line to toe, a very, very frail wire to do a tight-rope act on.[25]

However, at the same time, Mrs. Carter functions as a very un-modern woman, as *entrepreneuse*, stage-managing her daughter's sexual activities. Bella was beetle with a hard shell, her green silk might have been plate metal. She seemed metallic, as she sat there, refusing the cigarette, now lifting her glass, setting it down, and tilting Vermouth into the goblet. She moved with set precision, as if she knew her part very well, but was having stage-fright.[26]

Julia, as a separate creative being, can exist in her own right, but, in terms of the sexual relationship with Rafe, she and Bella are mirror images of each other, representing soul and body, spirit and flesh: a duality that the man is unable to reconcile ('he loves my body but you tyrannize his soul'). Neither Julia or Bella are people to Rafe, but versions of Woman:

> The funny thing was that facing Bella, Julia felt that she was looking at herself in a mirror, another self, another dimension but nevertheless herself. Rafe had brought them together; really they had nothing in common. They had everything in common. . . . She looked vampire-ish, the stage type of mistress, but no. She was eighteenth-century in that frock, she was something out of a play. They all were. . . . She and Bella were simply abstractions, were women of the period, were WOMAN of the period, the same one.[27]

Julia expresses overtly, and from the woman's point of view, a vision of adult life as dominated by the biological trap:

> It might be all right for men, but for women, any woman, there was a biological catch and taken at any angle, danger. You dried up and were an old maid, danger. You drifted into the affable *hausfrau*, danger. You let her rip and had operations in Paris (poor Bella), danger.[28]

However, the way out is the way Julia chooses, and is able, to take: 'There was one loophole, one might be an artist. Then the danger met the danger, the woman was man-woman, the man was woman-man.'[29]

Rico, though acknowledging the artist component in Julia's personality, refuses to relinquish his crude categorization:

> But Frederico, for all his acceptance of her verses, had shouted his man-is-man, his woman-is-woman at her; his shrill peacock-cry sounded a love-cry, death-cry for their generation.[30]

That is his problem; Julia the woman-artist has similar and other problems and must find her own way. That way is the way of the woman existing in and through words. In Cornwall, Julia works with the Greek dictionary; characteristically ambiguous, translating a Greek chorus, she is simultaneously 'self-effacing' and 'flamboyantly ambitious':

> The words themselves held inner words, she thought. If you look at a word long enough, this peculiar twist, its magic angle, would lead somewhere, like that Phoenician track, trod by the old traders. She was a trader in the gold, the old gold, the myrrh of the dead spirit. She was bargaining with each word.[31]

Julia is 'arrogant' and also 'humble' in the face of her own creativity: 'she wanted to coin new words.' At this stage of the game, Julia has arrived at the point where she rejects Rico as puppet-master: 'So Rico, your puppets do not always dance to your pipe. Why? Because there is another show.'[32] Nor is she willing to figure in Rico's picture, his 'self-portrait', his version of reality. Vane had called her *Personne*:

> I thought I was someone but he calls me *Personne*, Nobody. I am nobody when it comes to writing novels. But I will find a new name. I will be someone. I will write these notes and re-write them till they come true.[33]

Masculine values and masculine modes have to be set aside as does the conditioned desire to please men and gain approval:

> You might be angry with me. You might shrivel my hope. You might say I had no business writing of old shoes, ladies-bed-straw and the roots of the furze bushes. . . .
>
> Perhaps you would say I was trespassing, couldn't see both sides. . . .[34]

In the final analysis, truth resides in the solitary, female writing self: 'It is simply myself sitting here, this time propped up in bed, scribbling in a notebook, with a candle at my elbow.'[35]

2

Some women autobiographers solve the problem of autonomy by projecting themselves as pseudo-men, rather than as fully authenticated self-sufficient selves. Such is the case of Lillian Hellman whose ultimate accolade in *An Unfinished Woman* (1969) is to have been considered by Hemingway to have *cojones*.

136

Indeed, it is the suspicion that, in going out into the shelling in Madrid to make an important broadcast, Hellman may well have more courage than Hemingway that causes a rift in future years:

> When the broadcast was over and I was back at the hotel, Ernest knocked on my door. We had a few drinks. . . .
>
> (Although I saw Hemingway often in Madrid and a number of times in the years after, I don't think he liked me ever again, and I'm not sure what I felt about him, either.)[36]

A similar competitive spirit manifests itself in an episode with a Spanish chauffeur:

> My head had hit the side of the car as we careened. 'For God's sake,' I said, 'let me drive'. He said, 'A woman could not drive this road'. We had been over this several times during the day and my voice was angry now because my head hurt and I told myself I hadn't come to Spain to die in a car with Luis.
>
> I said, 'I've been driving a car since I was fourteen years old'.[37]

Hellman's crucial error, though, in her attempts to be one-of-the-boys, occurs when she makes unfavourable comments on a new Hemingway manuscript (*To Have and Have Not*):

> So I was pleased to be sitting up in bed, fighting a hangover, flattered that Ernest had brought his new book for my opinion. He sat by the window, drinking, looking through a magazine, mostly watching me as I read the book. I wanted him to go away and leave the book, but when it was good, which wasn't always, I forgot about him. . . . I went back and reread two or three pages.
>
> 'There are missing pages in these proofs.'
>
> Ernest said, 'Where?'
>
> He came to the bed and I showed him what I thought was a puzzling jump in story and in meaning.
>
> 'Nothing is missing. What made you say that?' His voice had changed, not to sharpness, but to a tone one would use with an annoying child or an intrusive stranger, and these many years later I can still hear the change.[38]

Hellman's reward for an attempt at honest criticism is a sexual snub. The genuine put-down is delivered by Dashiel Hammett to Hemingway: 'Why don't you go back to bullying Fitzgerald? Too bad he doesn't know how good he is. The best.'[39] On the other hand, Hemingway had been 'generous' about Hammett's

books: 'Hammett laughed. "Must mean I'm a bad writer." '
What's curious about this reported badinage is the total omission
of the fact that Hellman too is a writer. Hellman very seldom
mentions her own work, other than her journalism, and thereby
seems to ignore her presumed raison-d'être. Her primary purpose, in *An Unfinished Woman*, appears to be the fabrication of a
masculine-style identity, the presentation of herself as a brave,
hard-drinking tomboy who can battle it out with the best that
the male world can offer. Perhaps this identity comes from the
fact that she was an only child and needed to develop an
androgynous persona to satisfy the needs of both parents; in any
event, Hellman, as a child, perceived herself as both more
powerful and more helpless than is normal:

> Most certainly I needed a doctor to reveal for me the violence
> and disorder of my life, but I had always known about the
> powers of an only child. I was not meaner or more ungenerous or
> more unkind than other children, but I was off balance in a world
> where I knew my grand importance to two other people who
> certainly loved me for myself, but who also liked to use me to
> against each other.[40]

Hellman's knowledge that her father has other women fills her
with 'pity and contempt' for her mother; her rage is expressed
by throwing herself from the top of a fig tree and breaking her
nose. Only later, when Hellman has gone to live with Hammett,
does she feel remorse for the contempt she had had for her
mother's jealousy. In fact, the world of the emotions has little
place in Hellman's picaresque description of her eventful life.
Her picture of Hammett and the details of their life together
remains completely externalized. Any introspection concerning
love and writing is absent from this saga in which the experiences of abortion and breakdown are rendered with up-front
sang-froid. Hellman's method seems to consist of the Hemingway
iceberg style, with the iceberg itself pared away.

However, the tough persona reveals itself as the sham it is in
her central battles with Hammett, in which she is the pre-
programmed loser. Hammett is manipulative and sadistic, ruling
his disciple by fear:

> Many years later, unhappy about his drinking, his ladies, my
> life with him, I remember an angry speech I made one night: it

had to do with injustice, his carelessness, his insistence that he get his way, his sharpness with me but not with himself. I was drunk, but he was drunker, and when my strides around the room carried me close to the chair where he was sitting, I stared in disbelief at what I saw. He was grinding a burning cigarette into his cheek.

I said, 'What are you doing?'

'Keeping myself from doing it to you,' he said.

The mark on his cheek was ugly for a few weeks, but in time it faded into the scar that remained for the rest of his life. We never again spoke of that night because, I think, he was ashamed of the angry gesture that made him once again the winner in the game that men and women play against each other, and I was ashamed that I caused myself to lose so often.[41]

In another incident, Hammett provokes Hellman to spit in his eye and welcomes her success: 'That's my girl. Some of the time the kid kicks through.' The embarrassing self-consciousness of these exchanges masks the truth that Hellman's fake toughness and inability to delineate emotion point to an inescapable dilemma; Hellman has fabricated a persona whose abrasive camaraderie hides neurotic dependency. Hammett's remark, 'All I ever wanted was a docile woman and look what I got' does not express the irony Hellman intends, but irony of another sort. Hellman's submissiveness in manufacturing a false identity involves an inability to feel or name. Her summary of her regard for Hammett assumes the quality of bathos in view of the obvious fact that he dominated the greater part of her life: 'He was the most interesting man I've ever met.' In defence of Hellman's oblique approach to life, art and feeling, it could be said that she relies on the reader's elaboration, but relies on it overmuch. The most successful areas of her memory are the compelling portraits of the black women, Sophronia and Helen, with whom she had intense and complex involvements, the first in childhood, the other in adult life. It is here that Hellman proves her capacity, in spite of disclaimers, to find what she called 'truth'.

Hellman's intention in creating the embattled persona of *An Unfinished Woman* was to avoid being overwhelmed by the difficulties of a woman's life in the modern world. Her strategy was to take on the masculine world on its own terms. Mary

McCarthy, whose concern with the elusive nature of truth and the difficulties of memory was mentioned earlier, solved similar problems by the use of intelligence as a weapon of defence. She valued her catholic upbringing for the intellectual discipline and knowledge it brought her. Her mature attitude is to admit the benefits while rejecting the belief:

> If you are born and brought up a Catholic, you have absorbed a good deal of world history and the history of ideas before you are twelve, and it is like learning a language early; the effect is indelible.[42]

Although Mary McCarthy claims that she is writing a memoir and not a work of fiction and absolves herself from the obligation to provide psychological insight and motivation, *Memories of a Catholic Girlhood* deliberately blurs the distinction between fact and fiction. The same key episodes are represented both as they appear in memory and as they were in fact, significant differences being recorded. Indeed, McCarthy operates in her text the painterly technique of *pentimento* used by Lillian Hellman as title and substance for a further volume of reminiscences:

> That is called 'pentimento' because the painter 'repented', changed his mind. Perhaps it would be as well to say that the old conception, replaced by a later choice, is a way of seeing and then seeing again.

A key episode in *Memories of a Catholic Girlhood*—that of the tin butterfly—is a case in point: the child's desire is to control painful experiences by understanding them, and it is the adult's need also. Fate has deprived her and her brothers of their parents but injustice must not be added to the wrong. The fairy-tale nature of Mary McCarthy's early life—the child of indulgent, attractive parents who died in a 'flu epidemic; adoption into the care of an inadequate aunt and uncle, both brutal and cold; rescue by a Protestant grandfather and his Jewish wife—all these experiences are without logic and require immense skills of adaptation. McCarthy's childhood seems devoid of affection; separated from her brothers, she is unable to gain substitute siblings in her friends since her talents single her out and cause resentment. Falsely accused of stealing the butterfly and beaten for refusing to conform, Mary 'finally limped up to bed, with a crazy sense of inner victory, like a saint's, for I had not recanted, despite all they had done or could do to me'. The injustice that is the basis of this scene permeates Mary's sense of being unrecognized—of not being given due attention: 'It had come to me, suddenly, that I was neglected because the convent did not know *who I was*.' She seeks to remedy this situation with a dramatic loss of faith and an equally dramatic recovery of it.

McCarthy's story is a drama of adolescence; her hopes and fears are conventional ones but are highlighted by the bizarre and varied nature of her upbringing. It has often been said that female autobiographies stop short at the adult years because from that time on social and other expectations mean that women lose their identities in the pre-ordained rôles of wife and mother (though family life can often provide a hidden area of powerful irresponsibility). Mary McCarthy's memoir ends with references to her future college life and her first (failed) marriage; but the emphasis is on the growth of the writer's mind, and she uses significant visual detail to enforce her argument about the problematic nature of recall and the instinctive reordering of experience to make a better 'story'. The author's comments on her own unconscious shaping of her material provoke questions as to the relationship of 'fiction' to 'reality' and show that, in the very act itself, the potential autobiographer is subconsciously developing a myth; her task, as Hellman claims also, is to make what sense of it she can. Apart from purely biological events it has been said that this memoir could be the record of the early years of a sensitive and gifted man. The difference appears only in the final chapter 'Ask Me No Questions', in which Mary McCarthy confronts the taboo subject of her grandmother's personality and attempts an assessment of this complex female enigma and her own relationship to it. The opening sentence itself indicates that McCarthy will have to face issues earlier hidden under the witty account of archetypical childhood problems. 'Ask Me No Questions' initiates its discourse of disclosure in this way: 'There was something strange, abnormal, about my bringing-up; only now that my grandmother is dead am I prepared to face this fact.'[43] Telling the forbidden story of her grandmother's life involves McCarthy in an enterprise that is potentially dangerous for herself:

> Starting to tell that story now, to publish it, so to speak,
> abroad, I feel a distinct uneasiness, as though her shade were
> interposing to forbid me. . . . She would never forgive me for
> what I am about to do. . . .[44]

What McCarthy does is to reveal the total negativity of female
narcissism; her grandmother's life was one in which her body
was everything, her mind nothing, and this existence is gradually
perceived by the author, as her own sensibility develops from
childhood to maturity, to be a kind of play-acting that hides real
horror. McCarthy, as autobiographer, will avoid this fate by the
exercise of mind and will, moulding to a satisfactory and
pleasing pattern the material her experience as a woman gives
her. Her grandmother's body was 'the cult object around which
our household revolved'; in later years, this body was a relic to
which the family was devoted, a relic 'laved and freshened every
day in the big bathroom, and then paraded before the public in
the down-town stores'. The grandmother's punitive grief for the
death of her daughter and for her own 'tragedy' (a failed face-
lift) caused her to adopt a reclusive way of life and to impose it
on the family. 'Life itself was obliged to court her'; McCarthy's
grandmother's strategy for dealing with the world was to seduce
it (rather than to subject it to the exercise of perception, the
mode of operation chosen by McCarthy herself). Clerks and
shop-assistants were her suitors whom she defied to please her;
potential purchases were treated with the same teasing, almost
sexual, playfulness:

> She would set the hat or hats back on the table, as if she were
> through with them. . . . She was the same with her shoes and
> dresses: she would even coquette with a piece of meat; it was as
> though she would not give these things the satisfaction of letting
> them see that she liked them. To her, every piece of merchandise,
> suing for her favour, appeared to enter the masculine gender and
> to be subject, therefore, to rebuff.[45]

In spite of these perverted attempts at the control of her
environment, the grandmother is clearly a victim, dependent on
the impossible preservation of her physical beauty. Verbally,
she courts sympathy and affection by the telling of anecdotes in
which she is the constant loser; her story-telling is another form
of self-display:

142

She is always the loser in these anecdotes; she never gets the better of the situation with a biting retort, as she often did in real life. But because she is the heroine, she is usually rescued, in the nick of time.[46]

McCarthy's grandmother's ritualized behaviour only cracks on one occasion; significantly, it is the death of her sister which causes an almost animalistic reaction—in total contrast to the willed sophistication and pretence of the rest of her life:

My grandmother understood before I could tell her, before I had set down the telephone. A terrible scream—an unearthly scream—came from behind the closed door of her bed-room; I have never heard such a sound, neither animal nor human, and it did not stop.[47]

Emotionally, McCarthy understands that this is the clue to the mystery of her grandmother's life: 'it seemed clear to me that night, as I sat stroking her hair, that she had never really cared for anyone but her sister.' Intellectually, McCarthy has had a revelation about the quality of Jewish family feeling and the elements of 'classic Jewish mourning'. Finally, her grandmother's senility focuses on the very narcissism that has caused her essential loneliness; the concluding and conclusive image of *Memories of a Catholic Girlhood* is of the grandmother, 'wrought up', searching for a mirror. This search for validation and worth is the result of her presentation of herself as an aesthetic object and in itself creates her isolation:

She was lonely. This was the thing that made her seem so garish and caused people to turn their heads when she went by. Loneliness is a garish quality, and my grandmother's wardrobe and elaborate toilette appeared flamboyant because they emphasised her isolation.[48]

McCarthy's own concern in writing her memoir is to create a verbal, rather than a physical, artefact, defeating loneliness.

3

Many autobiographies address themselves to the question of marriage versus work; the family can be a trap which dissociates the woman from her real self and destroys her identity. This is not just a twentieth-century phenomenon; several nineteenth-century authors consider these problems in detail, in writing which is both direct and concealed autobiography. *The Yellow Wallpaper* (1892), for instance, charts the obsession and madness of a protagonist curiously more sharply defined than the 'real' personality in Charlotte Perkins Gilman's *Autobiography* (published in 1935, after her death). Both Charlotte Gilman's *The Yellow Wallpaper* and Kate Chopin's *The Awakening* (published in 1899) are deeply subversive documents, covert attacks on the institution of the nuclear family. The staccato style of *The Yellow Wallpaper* enunciates the deep emotional and mental disturbance of its protagonist, a disturbance that is nevertheless chillingly rational (as William Dean Howells described it in 1920, 'a story to freeze our . . . blood'). It seems that the mask of fiction released Charlotte Perkins Gilman from the inhibitions and guilts of 'straight' autobiography, so that, in fictional terms, she could attack convention and insist on the right and need of women to work. Marriage rendered women ineffectual and silenced them and yet, as Gilman stated in her *Women and Economics*:

> all that she may wish to have, all that she may wish to do, must come through a single channel and a single choice. Wealth, power, social distinction, fame,—not only these, but home and happiness, reputation, ease and pleasure, her bread and butter,— all, must come to her through a small gold ring.[49]

The origin of the heroine's neurosis in *The Yellow Wallpaper* is the stifling nature of marriage itself and the fact that she is 'absolutely forbidden to "work"'. Obviously, her own view is the correct one: 'Personally, I believe that congenial work, with excitement and change, would do me good', but the patriarchal system insists that her view must be wrong because it is hers. She is incarcerated in an 'atrocious nursery' and consequently 'hasn't felt like writing since the first day'; indeed, she is counselled against the exercise of her imagination:

> John has cautioned me not to give way to fancy in the least. He says that with my imaginative power and habit of story-making, a nervous weakness like mine is sure to lead to all manner of excited fancies, and that I ought to use my will and good sense to check the tendency.[50]

The heroine's sister-in-law keeps watch to prevent any writing taking place ('I verily believe she thinks it is the writing which made me sick!'). Since she is not allowed to do anything, her confidence and self-esteem disintegrate; she continues to try to express what she feels and thinks, but the effort is becoming too great. The success of the family in silencing and infantilizing the heroine results in complete alienation; she identifies with the imaginary woman imprisoned behind the wallpaper and with the creeping women of her hallucinations. As Elaine Hedges has commented, the suicide of Kate Chopin's heroine and the madness of the heroine of *The Yellow Wallpaper* are:

> all deliberate dramatic indictments, by women writers, of the crippling social pressures imposed on women in the nineteenth century and the sufferings they thereby endured: women who could not attend college although their brothers could; women expected to devote themselves, their lives, to aging and ailing parents; women treated as toys or as children and experiencing who is to say how much loss of self-confidence as a result. It is to this entire class of defeated, or even destroyed women, to this large body of wasted, or semi-wasted talent, that 'The Yellow Wallpaper' is addressed.[51]

Kate Chopin's *The Awakening* initially defines its protagonist as the property of her husband: 'You are burnt beyond recognition' ... 'looking at his wife as one looks at a valuable piece of personal property which has suffered some damage'. Mrs. Pontellier, in the course of the narrative, gradually emancipates herself from the rôles of wife and 'mother-woman':

> The mother-women seemed to prevail that summer at Grand Isle. It was easy to know them, fluttering about with extended, protecting wings when any harm, real or imaginary, threatened their precious brood. They were women who idolized their children, worshiped their husbands, and esteemed it a holy privilege to efface themselves as individuals and grow wings as ministering angels.[52]

Edna Pontellier, on the contrary, works to develop herself as a separate individual who does not exist for the benefit and use of others, but in her own right. She tells Madame Ratignolle that she would never sacrifice herself for her children, or for anyone:

> I would give up the unessential; I would give up my money, I
> would give up my life for my children; but I wouldn't give
> myself. I can't make it more clear; it's only something which I
> am beginning to comprehend, which is revealing itself to me.

In a symbolic scene, she flings her wedding ring down on the
carpet and tries to stamp on it and crush it, 'but her small boot
heel did not make an indenture, not a mark upon the little
glittering circlet.' Even the positive vision of marriage presented
by her friend Madame Ratignolle fails to inspire or impress her:

> Edna felt depressed rather than soothed after leaving them.
> The little glimpse of domestic harmony which had been offered
> her, gave her no regret, no longing. It was not a condition of life
> which fitted her, and she could see in it but an appalling and
> hopeless ennui.[53]

Edna, up to this time, has lived in a world of fantasy, deeply
introverted and introspective, her thoughts and dreams the only
possessions she can call her own. Her developing love for
Robert draws her into the real world of pain and longing; Kate
Chopin isn't operating as a moralist and there is no condemna-
tion of this situation. Edna must be true to the integrity of her
own needs, not submit to hypocritical social mores. Inevitably,
her husband's response to her growing self-assertion is to
suspect that she is mentally unbalanced:

> He could see plainly that she was not herself. That is, he could
> not see that she was becoming herself and daily casting aside that
> fictitious self which we assume like a garment with which to
> appear before the world.[54]

Edna's liberation continues as she takes a lover and moves to
her own house. Robert reappears, but the consummation of
their relationship is delayed by Edna's attendance at her friend's
latest childbirth: 'With an inward agony, with a flaming, out-
spoken revolt against the ways of Nature, she witnessed the
scene of torture.'[55] Returning, to take possession of Robert,
rather than being herself possessed, she finds him gone: 'Good-
by—because I love you.'

The metaphor of swimming has been used throughout the
novel to stand for freedom and autonomy, but proves to be
deeply ambivalent: 'She grew daring and reckless, overestimating

her strength. She wanted to swim far out, where no woman had swum before.'[56]

Edna has experimented with different life-styles, conventional marriage, the life of the artist, independence and unrestricted sexuality. Her suicide by drowning has its own sexual connotations:

> The water was deep, but she lifted her white body and reached out with a long, sweeping stroke. The touch of the sea is sensuous, enfolding the body in its soft, close embrace.[57]

Her experimentation ends in failure—she cannot cope with marriage, solitude or with an artistic vocation; in all areas she functions as a dilettante, lacking discipline and stamina.

The Awakening ends with the protagonist in a state of negative control, in charge of her own death, if not of her own life. In *The Bell Jar* (1963), Sylvia Plath's autobiographical heroine Esther Greenwood achieves an ambiguous success, being delivered from the mental hospital into the outside world but still guiding herself by the eyes and faces of her doctors, 'as by a magical thread'. She has been reborn, 'patched, retreaded and approved for the road'. Throughout *The Bell Jar*, Esther tries on and rejects various identities, or rather, she contemplates the many images of women available to her in her culture; none seem appropriate or even possible. There is no woman she wants to be and no man she wants to be identified with:

> That's one of the reasons I never wanted to get married. The last thing I wanted was infinite security and to be the place an arrow shoots off from. I wanted change and excitement and to shoot off in all directions myself, like the coloured arrows from a Fourth of July rocket.[58]

Esther, after each initiating plunge into a new experience, desires, like the persona of the Plath last poems, a purging purity. Her manipulative mother 'with her sweet, martyr's smile', defines her previous experience as 'a bad dream' but, 'To the person in the bell jar, blank and stopped as a dead baby, the world itself is the bad dream.'[59]

After the suicide of Joan, her alter-ego, Esther is able to begin to recover, narcissistically displacing her failures onto the other girl. As Joan is buried, Esther, 'took a deep breath and listened to the old brag of her heart. I am, I am, I am.'

If Esther learns anything, it is to reject false images of women and to resist other women who try to implicate her in their own suspect fictions: 'they all wanted to adopt me in some way, and, for the price of their care and influence, have me resemble them.' Esther's advance on Edna Pontellier's position lies in the fact that she rejects these surrogate selves, rather than the self she has managed to develop in the face of great cultural and emotional odds. Her negative memories are her psychological 'landscape', but, at the end of the book, she, at least, has the possibility of incorporating them into a more coherent self.

The Bell Jar ends hesitantly; not so a more recent auto-biographical work which exists on the level of fantasy and fact. In *The Woman Warrior* (1976), Maxine Hong Kingston constructs a myth of woman as swordsman, as instigator of a new martial art: 'When we Chinese girls listened to the adults talking-story, we learned that we failed if we grew up to be but wives or slaves.'[60]

The heroine puts on armour and goes out to do battle with her enemies; asked to identify herself, she claims, 'I am a female avenger.' On the literal level, the protagonist claims her identity in spite of the lack of value accorded her by her own community because she is a girl and by American society at large because she is a member of an ethnic minority. As with all the other woman practitioners of American autobiography discussed here, Maxine Hong Kingston, through the examination and recreation of myth, attempts the articulation of her 'real' self.

NOTES

I am indebted to the pioneering work of Patricia Meyer Spacks in *The Female Imagination* and to the perceptive introductions of Janet Hobhouse and Helen McNeil in the Virago editions of Stein and H.D.

1. *Everybody's Autobiography* (London, Virago, 1985), p. 53.
2. 'The Personal Life Deeply Lived' in *The American Autobiography*, ed. Albert E. Stone (Prentice-Hall, Inc., 1981), p. 163.
3. *The Autobiography of Alice B. Toklas* (Harmondsworth: Penguin, 1981), p. 228.
4. *The Geographical History of America* (New York: Vintage Books, 1973), p. 74.
5. *Memories of a Catholic Girlhood* (London: Heinemann, 1957), pp. xi–xii.

6. *Toklas*, p. 272.
7. *E.A.*, p. 278.
8. Ibid., p. 184.
9. Ibid., p. 277.
10. *Her* (London: Virago, 1984), p. 148.
11. Ibid., pp. 161–62.
12. *Paris Review Interviews*, ed. George Plimpton (Harmondsworth: Penguin, 1981), p. 383.
13. *Her*, p. 168.
14. Ibid., pp. 172–73.
15. Ibid., pp. 71–2.
16. *The Gift* (London: Virago, 1984), p. 1.
17. Ibid., p. 4.
18. Ibid., p. 139.
19. *Bid Me to Live* (London: Virago, 1984), p. xiii.
20. Ibid., p. 8.
21. Ibid., p. 11.
22. Ibid., p. 62.
23. Ibid., p. 77.
24. Ibid., p. 89.
25. Ibid., p. 97.
26. Ibid., p. 96.
27. Ibid., p. 103.
28. Ibid., pp. 135–36.
29. Ibid.
30. Ibid.
31. Ibid., p. 162.
32. Ibid., p. 164.
33. Ibid., p. 176.
34. Ibid.
35. Ibid., p. 177.
36. *An Unfinished Woman* (London: Quartet Books, 1977), p. 84.
37. Ibid., p. 78.
38. Ibid., pp. 65–6.
39. Ibid., p. 60.
40. Ibid., p. 11.
41. Ibid., p. 155.
42. *Memories of a Catholic Girlhood* (London: Heinemann, 1957), pp. xxxi–xxxii.
43. Ibid., p. 172.
44. Ibid., p. 175.
45. Ibid., p. 198.
46. Ibid., p. 196.
47. Ibid., p. 223.
48. Ibid., p. 199.
49. Quoted in *The Yellow Wallpaper*, ed. Elaine R. Hedges (London: Feminist Press, 1973), p. 57.
50. *The Yellow Wallpaper*, pp. 15–16.
51. *Afterword*, p. 55.

52. *The Awakening*, p. 16.
53. Ibid., p. 93.
54. Ibid., p. 96.
55. Ibid., p. 182.
56. Ibid., p. 47.
57. Ibid., p. 189.
58. *The Bell Jar* (London: Faber, 1966), p. 87.
59. Ibid., p. 250.
60. *The Woman Warrior* (London: Picador, 1981), p. 25.

7

'The Stance of Self-Representation': Moderns and Contemporaries in Afro-American Autobiography

by A. ROBERT LEE

1

Very soon after I went to live with Mr. and Mrs. Auld, she very kindly commenced to teach me the A,B,C. After I had learned this, she assisted me in learning to spell words of three or four letters. Just at this point of my progress, Mr. Auld found out what was going on, and at once forbade Mrs. Auld to instruct me further, telling her, among other things, that it was unlawful, as well as unsafe, to teach a slave to read. To use his own words, further, he said, 'If you give a nigger an inch, he will take an ell. A nigger should know nothing but to obey his master—to do as he is told to do. Learning would *spoil* the best nigger in the world. Now,' said he, 'if you would teach that nigger (speaking of myself) how to read, there would be no keeping him. It would forever unfit him to be a slave. . . .' These words sank deep into my heart, stirred up sentiments within that lay slumbering, and called into existence an entirely new train of thought. It was a new and special revelation, explaining deep and mysterious things, with which my youthful understanding had struggled, but struggled in vain. I now understand what had been to me a most perplexing difficulty—to wit, the white man's power to enslave the black man. It was a grand achievement, and I prized

151

it highly. From that moment, I understood the pathway from
slavery to freedom.
—*Narrative of the Life of Frederick Douglass, An American Slave,*
Written by Himself (1849)

When, under the imprint of the Boston Anti-Slave Office,
Frederick Douglass issued his landmark *Narrative*, he must have
hoped that it would serve a number of ends. First, irrefutably, it
would offer his rallying-cry against all the unconscionable abuse
of slavery, a call to moral if not physical arms in the cause of
abolition. Second, it would be his own act of witness, the
'narrative' quite uniquely of his birth, upbringing, survival
skills, hirings-out, and eventual dramatic escape north to New
England from Maryland. In both it would show America's
white, and ostensibly Christian, citizenry the profound travesty
implicit in having a slave population, slavery as known and
indicted by a recent ex-slave. His slim volume, in other words,
sought to speak unaffectedly but compellingly to a single
purpose: the closing down, for ever, of America's 'peculiar
institution'.

In this respect, too, the patent immediacy of Douglass's
account—and its evidentiary, plain-style manner—had their
part to play. Here was a transcript directly from life, slave-
drama written by a fugitive still in theory open to recapture.
There is certainly anything but hype on Douglass's part in his
refusal to name those who have helped him or to give the full
details of his escape for fear of reprisals and the compromise of
fellow slaves who might follow in his wake. Yet as celebrated as
the *Narrative* was to become in his own lifetime, especially given
Douglass's acclaim as an abolitionist orator, he could hardly
have predicted the kinds of deciphering (and now deconstruction) still later readerships would visit upon it. In confirming its
place for them also as the pre-eminent slave narrative, they
have insisted upon it as a generic or canonical Afro-American
text. Its confessional format, its identifying iconography and
motifs—not least the journey from darkness to light—enscribe
a crucial process of black self-becoming, the self recreating its
identity in precisely the way a literary text itself is edited and
composed. Douglass's double act of defiance, thereby, the
escape itself and the very style in which he makes account of

that escape, are to be seen as having laid down track for nearly all subsequent Afro-American autobiography. The above extract, then, yields a number of connecting departure points. It represents the *Narrative* at strength. It suggests something of the emblematic or generic other meanings behind Douglass's telling. And it offers precisely a forward perspective.

At one level Douglass does no more than recall his first forbidden steps into literacy under the 'kind' tutelage of his Maryland slave-master's wife. But he recalls, too, in terms of 'a new and special revelation' and the explanation of 'deep and mysterious things', his transforming recognition that access to the word—to its hitherto prohibited powers for him of defining self and reality—has had quite as much to do with his liberation as his clandestine flight northwards. For as much as he may have defied his literal enslavement by escaping underground to Boston, he sees, too, that actually up to the time of writing the *Narrative* he has remained subject to the subtler tyranny of having to construe himself on the basis of names and categories created by his one-time owners and even by the Quakers and abolitionists who have helped him to his freedom. In this sense he has continued, even after slavery, to be 'owned' by others.

As a slave, according to his *Narrative*, he had been forced to exist within the definitional orbit of 'slave', 'nigger', 'property', 'boy' or 'hand', together no doubt with others which convention did not permit him to print, terms always outside his own choosing and calculated only to de-individuate and possess. Even the term 'ex-slave' says virtually nothing about him as a self, merely another, however welcome, category. Not that he could relax into that category, either. Despite writing from Boston and a Free State he remains in law, as his sub-title indicates, *An American Slave*. Thus when, in a moment whose importance he especially invites his reader to ponder, he recalls his action of actually composing himself as 'Frederick Douglass' (from a choice which includes 'Frederick Augustus Washington Bailey', 'Stanley', 'Frederick Johnson' and plain 'Frederick') he shows how arbitrary has been his past naming, an 'identity' contrived as it were on the spot.

But on account of Mrs. Auld's teaching of the alphabet, understandably so alarming to her husband, there will indeed

153

be 'no keeping' Douglass as a slave. Under his new-made signature of 'Frederick Douglass', he can attempt not partly but wholly to remake the meaning of his life and experience, his *Narrative* or *Life*, indeed a 'story', but in quite equal measure a re-enactment of that story to his own new-found and further de-enslaving terms of reference. For the *Narrative*, we cannot but see, whatever its surface ingenuousness amounts to nothing less than Douglass's profound reconstitution and articulation as much to and for himself as to and for his readers. In this, it serves him and his successors as nothing less also than a new genesis, a new politics, of identity.

In this connection, too, the other component in his title, *Written by Himself*, takes on similarly more inclusive layers of implication. It does, to be sure, offer an immediate credential, a would-be personalized guarantee of a life lived cruelly first-hand under the terms of the South's 'peculiar institution', and not even at its worse down-river extremes at that given Maryland as a tobacco-producing rather than a cotton and chattel-slavery state in the Deep South. It clearly also suggests that Douglass deliberately wanted to comment on the fact that, as he has his Mr. Auld remind his wife, it was both 'unlawful' and 'unsafe' to allow slaves to write and read. But still more of import lay behind the phrase.

Douglass had recognized the abiding connection between literacy and liberation, the appropriation of the word back from those who hitherto have done the defining as being crucially as important to his self-meaning as the appropriation of his own physical body from south to north in 'the pathway from slavery to freedom'. As he further cites Mr. Auld, in words which would have not been amiss had they been spoken by Mark Twain's Pap Finn: 'If you teach that slave to read. . . . It would for ever unfit him to be a slave'. Douglass's *Narrative*, in other words, represents an illegal or outlaw text not simply because it violates slave laws about literacy or gives the account of an escape which could have rendered Douglass liable to recapture under the Fugitive Slave Bill (and to escape whose provisions he took off to England). It represents trans-gression of a profoundly more consequential kind, autobiography as the 'making' of the self in the face of that self's historic denial.[1]

2

The jump from Frederick Douglass (1817–95) to Richard Wright (1908–60), with whose two-volume autobiography *Black Boy* (1945) and *American Hunger* (post. 1977) the present essay properly begins, is a large one, and assumes a number of stopping-off places en route. Nevertheless, Wright as much as any other autobiographer in Afro-American tradition, returns us precisely to those concerns about self—and about self-representation—so unaffectedly set out by Douglass. Who has rights of definition over whom? What is it to speak, and write, in one's own 'black' voice, be the context that of slave-holding Maryland or that of a South Side and Depression Chicago? In what ways, for a black writer more than his or her white counterpart, does autobiography give access not only to a personal but a collective self, especially one forged in slavery and the wilful erasure of communal African beginnings? How, in addition, does a *written* account of black selfhood tie in with a culture whose styles of everyday expression, folklore, religion, humour, storage and release of experience, overwhelmingly have been oral? Despite all their evident differences, Douglass 'up from slavery' in the 1840s and Wright born the son of a Mississippi sharecropper, a Chicagoan by adoption in the 1930s, and destined to head the expatriate black literary colony in the Paris of the 1950s, both speak to this shared and continuing complex of questions. As, it quickly becomes evident, do still later black autobiographies. For black American autobiography, modern and contemporary, has been nothing if not also about the refinding and remaking of a usable language of self, both in individual terms and in the name of a larger Afro-America.

Douglass's *Narrative* also points ahead to how Afro-American autobiography has evolved as a form, a style of self-narrative. In subsequent narrative, 'enslavement' serves as a persistent metaphor, lives once written out of American history and now both literally and figuratively resolved to write themselves back in. One has only to think in time of Malcolm Little becoming the Malcolm X of his *Autobiography* (1964), of Maya Angelou's traumatized speechlessness as a child becoming the articulate self of her five-volume autobiography, or LeRoi Jones's radicalizing self-transposition into the Black Nationalist and latterly Marxist *griot* Imamu Amiri Baraka. Or, to return to Wright, the itinerant child whom the older man in his two-part autobiography re-invents as 'Richard'. Thus self-naming, the self as a 'text' to be written only by its sovereign owner, become recurring ingredients—a process symptomatically also at the centre of Ralph Ellison's *Invisible Man* (1952), still the high point of Afro-American fiction and not least because it too performs so cannily as 'autobiography'.

Nor indeed can one get from Douglass to Wright and his successors without acknowledging how these issues have shown up in intervening other black autobiography. Allowing for pioneer 'firsts' like *A Narrative of the Uncommon Sufferings and Surprising Deliverance of Briton Hammond, a Negro Man* (1760) or *The Interesting Narrative of the Life of Olandah Equiana, or Gustavus Vassa, the African* (1789), together with a number of so-called 'conversion' and 'captivity' narratives, three discernible tiers in the tradition require mention—especially in how they address the whole issue of self-representation.[2]

First, there has to be reckoned in all the other American slave-narrative, a huge archive of vivid (if at times overlapping) human witness and drama. The best-known by, say, William Wells Brown (1847), J. W. C. Pennington (1849), Henry Bibb (1850), Solomon Northrup (1853), John Thompson (1856), William and Ellen Craft (1860), Harriet Jacobs (1861), James Mars (1870), or Sojourner Truth (1875), in their respective ways, share with Douglass's *Narrative* the concern that liberation, true freedom, also means as far as possible the reconstruction of black selfhood in their author's own language.[3]

For quite as much as slave-narrative is 'about' lives under, or in escape from, literal Southern servitude, it also becomes for the ex-slave as in Douglass's case a further act of de-enslavement. In the very creation of the told life, as it were, void is replaced by identity, blank by signature. No longer, thereby, can the self be viewed as object and not subject, or through a coded, incarcerating slave language of ownership, colour, work-function, or brute sexual utility. Rather in the self-written narrative, the former slave authenticates, celebrates even, his or her liberation, possessing rather than being possessed by, the word. In these respects, not just Douglass but all his fellow makers of slave-narrative can be said to have taken Mr. Auld's 'ell' from his 'inch'. As, again, though in quite other styles, will Douglass's successors in the furtherance of Afro-American autobiographical tradition.

A second tier involves three turn-of-the-century classics. In *Up from Slavery* (1901), Booker T. Washington moves on from slave-narrative *per se* into what he himself explicitly terms 'autobiography'. Though born a slave in Virginia, and subject to the same arbitrary naming and semi-anonymity as Douglass ('Of my ancestry I know almost nothing'), the 'self' he shows to emerge is that of the assured race-leader, the presiding spirit of Tuskegee Institute and the postbellum Great Conciliator. It is, at every turn, a most carefully fashioned public self, supported by extracts from the press and his own correspondence, a *Life* meant clearly to exemplify his own precepts of unmilitant assimilation. Later black Americans have not judged him kindly in this, Washington as an Uncle Tom, too ready in his deference to the white-supremacist *status quo*. That he was more self-divided, impatient and adroit than *Up from Slavery* (and his other autobiography) suggests, shows up some of the complication of using the form as a public or exemplary mode, a point of continuing relevance in black-political, sports, and show-biz autobiography—be it, among others, Adam Clayton Powell, Sr.'s *Against the Tide: An Autobiography* (1938) or Shirley Chisholm's *Unbought and Unbossed* (1970), Joe Louis's *My Life Story* (1947) or Muhammad Ali's *The Greatest: My Own Story* (1975), Billy Holiday's *Lady Sings the Blues* (1956) or *Good Morning Blues: The Autobiography of Count Basie* (1985).

More to later taste, undoubtedly, has been the figure of W. E. B. DuBois and *The Souls of Black Folks* (1903), anything but slave narrative. DuBois speaks at once from outside and (by an act of self projection at least) from inside the legacy of slavery, a Harvard-educated black Yankee and historian, the coming figure behind the N.A.A.C.P., and the unappeasable voice—and self—of educated black militancy. His, at least on the evidence of *The Souls of Black Folk*, is the professional self observing in the manner of the social scientist (being *Dr.* DuBois was of importance), the musicologist of black Southern field songs and blues, the analyst of the failures of Reconstruction, and the acclaimed philosopher of the 'veil' of race and the

157

alleged 'twoness' of all Afro-Americans. Less frequently read, though in many ways an altogether more personalized expression of the man behind the public figure, is his trilogy, *Darkwater: Voices Within the Veil* (1921), *Dusk of Dawn: An Essay Towards an Autobiography of a Race Concept* (1940) and *The Autobiography of W. E. B. DuBois* (1968).

At a slight remove, there has to be invoked, too, James Weldon Johnson's *The Autobiography of an Ex-Colored Man* (1912), a novel rather than literal autobiography, a story of 'passing' and racial impersonation which opens a perspective not only on 'ragtime' America (whose spirit is again recalled in the Scott Joplin-like figure of Coalhouse Walker in E. L. Doctorow's *Ragtime* (1974)), but also on the rich imaginative possibilities of exploring the ways of the colour-line. Johnson's novel also anticipates a crucial tradition of still later fictionalized black autobiography, *Invisible Man* to be sure, but similarly important first-person narratives like John A. Williams's *The Man Who Cried I Am* (1967), Ernest Gaines's *The Autobiography of Miss Jane Pittman* (1971) and Gayl Jones's *Corregidora* (1975).

With the Harlem or New Negro Renaissance, a less adversary note is sounded. The general buzz and hopefulness caught in Alain Locke's manifesto/anthology, *The New Negro* (1925), carries over into nearly all the black autobiography which arises out of the 1920s.[4] None expresses this upward note better than Langston Hughes's *The Big Sea: An Autobiography* (1940) and *I Wonder as I Wander: An Autobiographical Journey* (1956), the black creative self as a species of *flâneur*, a harlequin or picaresque figure moving across a human landscape triumphantly more various than any prescribed by segregation or racist stereotype. James Weldon Johnson's *Along this Way* (1933) similarly assumes a self in possession of itself, an ease with the world not altogether surprising in a man of consequential mixed Caribbean stock, a black 'first' in being admitted to the Florida bar, the holder of American consulships in Venezuela and Nicaragua, a Professor at Fisk, and an internationally recognized lyricist and anthropologist. Johnson's accent throughout bespeaks authority, a self sure of its centre. Claude McKay's *A Long Way from Home* (1937), in turn, offers 'the distilled poetry of my experience', a life of politics, travel, writing, and the gamesome record both of his Jamaican beginnings and of his 'American' blackness as an experience both at home and abroad. In their considerably different ways, Hughes, Johnson and McKay embody the very spirit of the New Negro Renaissance, life and times in the black, Harlem-centred 1920s as the promissory note of a major change in racial fortune.

The Wall Street Crash and the Depression were to change matters utterly in this respect. For Richard Wright, who follows in their wake, the process has virtually to begin all over again. In the light of a South rekindled into Klan-led racial hate, and a North, a Chicago in Wright's case, ghettoized and impoverished, autobiography serves once more as a means of giving form to the black-American self in dispossession. 'Modern' Afro-American autobiography can so be said to begin with Wright, alongside, it might be argued, two others of his immediate generation, Zora Neale Hurston (1903–60) and Chester Himes (1909–84). In turn, with James Baldwin and Ralph Ellison as figures of transition, the 1960s yield a subsequent, 'contemporary' autobiography, the expression of a decade of Black Power. The insistence, more explicitly than ever before, again falls upon a re-conceived language and iconography of black selfhood, nowhere more tellingly than in the replacement of Negro by Black, the former discarded as a term of racial deference and the latter taken up as being thought in tune with a racial militancy beyond Civil Rights and the Christianized politics of integration set out in Martin Luther King's autobiography *Why we Can't Wait* (1964) and again in his wife Coretta Scott King's *My Life With Martin Luther King, Jnr.* (1969). Its undoubted centrepiece has to be *The Autobiography of Malcolm X* (1964), against which are to be measured the essays, narratives, self-contemplations of a generation which includes Eldridge Cleaver, George Jackson, Rap Brown, Stokely Carmichael, Bobby Seale, Huey Newton and Claude Brown. They, in their turn, can now be viewed through an ensuing tier of black autobiography which came to the fore in the 1970s, not least by Nikki Giovanni, Julius Lester, John Wideman, LeRoi Jones/Imamu Amiri Baraka and, most strikingly, Maya Angelou.

The tradition, evidently, has been, and is, a considerable one. Yet for present purposes one name more especially needs to be added to those so far given, that of Angela Davis, even into the 1980s a committed West Coast member of the American

Communist Party and the author of *Angela Davis: An Auto-biography* (1974). Charged amid all the drama of Black Power with 'murder, kidnapping and conspiracy', she recalls in *If They Come in the Morning*, a political anthology issued in 1971, her address to the California court: 'only in the stance of self-representation will I be able to properly and thoroughly con-front my accusers.' 'The stance of self-representation' I have consciously widened to serve as a gloss, a working departure-point, for all the autobiographies covered here, though not, it is hoped, at the expense of losing the phrase's historic legal resonance. For Davis's phrase could not supply a keener link back to Douglass's '*Written by Himself*', both steeped in legal implication and both an insistence on the undiminishing black need to be understood on terms not imposed from 'outside'. 'Self-representation', then, carries a more than usually heavy weight of meaning for how Afro-America has sought to articu-late both its individual and collective identity. And nowhere more defiantly, or engagingly, than in its tradition of auto-biography, be it indeed early, modern or contemporary.[5]

3

Towards the close of *Black Boy* (1945), Richard Wright sounds a note which especially recalls Douglass and other major writers of slave-narrative:

> Not only had the Southern whites not known me, but more important still, as I had lived in the South I had not had the chance to learn who I was.

'To learn who I was', to be sure, does not implicate Wright in an actual slave escape. But it does argue a similar shedding of imposed terms of reference along the lines implicit in Douglass's *Narrative*. Both *Black Boy* and the posthumous *American Hunger* (1977) bespeak a will to articulacy, a quite compelling impulse to name and so control for oneself the world at hand in all its difficulty and contradiction. Thus as much as his autobiography gives off an extraordinary eventfulness—the itinerant family moves across Mississippi, Arkansas and Tennessee and the eventual migration north into Chicago—Wright's emphasis also falls almost unfailingly upon his coming authorship. For in speaking time and again of his 'hunger', he is speaking of an artist's hunger, the compulsion to 'learn who I was' as an act of self-enscription, at one and the same time the 'black boy' of Southern writ, 'Richard' and Richard Wright.

Read one way, *Black Boy* can indeed be construed as almost all 'event'. The volume opens with a scene of arson, the boy's singular, visceral will to burn down the family house. It is this 'Richard', too, who strangles the kitten to spite the father who will eventually abscond, then mockingly display his new woman, and whom Wright will later recall as a spectral, uncomprehending black field-hand. The account fills out with remembrances of the child alcoholic, the intimidated witness to his mother's stroke, the victim of his Aunt Addie in all her pentecostal fury and of his mean, Adventist Grandmother, and the duped deliverer of Klan newspapers. This 'other self' of his childhood and adolescence is also the 'Richard' who sleepwalks, can strike back at his adult persecutors with an open knife, and who cheats, lies and hustles too much ahead of his time. His early work-experiences both at the optical company and the Memphis hotel bring him ever more implacably up against the Dixie colour-line. In none of these 'events' does 'Richard' operate from his own centre, merely in rôles which signal displacement, an enforced otherness.

But throughout Wright calls attention to the boy's nascent creativity, the literary self-in-waiting as it were. He offers a Whitmanesque catalogue of natural impressions brought on after the boy's beating for his part in the fire. He recalls the magic he associated as a child with the riverboat *Kate Adams*. He thinks back on the impact of the sumptuous 'conjure' and folklore of his black boyhood, from the sexual slang to 'the dozens' to the communal parables and stories. He re-tells his insistence on reading his own class-address as against that of his Tom-like High School Principal. And, finally, he underscores the 'redemption' he found in reading Mencken and through him a whole circuit of major literature. Nor, for nothing, does he also recall the segregated Southern library which necessitated the subterfuge of the forged ticket—reading, and eventually writing, as proscribed activity, a kind of black cultural out-lawry. The literary prospect so long denied him becomes his for the taking. 'The South', too, whatever its actualness in his life, he now transforms into a site lodged deep within the imagination, at once a remembered sense of place and a usable past. It is this transformation, too, that he has in mind when he writes, 'I knew I could never really leave the South'—a view his fiction amply vindicates. 'Richard' so becomes Richard Wright, the author as successor to his own 'character'.

The same process continues over, or is re-enacted, in *American Hunger*. Chicago, even as he arrives, for all its stockyard, wind-swept reality, and even its black South Side, strikes him as also 'an unreal city'. Once again he finds himself an oddly displaced person, in no one job or rôle for any length of time, whether with the Hoffmans, at the Post Office, in the John Reed Club or at the outer fringes of the Communist Party. More and more he shows how the self he most recognizes to have been his own is that of the writer, the custodian of his own naming of things. He vows, or says he vowed at the time, to give utterance to 'the area of No Man's Land into which the Negro mind in America has been shunted'. He refers, insistently, to 'my excessive reading', to 'stabs of writing' and to pages 'full of tension, frantic poverty and death'. He thinks of the 'language' of his difference from the white shopgirls with whom he works, from the white medical researchers at the laboratory, from the C.P. brethren and the 1936 May Day marchers, and even from many of his fellow blacks. To one Marxist, in a nice irony, he is denigrated for seeming 'to talk like a book'. But he is impressed also by those Soviet Marxists who have sent phonetic experts into the hinterlands to capture the speech of peasantry who under Czarist repression have hitherto been 'tongueless people'. He also gives something of the origins of his own first short stories, among them 'Big Boy Leaves Home', 'Down by the Riverside' and 'Long Black Song', stories at once grounded in fact and yet shaped into parable and near-folklore.

American Hunger, like *Black Boy* before it, uses autobiography to enact a process whereby all Wright's past promptings to self-articulation are finally and defiantly written into being. In this he avails himself of the volume's perhaps most haunting image, that of the dogs in the laboratory whose vocal chords have been cut and 'who would lift their heads to the ceiling and gape in soundless wail'. Wright's 'self-representation' in both volumes enacts how he has put his own 'soundlessness' to rest,

162

dramatically made vocal that within him which previously has been unvoiced. Both parts of his autobiography, in sum, yield nothing other than a Portrait of the Artist, 'Richard' as the begetter of Richard Wright as surely as 'Stephen Daedalus' can be said to have begotten James Joyce.

'Like the dead-seeming, cold rocks, I have memories within that came out of material that went to make me. Time and place have had their say.' On that 'down-home', typically beckoning note Zora Neale Hurston opens her *Dust Tracks on a Road* (1942). But for all that hers has rightly come to be regarded as the most consequential of all pre-1960s auto-biography by a black woman, it has also been hedged with controversy. Did she, as her biographer Robert Hemenway and others have alleged, fudge much of the detail of her life?[6] Is her autobiography indeed 'less than frank', 'a kind of camouflage', too unwilling to 'explain racial segregation' or to disclose the entire reality of her own racial experience? To an extent the answer has to be yes; there are omissions, some massaging of the apparent facts, and on occasion a no doubt too kind reading of white racial malpractice and patronage.

But what redeems *Dust Tracks on a Road* is not just 'style' as Hemenway also alleges, but Hurston's massively subtle and exemplary feats of organizing her other material. For she tells her life as itself an instance of the very folk culture which she knew both as an insider brought up in Eatonville, Florida (the first all-black incorporated township in America) and as the anthropologist with a hard-won training at Barnard College and Columbia under the tutelage of the likes of Franz Boas and on field-trips in Haiti and the West Indies. The extraordinary good ease of her writing, her resorts to the sayings of her upbringing—'I have been in Sorrow's kitchen and licked out all the pots' is probably as well-known as any—shows through at every turn. For her autobiography yields both a life-story and an act of homage, a life as wholly particular as any and evi-dently more sweet than sour though never other than both, and at the same time a celebration of the black culture that bred her. Muted, easeful of her white readership's sensibilities at least, Hurston's critique of the American colour-line may be.

163

But that should not be confused with her kindly, generous cross-racial willingness to let the non-black reader in and to be engaged and educated by the account she has to offer.

The 'stance', equivocal as it has been to some, she sustains with great adroitness. She may especially have infuriated a number of black contemporaries and a later round of black-nationalist critics by her coolness to 'race solidarity' ('And how can Race solidarity be possible in a nation made up of so many elements in the United States?'). She may, too, have inveighed impatiently against 'this Negro business', against black as well as white 'race clichés', and against the assumption of any one single black identity ('There is no *The Negro* here'). But who would doubt the warmth and nourishing insider-ness she feels for her own black roots? When, for instance, she recalls with some pain her father's attitude to her in childhood, she does so with a clear appreciation of the inventiveness of black idiom: 'A little of my sugar used to sweeten his coffee right now. That is a Negro way of saying his patience was short with me.'

This same stylish recreation of idiom recurs. Of her 'visions' in childhood she says: 'A cosmic loneliness was my shadow.' She glosses her own poetizing habits in Eatonville as follows: 'My phantasies were fighting against the facts.' Of her furious grappling-match with her stepmother, she avers: 'This was the very corn I wanted to grind.' For all her later 'vagrancy' and her 'for ever shifting', as she calls it, 'I was a Southerner and the map of Dixie was on my tongue.' Under Boas and her teachers she took on the academic research into folklore and black myth; yet she can still also describe herself in more homely manner as 'delving into Hoodoo, a sympathetic magic'. In remembering the publication of her first stories and books like *Jonah's Gourd Vine* (1934) and *Mules and Men* (1935), she observes not a little startlingly: 'You know that feeling when you found your first pubic hair.' Of her friendship with Ethel Waters she writes: 'I am her friend and her tongue is in my mouth.'

These, and a dense tissue of similar sayings, mark out *Dust Tracks on a Road*, not least as she recalls Cudjo Lewis, the last ex-slave born in Africa and still alive in her time; or the Eaton-ville of her near-mythic kinsfolk ('Papa said he didn't have to do but two things—die and stay black'); or her own love-affairs ('I did not just fall in love. I made a parachute jump'); or, even, her refusal to be trawled into a uniform American 'blackness' ('And why should Negroes be united? Nobody else in America is'). Similarly, in her willingness to tackle sexual as well as racial materials, she writes with an edge as acerbic as anything in Dorothy Parker ('I may be thinking of turnip greens with dumplings, or more royalty checks, and here is a man who visualizes me on a divan sending the world up in smoke'). Robert Hemenway rightly calls attention to the 'paradox of the public and private Zora Neale Hurston'. Even an otherwise fervently admiring Alice Walker speaks about 'oddly false-sounding' elements in *Dust Tracks*.[7] But that, nonetheless, cannot detract from the best of her autobiography. At strength she shows all her characteristic verve, her own affirmations and nay-sayings.

If any especial motifs recur in Chester Himes's two volumes of autobiography, *The Quality of Hurt* (1972) and *My Life of Absurdity* (1976), they are in fact indicated at the outset in his very title-phrases: hurt and absurdity.[8] For few black literary narratives can have reflected a career more punitive, violent or, even at the time of writing, more unresolved. Himes's stance, throughout, is to tell, stably, a life of marked instability, that of a personality on his own admission 'argumentative, bad-tempered, and unsympathetic'. His opening volume admits quite freely to 'the eccentricities of my creativity', 'blind fits of rage'; its successor to 'the absurdity of my life', 'my sensitivity towards race', the endeavour 'to find a life into which I could fit'. Yet Himes writes anything but mere pathology. Far from it; his autobiography directs us well beyond himself into a world of change, personalities and event, indeed in this latter respect, a world as eventful as the Coffin Ed Jones/Grave Digger Johnson Harlem detective series which first saw print under the Gallimard imprint as *romans policiers* in the 1960s and through which his reputation has had its best-known success.

The Quality of Hurt covers the years from his birth in 1909 in Jefferson City, Missouri, to his European exile in the early 1950s. The stopping-off places en route read like pages from his own fiction: the cruel decay of his parents' marriage (which he used in *The Third Generation* (1954)); the freak blinding in a gun-

165

powder incident of his brother Joseph which haunted Himes throughout his life (Joseph Himes went on to a distinguished career in sociology at the University of North Carolina); his own back injury in a lift shaft and his being cheated of proper compensation; his time at Ohio State University where his gambling and Cleveland hustling background quickly got him into trouble (he had hung about with an exotic character named Bunch Boy); and the bizarre chain of events which led to his sentence for a jewel theft in 1929. His seven tough years in jail he would put to account in *Cast the First Stone* (1952), especially a murderous prison fire. Released in 1936, he married Jean Johnson, wrote a series of prose poems for the *Cleveland Daily News*, worked under the auspices of the F.P.A. on a history of Cleveland, continued to produce the crime and prison stories he had begun while still serving his sentence, spent time on Louis Bromfield's community farm at Pleasant Valley, Ohio, and saw the publication of his first novel, *If he Hollers Let him Go* (1945).

His different women, cars, cats, houses, apartments and encounters, enforce the impression of a man likely to respond to experience with the sharpest nervous intensity. Of the shifts in his life, he remarks: 'I can truthfully say there has been nothing permanent in my life but change.' During his time with Alva Trent, a principal source for Elizabeth Hancock in the novel for a long time available only in French, *Une Affaire de Viol* (1963), he helped to write *her* autobiography, *The Golden Chalice*, unfortunately never published. *The Quality of Hurt* takes Himes through to his meetings in Paris with Wright and Baldwin, on to Spain (he describes a tetchy encounter with Robert Graves in Mallorca) and London, where he found the racism and general seediness especially depressing—not least because he was in the company of a white woman. The volume closes with a confession of continuing 'hurt', a man still to find any sure point of stillness amid the flurries of travel and relationship.

Two observations in particular mark out the volume. In the first, Himes offers his stand as a writer:

> No matter what I did, or where I was, or how I lived, I had considered myself a writer ever since I'd published my first story in *Esquire* when I was still in prison in 1934. Foremost a writer. Above all a writer. It was my salvation, and is. The world can deny me as an ex-convict, as a nigger, as a disagreeable and

unpleasant person. But as long as I write, whether it is published or not, I'm a writer, and no one can take that away. 'A fighter fights, a writer writes,' so I must have done my writing.

The other, a run of insights made while describing the circumstances in which he wrote the intimately autobiographical novel, *The Primitive* (1955), gives a measure both of Himes's personal contrariness and his estimate of what blackness in America and beyond can mean. The phrasing, intendedly or not, nicely echoes Crèvecoeur:

> The American black is a new race of man; the only new race of man to come into being in modern time. And for those hackneyed, outdated, slavery time racists to keep thinking of him as a primitive is an insult to the intelligence. In fact, intelligence isn't required to know the black is a new man—complex, intriguing, and not particularly likeable. I find it very difficult to like American blacks myself; but there's nothing primitive about us, as there is about the most sophisticated African.

That kind of contrariness, and the hurt which underlies it, does not sit easily in any camp.

My Life of Absurdity continues the momentum: the moves back and forth between Europe and America; the Paris café circles once more; the edgy friendships with Wright, Carl Van Vechten, George Lamming, Jean Giono, Marcel Duhamel, Malcolm X, younger fellow writers like John A. Williams, Melvin Van Peebles, and still subsequently, Nikki Giovanni; his rise to fame with the *Série Noire* thrillers; the continuing travels and amours; his eventual second marriage to Lesley Packard, a white Englishwoman and journalist with whom in his last years he made his home in Spain; his disabling stroke in Mexico; the penchant for fast cars; and his emotional purchase of a permanent house in Jávea. Himes hardly wrote a life which can be said to have come to order. Perhaps he found that impossible. 'No American', he alleges, 'has ever lived a life more absurd than mine.' His further comments on blackness, on expatriation, and on the writer's psychology and craft, give additional detail to that 'absurdity'. That Himes remained, by his own account as much as any other, cantankerous, easily angered, as hard on black brothers as well as white Europeans and Americans, in all as 'hurt' and 'absurd' as he professes, gives both volumes of autobiography a quite compelling interest. In suggesting 'the black man is a harlequin', he also offered as pertinent a clue as any to his own life.

4

No black autobiography better signals the transition from modern to contemporary than that of Malcolm X. Which is not for a moment to pass over James Baldwin, especially the epochal, self-testifying pieces which won him his early reputation, *Notes of a Native Son* (1955), *Nobody Knows my Name* (1961) and *The Fire Next Time* (1963). Of Baldwin's own literary generation, perhaps only Norman Mailer has shown the same ability to make the self a sounding-board for the passage of history, American racial turmoil and change as played out through a unique witnessing sensibility. Nor is it to ignore the stately presence of Ralph Ellison, his novel *Invisible Man* (1952) as always, but also his many essays, especially those which touch upon his own life—be it his Oklahoma upbringing, his education and young adulthood in the South, his observations on his own craft and that of other writers, his interests in Jazz, sculpture and the iconographies of blackness, or his notes upon the Harlem he has long made his home. These bestow an important personal dimension on the work collected as *Shadow and Act* (1964), and latterly, *Going to the Territory* (1986). But however unignorable, neither Baldwin nor Ellison, in any strict sense, has been an autobiographer.

Nor, given the 1960s of Civil Rights, Black Power, and the demands for a clenched-fist black art to match, was either seen as politically at one with the temper of things. Baldwin came under indictment for his continuing faith in liberalism, castigated not only for his 'accommodationism' but as Eldridge Cleaver notoriously alleged for his not unrelated sexual orientation towards white men. Ellison, to his black-radical critics, simply appeared too aloof, too mandarin and actually conservative, to be of political use. Travesties these accounts may have been, but they arose from the conditions of their time and place. For a clearer agenda beckoned: change in the American racial *status quo* by the deed, by a politics of confrontation and violence. And the text to hand—more so even than the broadsheets of

S.N.C.C., C.O.R.E., the Black Panthers and the rest—was to be found in *The Autobiography of Malcolm X* (1964). Here, in all its dire prophetic accuracy ('If I'm alive when this book comes out, it will be a miracle'), lay a call to arms, a history of the making of black insurrectionary identity, an 'exemplary' life. Other 1960s-bred black autobiography was to play its supporting rôle, but a black-American 'stance of self-representation' as embattled, as headily and articulately combative, was without precedent.

Consider, for instance, the history bound up in Malcolm's name-changes. 'Malcolm Little' is the self who leaves Omaha, Nebraska for Detroit, and then, via his step-sister Ella, moves on to Boston, the drop-out, the conked and zoot-suited adolescent ('my first really big step towards self-degradation'), quick to move into drugs and street crime and hustle of every stripe. 'Red' becomes his community name, the 'mariny', light-skinned hoodlum youth. In Boston he becomes 'Homeboy', his step-sister's ward. Once in Harlem ('I had seen a lot, but never such a dense concentration of stumblebums, pushers, hookers, public crap-shooters, even little kids running around at midnight begging for pennies') he becomes 'Detroit Red', a Numbers man, pimp, drugs-pusher and eventual house-thief. The continuing 'robberies and stick-ups' ('I can't remember all the hustles I had during the next two years in Harlem') land him, at not yet 21, with a ten-year sentence, seven of which he serves under the name of 'Satan' as given him by his cellmates for his blasphemy and anti-Christianity. But there, too, he first hears of 'something called "The Nation of Islam" ', the next stage in his name/life changes.

Correspondence with Elijah Muhammad, a ready belief that Christianity had 'taught the "negro" that black was a curse', a convert's remorse at 'the very enormity of my previous life's guilt' and self-education from prison library books, leads on release to his Black Muslim incarnation—first as 'Brother Malcolm', then 'Malcolm X' and eventually 'Minister Malcolm X'. This 'self', in turn, becomes the self seized upon and reworked by the media, that of the fantasized Muslim black racist and hatemonger who brings down upon himself an ever hungrier American T.V., press and campus following. The 'stance' he himself believed to be putting on offer he summarizes as follows for his co-writer and amanuensis Alex Haley:

> I'm telling it like it is! You never have to worry about me biting my tongue if something I know as truth is on my mind. Raw, naked truth exchanged between the black man and the white man is what a whole lot more of is needed in this country—to clear the air of the racial mirages, clichés, and lies that this country's very atmosphere has been filled with for four hundred years.

Recalling his life under the Honorable Elijah Muhammad's direction—and his preaching not only of black separatism but the whole 'devil' counter-theology of Yacuub and satanic whiteness—he sets the ground for what, in the discovery of Muhammad's adulteries and his own *Hajj* to Mecca, will become 'my psychological divorce from the Nation of Islam'. In his further transforming encounter with 'orthodox Islam', a religion as he learns essentially tolerant and inclusive of all races, he recognizes the error of his past Muslimism (Prince Faisal tells him ' "the Black Muslims have the wrong Islam" '). Re-born into this new Islamic self he becomes 'El-Hajj Malik El-Shabazz', the same figure who journeys on to Beirut, Cairo, Ghana, Liberia, Senegal, Morocco and Algeria and whom the Nigerian Yoruba will call 'Omowole', 'the son who has come home'. Back in the America where his break with Elijah Muhammad has become ever more dangerous, he seeks the establishment of his own 'Organization of Afro-American Unity', the ecumenical beneficiary of his *Hajj*. 'A marked man', as Haley witnesses him saying, this last and subsequent Malcolm dies by the bullet, at one, tragically, with the Malcolm who earlier has observed, 'I hope the book is proceeding rapidly, for events concerning my life happen so swiftly.'

The 'self' which Haley so elicits and for which Malcolm himself provides an overlay of glosses, the *Autobiography* shows to exist doubly both in time past and present, the human sum of a forty-year span yet to the end still powerfully in process of finding its essential centre. One can, as above, trace that self through Malcolm's naming. Or through the different women who make up his life: his mother so traumatically recalled; the strong figure of his Boston kinswoman, Ella; his first true girl-friend Laura for whose demise through drugs and prostitution he holds himself accountable; the white woman 'Sophia'; the myriad other chippies and streetwomen; and ultimately, Sister Betty X, the respected Muslim black woman who becomes his wife and the mother of his children. The odd, almost contrary puritanism, which characterizes his relationship with women, offers as he himself acknowledged an important clue to his personality.

Or, one can turn to the settings which will also characterize other 1960s black autobiography: the street, the tenement, the pool-halls, the ghetto at large, and above all, the penitentiary. Other prison names will become benchmarks—San Quentin, Soledad, Attica. But though in Malcolm's case his jails do not carry the same resonance, respectively Charlestown State Prison, the Concord Prison and the Norfolk Prison Colony, they prototypally do offer both a major phase of his life and a source of recurrent imagery (' "The white man is a devil" is a perfect echo of the black convict's lifelong experience'). As much as Malcolm's *Autobiography* bears witness to the politics of separatism, to the imperative of ditching white versions of black, to his own self-transformations, it at the same time offers the most dynamic theory of black personality, an Afro-American life once again unfixing and literally rewriting the terms of its own identity.

Other forms of radical, convict or ghetto autobiography follow in abundance in Malcolm's wake, a litany of black self-interrogation and dissent. Few did so less accommodatingly than Eldridge Cleaver's West Coast prison and Black Panther essays, *Soul on Ice* (1968), *Post-Prison Essays and Speeches* (1969) and *Conversations with Eldridge Cleaver* (ed. Lee Lockwood, 1970). It was Cleaver, especially, who on hearing of Malcolm's assassination wrote from his Folsom, California, cell: 'We shall have our manhood. We shall have it or the earth will be levelled by our attempts to gain it.' But that 'manhood' was not only to be of a political kind. The 'self-representation' he finds in his own writing equally serves him as a means to 'save myself', to slough off the Cleaver 'who came to prison'. Nor was Cleaver the only Black Panther to have written from the legal margins. In Bobby Seale's *Seize the Time* (1970) and *A Lonely Rage* (1978) and Huey Newton's *To Die for the People* (1972), though without Cleaver's flair, a further witness is given to black radicalization, a process with necessary reference to the F.B.I., police shoot-outs, street violence and arms. These, in turn, invite comparison with other 'confessional' and radical lives like H. Rap Brown's *Die Nigger Die!* (1969) or Hoyt Fuller's *Journey to Africa* (1971).

171

The black 1960s, California-style at least, also found auto-biographical expression in two further and linking works, *Soledad Brother: The Prison Letters of George Jackson* (1970) and Angela Davis's *An Autobiography* (1974). Not only do they re-enact lives made revolutionary by racial oppression, they testify to the alliance their authors forged in life, Jackson the self-taught, obdurate and existentialist lifer cut down by the bullets of his Soledad guards, and Davis, the Marxist 'sister' revolutionary whose black-bourgeois origins nonetheless took her on to Communist Party membership and an ideology much shaped by Herbert Marcuse. To these should be added the fictionalized 'ghetto' autobiographies of Claude Brown's *Manchild in the Promised Land* (1965) and Piri Thomas's *Down these Mean Streets* (1967), the former the history of a Harlem Street adolescence and the latter that of a life inside 'barrio' Puerto Rican Harlem. 'Stances of self-representation' of necessity differ across this 1960s spectrum. But they all collectively can be said to have found a precedent in Malcolm's *Autobiography*, the contributing disclosures of a newly found and newly released black American selfhood.

5

Nor has the impulse to 'represent' that selfhood autobio-graphically and in all its continuing variety in any way abated. The 1960s legacy of reconstruing self and blackness, for instance, presses hard behind Nikki Giovanni's *Gemini: An Extended Autobiographical Statement on my First Twenty Five Years of Being a Black Poet* (1971). Its emphasis upon the 'black' creativity in her own life is made inclusive not only of her literary inclinations but of the wider contributions of style and strength of the black community at large and most especially of its black women— above all those of her own Knoxville, Tennessee family. At a quite other reach, a Life told as inventively as his *Jazz*, stands *Beneath the Underdog: His World as Composed by Mingus* (1971), Charlie Mingus's collaborative but wonderfully unusual and at times surreal self-chronicles. Less performative, though no less singular, has to be Vincent O. Carter's *The Bern Book* (1973), the cryptic self-anatomy of a Kansas City exile who becomes 'the only black man' in the Swiss capital.

Three 'literary' autobiographies also add formidably to the stock: Julius Lester's *All is Well* (1976), the history of a life which comes to adulthood in the ferment of the Black Power era and eventually finds its balance in the Catholic quietism of Thomas Merton; John Edgar Wideman's *Brothers and Keepers* (1984), the 'dual' family narrative of Wideman himself as the assured University of Pennsylvania and Oxford-trained novelist, and of Robbie Wideman, his street-raised, 'vernacular' brother, currently serving life for murder in Pennsylvania's Western Penitentiary; and *The Autobiography of LeRoi Jones/Amiri Baraka* (1984), the dense, formidable account of a Black Newark and New York 'growing up' within an American 'maze of light and darkness'. Though he designates his autobiography 'partial evidence', Jones/Baraka could not have contrived a more activist life, prodigious in its literary output and as his composite name signifies one of shifting identities from Beat to Black Nationalist to Marxist. Few writer/radicals have been more responsive to, or implicated in, the drama of racial change in America in the post-war period, a 'self-representation' equally in art and politics.

But still one other autobiography, or autobiographical sequence, needs to be brought into the account, Maya Angelou's five volumes of self-portraiture, a rare and vivid *Life* told from its Southern beginnings in Stamps, Arkansas, and brought forward across fifteen years of writing to her experiences in post-colonial West Africa. Hers, too, signals a forward move from the 1960s and its male-centred versions of 'militancy' and 'confrontation', a portrait of sexual as much as racial identity. Which is not to underplay the lively circumstantial reference to origins and experience lived vitally inside her blackness. But her emphasis as much also falls upon gender, the 'stance' of a black writer-performer as equally explorative of her womanhood as of her colour.

'In Stamps the segregation was so complete that most Black children didn't really, absolutely know what whites look like.' Such is the note on which Angelou opens *I Know Why the Caged Bird Sings* (1970). Her first memories are of dreaming she is a white child, a contradiction all her subsequent history will make abundantly plain. At 8 she is raped by her mother's black fancyman, Mr. Freeman, ('A breaking and entering when even the senses are torn apart. . . . I thought I had died'), a trauma which leaves her literally speechless for years. The writerly self she was to manifest lay closed inside this silence, one eased only by her Grandmother's support and that of her brother Bailey. Existing, too, amid a circle of competing names—'Margaret', 'Marguerite Johnson', 'Ritie', 'My', and eventually 'Maya', she moves out to her mother in California ('foggy days of unknowing for Bailey and me'), gives vent to 'my newly awakening sexual appetite' by the birth of her son Guy while still in her teens, and poignantly recalls the 'end' of childhood. She speaks, in retrospect, too, of the shaping powers about her, a 'tripartite crossfire of masculine prejudice, white illogical hate and Black lack of power'. Against that, the self she most senses within her has yet to find its 'representation'.

Gather Together in my Name (1974) starts amid the euphoria of America's World War II victory. Not that she herself had access to that euphoria ('I was seventeen, very old, embarrassingly young, with a son of two months . . .'). Job-seeking up and down the West Coast, at one point seeking entry to the Army, she embarks upon a series of near Gothic adventures, the high points as a 'Madam' in a brothel serviced by two lesbian women and as part of a nightclub dance act with one R. L. Poole. None of her different men, nor her different employment— waitressing, cooking Creole food, part-timing at the edges of show business, gives her definitive meaning. 'My life had no center', she acknowledges. Her sexuality becomes the only commodity left, and she begins her 'first slide into the shiny world of mortal sin', 'tricking' for Hispanic clients, the property of an exotic pimp named LD. As she says laconically: 'Survival was all around me but it didn't take hold.'

All three successive volumes witness to the increasing repossession of her life. *Singin' and Swingin' and Gettin' Merry Like Christmas* (1976) depicts her love-affair with a white Greek-American, her subsequent career as a 'shake' dancer in San Francisco, her theatre triumph in *Porgy and Bess*, and her picaresque times on tour in Europe. Still 'an assembly of strivings', her life takes increasing definition in motherhood, the protective intimacy she finds with her son. *The Heart of a Woman*

(1981) offers no lessening in the picaresque: the move to New York and a life lived amid the Harlem literary set, a singing career at the Apollo Theatre, participation in Martin Luther King's S.C.L.C., a starring rôle in Genet's *The Blacks*, and her unlikely marriage and life in London and Cairo with the South African freedom politician Vusumzi Make. Despite her son's near fatal accident in a crash, she witnesses his enrolment at the University of Ghana, a mother in her pride. *All God's Children Need Traveling Shoes* (1986) brings her African odyssey up to date, an affectionate memoir of Ghanaian culture and landscape, of the black literary circle headed by the expatriate and novelist Julian Mayfield, of Malcolm X's visit, and above all of her profound sense of continuity with the African women in whose lineage she places herself ('Despite the murders, rapes and suicides we had survived'). Race, culture and gender so blend, a life brought close to its own historic self-understanding. Maya Angelou's 'self-representation' triumphs precisely and fundamentally in this eclecticism, an Afro-American autobiography if ever there were to confirm the continuing strength of *Lives*—in an adaptation of Frederick Douglass's phrase—'written by myself'.

NOTES

1. No doubt because he thought the story could never wholly be told in all its completeness, Douglass went on writing—and rewriting—his Life. See, therefore, Frederick Douglass, *My Bondage and my Freedom* (New York, 1855) and *The Life and Times of Frederick Douglass* (Hartford, Connecticut, 1881).
2. A recent study which tackles both 'conversion' and slave narratives is William L. Andrews *To Tell A Free Story: The First Century of Afro-American Autobiography, 1760–1865* (Urbana: University of Illinois Press, 1986). Also of use is William L. Andrews (ed.), *Sisters of the Spirit: Three Black Women's Autobiographies* (Bloomington: Indiana University Press, 1986).
3. Anthologies and editions of slave narrative have proliferated. Of particular note are: Arna Bontemps (ed.), *Great Slave Narratives* (Boston: Beacon Press, 1969); Gilbert Osofsky (ed.), *Puttin' on Ole Massa: The Slave Narratives of Henry Bibbs, William Wells Brown and Solomon Northrup* (New York: Harper, 1969); Norman R. Yetman (ed.), *Life Under the 'Peculiar Institution': Selections From the Slave Narrative Collection* (New York: Holt, Rinehart and Winston, 1970); John F. Bayliss (ed.), *Black Slave Narratives* (New York: Collier

Books, 1970); and especially George P. Rawick (ed.), *The American Slave: A Composite Autobiography*, 8 volumes (Westport, Connecticut, 1971–). Also of relevance: Charles Nichols: *Many Thousand Gone: The Ex-Slaves Account of their Bondage and Freedom* (Leiden: Brill, 1963; Bloomington: Indiana University Press, 1969), and Julius Lester, *To Be A Slave* (New York: Dice Press, 1968).

4. Alain Locke (ed.), *The New Negro: An Interpretation* (New York: A. and C. Boni, 1925; reprinted New York: Athenaeum, 1968; New York: Arno, 1968; New York: Johnson, 1968).

5. In writing this essay I have benefited from the following: Rebecca Chalmers Barton, *Witnesses for Freedom: Negro Americans in Autobiography* (New York: Harper and Brothers, 1948); *The Negro In America: A Bibliography*, compiled by Elizabeth W. Miller, 2nd edn. by Mary L. Fisher (Cambridge, Massachusetts: Harvard University Press, 1966, 2nd edn., 1970, pp. 69–74); Russell C. Brignano, *Black Americans in Autobiography: An Annotated Bibliography of Autobiographies and Autobiographical Books Written Since the Civil War* (Durham: Duke University Press, 1974); Sidonie Smith, *Where I'm Bound: Patterns of Slavery and Freedom in Black American Autobiography* (Westport, Connecticut: Greenwood Press, 1974); Stephen Butterfield, *Black Autobiography in America* (Amherst: University of Massachusetts Press, 1974); Elizabeth Schutz, 'To be Black and Blue: The Blues Genre in Black American Autobiography', *Kansas Quarterly*, Vol. 7, No. 3 (Summer 1975), 81–96, and reprinted in Albert E. Stone (ed.), *The American Autobiography* (Englewood Cliffs, New Jersey: Prentice Hall, 1981); Robert B. Stepto, *From Behind The Veil: A Study of Afro-American Narrative* (Urbana: University of Illinois Press, 1979); C. W. E. Bigsby, *The Second Black Renaissance: Essays in Black Literature*, especially Chapter 7, 'The Public Self: The Black Autobiography'; Albert E. Stone, *From Henry Adams to Nate Shaw* (Philadelphia: University of Pennsylvania Press, 1982), especially Chapters 2, 4 and 7; Gordon O. Taylor, *Studies in Modern American Autobiography* (London: Macmillan Press, 1983), especially Chapter 2; and Henry Louis Gates, Jnr., *Black Literature and Literary Theory* (New York and London: Methuen, 1984).

6. See Robert E. Hemenway, *Zora Neale Hurston: A Literary Biography* (Urbana: University of Illinois Press, 1977). Also 'Introduction' to Robert E. Hemenway (ed.), *Dust Tracks on a Road* (Urbana: University of Illinois Press, 1984).

7. 'Foreword' to Robert E. Hemenway (ed.), *Zora Neale Hurston*, op. cit. See also Alice Walker's essays on Hurston in *In Search of our Mother's Gardens* (New York: Harcourt Brace Jovanovich, 1983).

8. Parts of this section appeared in an earlier form in A. Robert Lee, 'Hurts, Absurdities and Violence: The Contrary Dimensions of Chester Himes', *Journal of American Studies*, 12 (April, 1978) 99–114. See also Chapter 6 in Stephen F. Milliken, *Chester Himes: A Critical Appraisal* (Columbia: University of Missouri Press, 1976).

9. For a context of recent criticism and scholarship, see Claudia Tate (ed.), *Black Women Writers at Work* (New York: Continuum, 1983); Mari Evans (ed.), *Black Women Writers (1950–1980): A Critical Evaluation* (New York: Anchor Books, 1984); and Paula Giddings, *When and Where I Enter: The Impact of Black Women on Race and Sex in America* (New York: William Morrow, 1984).

8

Authenticity and Text in American Indian, Hispanic and Asian Autobiography

by DAVID MURRAY

1

Literary discussions of autobiography have mostly operated within the assumptions of Western literate societies about the nature of self and of text, but the American 'ethnic' auto-biographies examined in this essay offer a fundamental challenge, implicitly or explicitly, to those assumptions. 'Auto-biography', in as far as it concerns 'ethnic' lives, has been used to describe a wide range of text, ranging from memories elicited from an Indian tribesman, which have been translated, edited, re-arranged and published with notes and appendices by someone else, to works by Indians, Chicanos and Asians entirely written in English by their subject. These differences would seem to raise questions about relative authenticity, but the approach of this essay is to place such issues in a wider context by seeing all of these works as *texts*, which are the products of two unequally-related cultures.

Recent critical emphasis on issues of textuality, the increased awareness of the ways in which the 'I' becomes the 'other' through language, and the consequent problematic relation between this notion of text and the claims for certain sorts of authenticity contained within autobiography become particularly relevant here. This is because the cultural and social imbalances mean that the production of the text often operates to turn the speaking *subject* into an *object*, whether for study, entertainment, or the frissant of the exotic.

In this essay I deal with texts selected to represent the range of problems raised rather than to give a representative cross-section in terms of groups or subject-matter, and to this end I shall begin by developing a model based on the most problematic Indian texts and showing how it can usefully be applied even to later more recognizably literary autobiographies. This inevitably means that Indian materials will predominate in the essay, but there has been, in any case, very little Hispanic or Asian material of such relevance to my argument until comparatively recently. It must be stressed from the outset, though, that while I believe my argument can be applied to texts from these three different cultures, it is not my intention to underplay the enormous differences between, and even within, these cultures or their different relations to white literate America.

Indian autobiographies quite clearly present immediate problems of classification. What are we to make of works which announce themselves as autobiography but also claim on their title page to be 'by' a white editor, or by an editor who has conflated two separate lives into one, without fully acknowledging his own rôle in the process? The convention being broken here is the normal expectation that in an autobiography the same person is the subject of the narrative and its narrator, even if not the physical transcriber of it, and these anomalies are the consequence of the peculiar conditions required for the production of most Indian autobiographies—namely, the collaboration of several people–the subject, a white editor or anthropologist and, often, another Indian acting as translator. The texts thus produced are inevitably multi-voiced, hybrid products in which we can hear in varying degrees the 'speaking' subject but only through the ramifications and conventions of the written text.

Rather than criticize such works on grounds of historical or anthropological accuracy, it would seem to me more productive, using a number of perspectives from recent critical theory, to look at the whole range of such works as a distinct type of text. Arnold Krupat has usefully suggested that the term

178

'Indian autobiography' should apply specifically to those texts which exhibit 'bicultural composite authorship'.[1] This entails seeing them not as a corrupted and inferior form, but as a new form which reflects precisely the cultural limitations and contradictions inherent in a situation where oral and literate cultures meet. Krupat distinguishes these texts from what he calls 'autobiographies-by-Indians' where the composition of the text has a single source, but it would be wrong, in distinguishing the two types, to assume that the second, apparently more pure, form is not equally implicated in cross-cultural complicities and contradictions. By establishing first in their clearest manifestations the different voices in 'bicultural composite' texts, it should be possible to extend the analysis to single-source texts and then extend it to selected Hispanic and Asian works with the intention of showing the inevitable presence of conflicting and collaborating voices, even when emanating from only one source.

2

Biographies of famous Indians have long been popular, but apart from a few accounts actually written in English by converted and 'civilized' Indians, which follow the form of the providential narrative,[2] and some fragments and memoirs, it is not until *The Life of Black Hawk* (1833) that we find an account which purports to be an Indian's own life history.[3] Here we find many of the ingredients which are to recur in later autobiographies—the denial of any significant rôle, by the white editor, the claim to be presenting the authentic Indian himself, but also, in the text itself, the unmistakable hand of editor or translator—producing something which conforms to the literary standards of the times. The conventional stylistic flourishes are the editor's, even if the sentiments may be Black Hawk's, and in this case, the high-flown rhetoric has the effect of fitting Black Hawk into the mould of the defeated but noble redskin, a figure with great appeal to the popular imagination.

This popular view went hand in hand, of course, with the opposing view of Indians as savage monsters, and after the sensational newspaper reporting of his desperate fight for survival against American troops, Geronimo became the perfect exemplar of this view. When he published *Geronimo: His Own Story* in 1906, therefore, the editor S. M. Barrett, was at pains to put it in context. As prisoner-of-war, Geronimo agreed to tell Barrett his story but only if he could tell it all, and in his own way. There were official military objections, and Barrett's apprehension about associating himself too closely with Geronimo's views results in a series of anxious footnotes dissociating himself from Geronimo's version of historical events, and even, at one point, the insertion of a whole chapter to redress what he sees as the historical balance. These clearly-labelled intrusions by Barrett would seem to imply that we have here Geronimo's own voice—sufficiently his own, at least, to make whites nervous. Certainly there are forceful and uncompromising sections, and there are times when it seems as if two views are struggling against each other to be heard, but both voices are speaking English, and it is Barrett's English. Can the following be Geronimo on religion, for instance? 'In our primitive worship only our relations to Usen and the members of our tribe were considered as appertaining to our religious responsibilities.'[4] In addition, the arrangement into chapters and topics and the chronological order is Barrett's. Geronimo's manner of story-telling was distinctive. According to Barrett, he would not talk when a stenographer was present, nor wait for questions or corrections and would only tell at any one time what he wanted, but he would be prepared on a later occasion to hear his account re-read (in Apache) and to clarify and amplify it. Even so, he rapidly tired of the activity and completed it only to keep his word, so that the final product is, as John R. Leo puts it, 'an extraordinary mix; a text that was never meant to be except by the "writer" who is not its source'.[5] The chapter-titles are clearly Barrett's, a *textual* convention, but the book begins with several chapters outlining the beginnings of the Apache through mythology and tribal history, which has the effect of placing Geronimo's life firmly in a context that is *not* that of his white reader. Similarly, Geronimo nowhere seems interested in exercising introspection. He gives a record of events and his main purpose seems to have been to put the record straight rather than explore or even justify his own character and feelings, which would not be separable for him from actions and situations. In order to give even this version, though, he has to go against Apache practice in that he talks of the dead.

Geronimo is a particularly striking example of the trans-formations forced upon, and the uses made, of Indians in the American popular imagination and media as they moved from independent, alien and, therefore, profoundly threatening figures during the nineteenth-century to defeated, anachronistic sur-vivors, material for the exercise of suitable white emotions, whether the frissant of horror or idealized nostalgia or pity. Indians became comprehended within white linguistic and cultural categories—what Leo calls 'the encirclement of signs', and his article sets Geronimo's—or Barrett's—text usefully in this context. He sees Geronimo as ultimately escaping this encirclement, as taking on the system of values which imprisoned him, and using it for his own ends by exploiting his notoriety in the rapidly growing media—selling original photographs, riding in Roosevelt's inaugural parade, for instance. In this way, *His Own Story*, is Geronimo's way of subverting the system of values into which he is being subsumed precisely by cooperating with it. It is, as Leo says, 'the story of Geronimo's refusal to be enclosed'.[6]

It is important, then, to place the upsurge of interest in Indian material generally, both at popular and scholarly anthropological levels, in relation to the actual decline in autonomy and independence of Western Indians.[7] As they became *subject* peoples, they became, ironically, *objects* of white attention, comprehended in all senses. Texts such as Geronimo's seem to reverse the stereotype of the partnership of white man and Indian found in popular literature, in that 'the white man is silent, while the Indian, no longer a mute or monosyllabic figure, speaks for himself.'[8] Or *seems* to, because the text is not the voice, even if the white producers of the text are reluctant to admit it. John Neihardt's decision to call his celebrated text *Black Elk Speaks* (1932) illustrates this to perfection. His intention is solely to provide a medium through which Black Elk can speak, and to this end he creates a style which successfully incorporates what we have come to *expect* a dignified old Indian to sound like, were he to write in English. As with Geronimo, we have a composite authorship, but whereas Barrett intrudes and is at pains to dissociate himself from Geronimo, Neihardt puts himself and all his skills at the disposal of what Black Elk says—or what he *would* have said. Recent scholars have shown that some of the most celebrated and quoted passages are entirely Neihardt's,[9] and, in fact, his account of the creation of the text makes the composite authorship clear. He referred to it later as 'a work of art with two collaborators, the chief one being Black Elk',[10] and later changed the title page from 'as told to' to 'as told through', which reflected more clearly what he saw as his achievement in recreating 'the mood and manner of the old man's narrative'.[11]

Black Elk as a Lakota Sioux in the second half of the nineteenth century lived through the destruction of his tribe's economic and political independence, and he gives a vivid account of this, but he was also from an early age subject to visions, which marked him out within the tribe as possessing special spiritual powers. The book thus blends the historical and the spiritual to present a moving account of a world-view in which all aspects of existence are integrated into a whole, but which seems ultimately powerless to present the remorseless disintegrating forces of white civilization. This gives Black Elk's account an epic sweep and grandeur untypical of autobiographies, in that the individual becomes almost incidental, even though fully realized and human, but as Paul A. Olson has shown Neihardt, already working on an epic of the West, was particularly attuned to this use of history as allegory.[12] Whether we are responding to a Sioux vision and transcending our own cultural limitations or just responding to a predefined cultural category which we recognize as 'primitive' is perhaps impossible to decide, but knowledge of the marked shifts in popularity of different versions of Indianness should encourage a distinct scepticism about our ability to recognize or respond to something presented as transcendent of our own cultural limits, and the belated popularity of *Black Elk Speaks* in the 1960s has, therefore, to be seen in the context of the growing counter-cultural predilection for the irrational, supernatural and primitive which led to an increasing interest in, and idealization of, Indian culture.

Neihardt's intention was to show the *universality* of Black Elk's message, and this has been a common aim in literary treatments of Indians, but the development of modern anthropological interest in Indian life-histories was initially fuelled by very different motives. Under the influence of the great Columbia University anthropologist, Franz Boas, these life-histories came to be seen as an ideal way of recording the minutiae of life in a specific culture from a native perspective. What was required, then, was not the exceptional individual or the transcendent, supra-cultural experience, but the average and ordinary. Thus in his edition of the *Autobiography of a Winnebago Indian* (1920), Paul Radin introduced his subject as a 'representative, middle-aged individual of moderate ability',[13] an approach typical of that of many other anthropologists, as was his claim in a later work to have played a minimal rôle in the production of the text. Radin's concern was for scientific objectivity, which led him to misrepresent or underestimate his actual editorial and translating rôle. From his first scholarly publication in 1913 complete with parallel Winnebago text, through to *Crashing Thunder*, published for a more popular readership in 1926, Radin continually recorded and reworked several sets of material. Krupat demonstrates clearly the way Radin polished his translations and apparently even combined materials from different life-stories, but also cautions against discounting these texts as therefore more literary than scientific. All ethnographic accounts, he insists 'like histories and as well as fictional narratives, are texts and . . . no text can innocently represent the "order of things" independently of the orders of language'.[14]

Radin's pioneering work with the Winnebago was characterized by a profound concern to capture what is *distinctive* about that culture and its members, but, inevitably, he needs to express this distinctiveness in ways understandable within *our* conventions, since the alternative may simply be incomprehensibility, and he talks interestingly about our expectations of autobiography in his preface to *Crashing Thunder*. Our conventions, he asserts:

> effectually bar any true revelation. No man who regards his thoughts, feelings, and actions of sufficient importance for him to note them down in a diary or autobiography ever admits . . . that his life has not been a unified whole or that it did not gradually lead to a proper and early heralded climax.[15]

By contrast, this narration lacks any retrospective unity, and this is particularly interesting in that this particular narrative records

a conversion experience. After several inconclusive attempts to
have a vision as prescribed by traditional Winnebago religious
practice, Crashing Thunder eventually experiences this by
means of peyote, and becomes an adherent of the Native
American Church. His story's lack of retrospective patterning
is, therefore, in very marked contrast to the convention of
American providential autobiographies, and Radin praises
precisely the lack of reflexiveness and self-awareness which
would be seen as a deficiency in a conventional white autobiography. In his introduction to a Navaho autobiography, *Son
of Old Man Hat* in 1938, it is interesting to find the linguist
Edward Sapir making similar claims:

> It is in no sense the study of a personality. It is a sequence of
> memories that need an extraordinarily well-defined personality
> to hold them together, yet nowhere is this unique contribution
> obtruded upon us. We are in constant rapport with an intelli-
> gence in which all experiences . . . are held like waving reeds in
> the sensitive transparency of a brook.[16]

The desire to give the subject's *own* account, but to con-
textualize it, and explain how it was produced, often creates the
effect of a multi-layered sandwich. Nancy Lurie, for instance,
following in Radin's footsteps, played a similar rôle in the
production of *Mountain Wolf Woman: Sister of Crashing Thunder*
(1961),[17] and in the resulting text we are given a foreword, a
preface, a text with extensive footnotes, then the first brief
version of her life given by Mountain Wolf Woman which she
extended when she saw Lurie's disappointment—indicating
the influence of white expectations in the creation of such texts.
After all this, there is commentary on both texts by Lurie. If we
ask about the relative *authenticity* of these various accounts, we
can hardly avoid acknowledging certain problems. What rôle,
for instance, does a letter from Mountain Wolf Woman written
in poor English and reprinted in Lurie's introduction, play in
the combination of voices? It has a very different sort of claim to
authenticity from that of the rest of the text which was spoken in
Winnebago but is given to us in an English which is not like
that of the letter. We are offered either her poor written
English—which leaves us at a distance from her 'real' voice,
though is *her* own actual product, or a translation of her

speaking Winnebago which uses all the (white) literary and
scholarly resources available to recreate the 'real' speech and all
its resonances.

The same sandwich effect is often found even when the
subject speaks good English, as is the case with the Hopi
Indian, Don Talayesva, in his *Sun Chief: The Autobiography of A
Hopi Indian* (1942). The editor, Leo Simmons, gives a full
account of the production of Talayesva's story which is

> a highly condensed record in the first person and almost always
> in Don's own words. . . . The report is not free narrative but
> selected and condensed narration, interwoven with additional
> information obtained by repeated interviewing.[18]

He also appends several chapters of analysis of this life-history
and life-histories in general, so that we have the opportunity to
judge him and his approach as well as Don Talayesva, and this
is relevant to a notoriously sensitive issue raised in the book, the
reluctance of Hopi and other Indians to reveal details of
ceremonials to outsiders.[19] Simmons' account of overcoming
Talayesva's reluctance is noticeably devoid of any introspection
on his part about the propriety of his actions, and throws into
relief the issue of whether Talayesva is *subject* and making his
own choices, or *object* to be studied and manipulated. The
stance of scientific objectivity is revealed in all its limitations
here and in the style of his introduction, with its obliteration of
his own rôle through passive constructions. ('Increasing interest
was shown in Don's personal experiences. . . . It was explained
in great detail that . . .') and most notably in the breathtaking
and dangerous proposition that we are more objective in
dealing with what is alien than what is familiar:

> The subject was selected from an alien society, and within a
> culture greatly contrasted with our own, in order to insure
> objectivity and to emphasise the molding impact of culture upon
> personality.[20]

A vivid picture does, nevertheless, emerge, through Talayesva's
life-story, of conflicts and changes caused by the intrusion of
whites and their values into probably the most traditional
Indian culture. His matter-of-fact narration of his dreams
reveals both the fascination and the fears generated by his own
white contacts. He dreams, for instance, of being arrested for

'writing false reports to Washington' but defends himself so well that he is sent back to school, at 50, to become a judge. In the back room of the school a white woman helps him take a bath, with erotic embraces thrown in. In another dream, the Chief has been arrested for performing his ceremonial duties. Talayesva discovers him 'imprisoned in a large box with his head sticking out a hole, and a man was standing over it with a big sharp knife, ready to chop it off'.[21] He rescues the chief by arguing the Hopi right to practise their own religion, thus acting the rôle of mediator in the dream which he took on in his life and in the creation of his autobiography.

Don Talayesva's response to white culture is an ambiguous one, walking the line between being taken over and taking over,[22] and the autobiographies discussed have reflected this, often not so much in the substance of the narratives as in their bicultural hybrid form, where the different registers of language sometimes combine and sometimes struggle for dominance. Even in the case of books clearly authored by one person in the more conventional way, this issue of conflicting language does not disappear, since the two cultures are then incorporated and remain unreconciled within the single author and his text. Charles Eastman, who became a distinguished Indian spokesman and public figure earlier in this century, was sufficiently 'civilized' to write his own autobiography, and the two volumes he published in 1902 and 1916, *Indian Boyhood* and *From the Deep Woods to Civilisation: Chapters in the Autobiography of an Indian*, provide an account of what we would call acculturation, but what Eastman in the terms available to him at the time sees as the development from savagery to civilization. The big point of transition is the event with which the first book, *Indian Boyhood* ends. Brought up as a traditional Sioux, believing that his father had been killed by whites and fully expecting to avenge that death, the young Ohiyesa, as he then was, is suddenly confronted with a man dressed in white clothes who announces himself as his father. He had not been killed, but has been converted to Christianity and is determined that his son should grow up in white ways. Eastman describes this in terms of death and rebirth: 'I felt as if I were dead and travelling to the Spirit Land: for now all my old ideas were to give place to new ones.'[23] He says little more at this point about what must have been a traumatic shock, and this is consistent with the style and purpose of this first book, which is really an idyll, a picture of Indian life seen through the experiences of a child. Instead, to supplement the reminiscences, we are given myths and coup-stories, the whole account written in the conventional language used by whites (and civilized Indians, apparently) to describe such things: 'As he approached them in his almost irresistible speed, every savage heart thumped louder in the Indian's dusky bosom.'[24]

From Deep Woods to Civilisation, written fourteen years later, begins where the first volume ends, re-telling the events of the pivotal day when he regains a father, but a 'white' one. In this we are made immediately aware of the tensions and contra-dictions which characterize that moment and much of the rest of Eastman's life:

> I could not doubt my new father, so mysteriously come back to us, as it were, from the spirit lands: yet there was a voice within saying to me, 'A false life! a treacherous life!'[25]

Eastman goes on to succeed in the white world, but he also becomes an Indian spokesman, increasingly critical of white policies and these conflicting loyalties run through his book at all levels. At one level we are given a success story, presented as a parallel movement from innocence to experience and from savagery to civilization. We even see him collecting 'rare curios and ethnological specimens for one of the most important collections in the country' by using his knowledge of Indian customs to swindle their present owners out of them—a method he complacently refers to as 'one of indirection'.[26] Eastman seems here to play the exploitative white with no awareness of the irony of his position, but elsewhere in the book, and running counter to the primitive-civilized movement, is a growing realization that white society does not embody those values of Christianity for which he has been made to renounce his past. The contradictions are too pressing to be ignored since they affect his entire sense of himself, and his tortuous final para-graph only reflects, rather than solves, the contradictions:

> I am an Indian: and while I have learned much from civilisation, for which I am grateful, I have never lost my Indian sense of right and justice. I am for development and progress along social

and spiritual lines, rather than those of commerce, nationalism, or material efficiency. Nevertheless, so long as I live, I am an American.[27]

It is as if here words and names have become like counters, so that he can only vacillate from one spurious 'identity' to another, rather than *think* with the terms available, and this is directly related to Eastman's and his educated Indian contemporaries' problems at that historical point, in finding a means of self-definition. Eastman has taken over a terminology, revolving round the opposition savage-civilized, which is just not usable to describe what has happened to him, with the result that he can only simplify a complex process into a series of crude oppositions. As a result, in the genteel English which he uses, Indians inevitably are presented as 'other', and he even describes his own feelings in atavistic terms: 'the sweet roving instinct of the wild took forcible hold upon me once more.'[28]

These stereotypes, used by 'friends' as much as by enemies of the Indians, have continued to create problems for any Indians attempting to define their position or identity. As the Indian activist, Vine Deloria, has stressed, 'to be an Indian in the twentieth-century is to be unreal and ahistorical',[29] and recent Indian writing has presented an impressive exploration of these issues.[30] The fullest and best-known are N. Scott Momaday's attempts at finding literary forms which can do justice to both personal and tribal past and present. Rejecting the concept of individual identity as a separating and enclosing of what is unique in a person, Momaday recreates out of his own memory and the Kiowa oral traditions of tribal history, a fuller sense of who he is.

The Way to Rainy Mountain (1970) uses three strands of narrative—what Momaday describes as 'the mythical, the historical and the immediate'[31]—so that the re-telling of the Kiowa tales of migration on to the Great Plains is intertwined with personal reminiscence and commentary. A new awareness of place itself, of where he is now situated, as well as of the past, is crucial to Momaday's new imagining of himself. The act of imagining is not, for Momaday, a way of escaping reality, but of constituting it, and our own position in it, in its true fullness which has been reduced by our acceptance of reductive categories of reality and of self. In *The Names* (1976), although the immediate focus is much more on family history, the same combination of tribal and personal memories are used, often by imagining himself into the position of an ancestor. Amongst the many family photographs in the book is one of Momaday's mother, whose actual Indian blood was fairly minimal, in full and stylized Indian dress, and he explains her decision to see herself as Indian rather than as Southern belle:

> That dim native heritage became a fascination and a cause for her, inasmuch, perhaps, as it enabled her to assume an attitude of defiance, an attitude which she assumed with particular style and satisfaction; it became her. She imagined who she was. This act of the imagination was, I believe, among the most important events of my mother's early life, as later the same essential act was to be among the most important of my own.[32]

By seeing identity in terms of choice and imagination, rather than in terms of blood or savage/civilized, or even degree of acculturation, Momaday testifies to a new awareness by modern Indians that they need not accept the terms in which they have been categorized. Momaday's own way of recreating a self, by language, is, of course, one which brings him as much into the community of other *writers*, past and present, as other Indians. In referring to himself as a 'Man Made of Words',[33] he recognizes that these words bring with them cultural and political connotations, but stresses his ability to exploit them for his own ends. To insist that Momaday inevitably takes over pre-existent cultural and stylistic conventions and sometimes, perhaps, gets trapped by them, is not to decry his work or that of others writing in English, and especially not in the name of a chimerical authentic 'Indianness', but to assert again the main argument of this essay: that the authority of language and text can take on particularly challenging but potentially debilitating forms as a means of expression for individuals or groups usually excluded from it.

3

That this problem is by no means unique to Indians is illustrated by the carefully named *Hunger of Memory: The Education of Richard Rodriguez, An Autobiography* (1981). The child of Spanish-speaking Mexican immigrants in California, Rodriguez learns English and gains success in the academic world, but his book is a powerful and moving explanation of what is lost as well as what is gained. Returning home he experiences dislocation and distance:

> I could not cast off the culture I had assumed. Living with my parents for the summer I remained an academic—a kind of anthropologist in the family kitchen, searching for evidence of our 'cultural ties' as we ate dinner together.[34]

What is distinctive about Rodriguez, though, and what has made his book the subject of fierce controversy, is that he sees this loss as an inevitable part of the acquisition of a sense of a public self, which is gained by mastery of *language*. Crucially, he sees this separation of the family and the public realm as not one which should or even *could* be healed by the use of the family language—in this case, Spanish—in American schools. This has brought him into conflict with proponents of bi-lingualism and, combined with his general scepticism about affirmative action politics, has led to him being categorized as a reactionary, but this is to simplify his rigorously-argued position. Because he sees the alienation caused by education as applying equally to white working-class children, who also acquire a new relation to language, even if not a new language, he sees it as misguided to apply affirmative action on grounds of race rather than class, and feels that bilingual classes actually keep children disadvantaged by keeping from them the necessary realization of 'the right—and the obligation—to speak the public language of *los Gringos*'.[35] Rodriguez refuses the illusory comforts offered by being a representative of his people—of speaking for them:

> I do not give voice to my parents by writing about their lives. I distinguish myself from them by writing about the life we once shared. Even when I quote them accurately I profoundly distort my parents' words. (They were never intended to be read by the public). So my parents do not truly speak on my pages.[36]

Rodriguez sees the public nature of language and especially of writing, as, paradoxically, the instrument of self-discovery, and he relates this directly to his own act of autobiography. On the one hand, writing supplants the private with the public: 'The reader's voice silently trails every word I put down. I re-read my words, and again it is the reader's voice I hear in my mind, sounding my prose.' This, though, actually helps to define the private: 'By finding public words to describe one's feelings, one can describe oneself to oneself. One names what was previously only darkly felt.'[37] For Rodriguez, writing is ultimately an act of individualism, and his scepticism about ever regaining or representing the group intimacy of family or race by means of it offers an implicit challenge to the more optimistic claims of Indian writers. Certainly, in Rodriguez, there is awareness of the impossibility of imagining himself into the minds of his less literate contemporaries, let alone his ancestors. In particular, he refers to no *literary* antecedents. This is understandable, in that although there are other Chicano autobiographies, they are mostly bicultural composites[38] like the Indian ones discussed above, or, in the case of Ernesto Galarza's *Barrio Boy* (1971),[39] a written account of moving from barrio to public success in American society which never questions its ability to be representative.

4

To deal so briefly with Chicano autobiography is not, of course, to underestimate the diversity and richness of the experience dealt with, but reflects only the concern of this essay with literary modes rather than subject-matter, and the same must be made clear about any brief treatment of the even wider range of Asian-American experiences expressed in autobiographical forms.[40] The early autobiographies, because of the restriction of literacy to the aristocratic educated classes, tended to be written by scholars and diplomats and were as much concerned with distinguishing the educated (and, therefore, acceptable) Asians from the ignorant Asian immigrant workers, as they were with distinguishing between Asian and American cultures. The primary impulse, and this continues into second-generation autobiographies, is to stress the acceptability of the writers, and people like them, within the cultural values of America. Such Chinese-American books as Pardee Lowe's *Father and Glorious Descendant* (1943) and Jade Snow Wong's *Fifth Chinese Daughter* (1950), and the Japanese-American Monica Sone's *Nisei Daughter* (1953), are aimed at a white audience and are, therefore, working with a clear knowledge of the white

191

stereotypes, and while the aim is clearly to use the fullness and detail of a life to disperse the stereotype, the books in different ways accept the need for self-justification in American terms. One can be charmingly exotic (within acceptable and recognizable patterns) and/or successful in white ways, and the general 'success' of Asian-American groups in assimilating has tended to mean that this is the vision of Asian-American life most often presented and published. An interesting exception is Carlos Bulosan's *America is in the Heart* (1946), which is an account of Filipino migrant workers through Bulosan's own experiences. Here the book is again directed at white sympathies, but is much more critical of American policies and more consciously representing a group which is usually totally without a public voice.

This awareness of a huge range of experience totally unknown to white Americans, and the consequent reliance by whites on cultural racial stereotypes, operates as a constant presence in these autobiographies. There is a desire to undermine the stereotype, but, until recently, there has also been a desire to show even so the acceptibility of the culture described, and this has been clearly related to the overt political discrimination against these groups at different times. One of the effects of this discrimination has, of course, been to turn the group in on itself, and Maxine Hong Kingston faces one of the contradictions of her situation in writing about her own and her family's life in the opening sentence of *The Woman Warrior* (1977): ' "You must not tell anyone", my mother said, "what I am about to tell you." '[41] She then recounts the story of her aunt, whose ill-treatment at the hands of self-righteous villagers, led to her drowning both herself and her new-born baby. In doing so, Kingston is going against the silence by which the family erased this part of its past, and she stresses her rôle as writer and outsider:

> My aunt haunts me—her ghost drawn to me because now, after fifty years of neglect, I alone devote pages of paper to her, though not origamied into houses and clothes.[42]

The dual concern of *Woman Warrior*, here made clear from the beginning, is with the difficulty of being Chinese in America, but also with the difficulty of being a woman in either Chinese *or* American society. Kingston's response is to bring up to the surface buried or disregarded aspects of the past, as stories to be learned from, so that her book is a powerful mixture of personal memories, and vividly re-told, or re-invented, myths and stories. As with Rodriguez, she notes the conflict between the public American world and the private world of home and childhood, but she also recognizes the problem of deciding what is unique and what is typical:

> how do you separate what is peculiar to childhood, to poverty, insanities, one family, your mother who marked your growing with stories, from what is Chinese? What is Chinese tradition and what is the movies?[43]

Chinese tradition offers Kingston two opposed images of women, the slave and the liberating warrior. The contempt for women, and repression of them is powerfully documented at the personal and historical level in her book, even extending to the language women themselves used: 'There is a Chinese word for the female 'I'—which is 'slave'. Break the women with their own tongues!'[44] Kingston's recognition of this bondage within language and her ability to connect it with more traditional images of female submission, ('Even now China wraps double binds around my feet'[45]) allows her to turn the story of the woman-warrior who rescues her village into a story which is also about writing. In the story the woman warrior has a list of grievances to be revenged cut into her back, and using the deadly-serious and extended puns which are characteristic of her writing in its bridging of literal and metaphorical, Kingston relates herself to the woman warrior:

> The swordswoman and I are not so dissimilar. May my people understand the resemblance soon so that I can return to them. What we have in common are the words at our backs. The idioms for *revenge* are 'report a crime' and 'report to five families'. The reporting is the vengeance—not the beheading, not the gutting, but the words. And I have so many words—'chink' words and 'gook' words too—that they do not fit on my skin.[46]

That the story to be told is not exclusively that of women is shown very clearly by Kingston's next book, *China Men* (1980) which, using the same potent mixture of personal and traditional experiences and myths, concentrates more on her male ancestors, their journeys from China and their experiences in America. She says in an interview, 'What I am doing in this new book is claiming America',[47] and her own linguistic stratagems in the writing of these books are expressly designed for this task, making language yield up its many cross-cultural meanings to the writer and the reader. She creates in her writing, then, a community of writer and reader on equal terms which is far removed both from the speaking subject presented as anthropological object found in early Indian autobiographies, and from the self-conscious representation of the acceptably civilized and/or the marketably exotic. It is not that the dialogic nature of the writing reflecting the multi-voiced cultural situation has ceased—in fact, Bakhtin's account of the inevitably heteroglossic nature of language describes Kingston's style perfectly:

> The word, directed toward its object, enters a dialogically agitated and tension-filled environment of alien words, value judgements and accents, weaves in and out of complex interrelationships, merges with some, recoils from others, intersects with yet a third group.[48]

It is rather that the subject of the autobiography is now able to control and exploit the implications of the dialogue within her text rather than being the victim of it. How far this ability reflects a political situation and increasing audibility for underheard cultural voices in America, or how far it reflects the power of an individual artist to exploit and control his or her world through language, involves larger questions about language and ideology,[49] but I hope this essay has, at least, demonstrated that any answer to these questions must begin with the inevitably heteroglossic character of language and the impossibility of separating it out from its political and cultural context.

NOTES

1. 'The Indian Autobiography: Origins, Type and Function' in *American Literature*, 53, 1 (March, 1981), 24. repr. in Brian Swann (ed.) *Smoothing the Ground: Essays on Native American Oral Literature* (Berkeley: University of California Press, 1983). Arnold Krupat's *For Those Who Come After: A Study of Native American Autobiography* (California University Press, 1985) was

published too late for me to consult but will clearly become an essential text for any study of this material.

2. See, for instance, *A Son of the Forest: The Experience of William Apes, A Native of the Forest, Written by Himself* 2nd edn. (New York, 1831). For full bibliographical details and expert synopsis and commentary, see H. David Brumble III, *An Annotated Bibliography of American Indian and Eskimo Autobiographies* (University of Nebraska Press, 1981).

3. *Black Hawk: An Autobiography*, ed. Donald Jackson (Urbana: University of Illinois Press,1964).

4. *Geronimo: His Own Story*, ed. S. M. Barrett (1906), newly edited by Frederick W. Turner III (London: Abacus, 1974), p. 136.

5. John Robert Leo, 'Riding Geronimo's Cadillac: *His Own Story* and the Circumstancing of Text', *Journal of American Culture*, 1, 4, (Winter, 1978), 822.

6. Ibid., 834.

7. The early popularity of captivity narrative offers an ironic reversal of the textual activities described in this essay, in that these early narratives described a white being captured by Indians, being enclosed in Indian culture, whereas the later texts describe and enact the enclosing of the Indian within white cultural forms, even if not white society.

8. Krupat, op. cit., p. 37.

9. See especially Sally McCluskey, '*Black Elk Speaks*: And So Does John Neihardt', *Western American Literature* 6, 4 (Winter, 1972). Also Paul A. Olson, '*Black Elk Speaks* as Epic: A Ritual Attempt to Reverse History'. in *Visions and Refuge: Essays on the Literature of the Great Plains*, ed. Virginia Faulkner and Frederick C. Luebke (Lincoln: University of Nebraska Press, 1982), and Michael Castro, *Interpreting the Indians: Twentieth-century Poets and the Native Americans* (Albuquerque: University of New Mexico Press, 1983), pp. 79–97.

10. Quoted in McCluskey, op. cit., 238.

11. John G. Neihardt, *Black Elk Speaks* (New York: Pocket Books, 1972), p. xii.

12. Olson, op. cit., p. 5.

13. Paul Radin, *Autobiography of a Winnebago Indian*, 1920, (New York: Dover), p. 2.

14. *Crashing Thunder*, p. xiii.

15. Ibid., p. xxvi.

16. *Son of Old Man Hat: A Navaho Autobiography* recorded by Walter Dyk, introduction by Edward Sapir (New York: Harcourt, Brace & Co., 1938), p. viii.

17. *Mountain Wolf Woman: Sister of Crashing Thunder*, ed. Nancy O. Lurie (Ann Arbor: Michigan University Press, 1961).

18. *Sun Chief: The Autobiography of a Hopi Indian*, ed. Leo W. Simmons (New York & London: Yale University Press, 1942), p. 7.

19. See, H. David Brumble III, 'Anthropologists, Novelists and Indian Sacred Material' in *Canadian Review of American Studies* 11, 1 (Spring, 1980), 31–48, repr. with a reply by Karl Kroeber in Swann, op. cit.

20. Simmons, op. cit., p. 1.

21. Ibid., p. 378.

22. For a similar balancing act from a member of a very different culture, see *Guests Never Leave Hungry: The Autobiography of James Sewid. A Kwakuitl Indian*, ed. James P. Spradley (New Haven: Yale University Press, 1969), p. 3.

23. Charles A. Eastman, *Indian Boyhood* (New York: Dover Publishing Inc., 1971), p. 246.

24. Ibid., p. 36.

25. Charles A. Eastman, *From the Deep Woods to Civilisation: Chapters in the Autobiography of an Indian* (London & Lincoln: Univesity of Nebraska Press, 1977), p. 7.

26. Ibid., p. 166.

27. Ibid., p. 195.

28. Ibid., p. 175.

29. Vine Deloria, *Custer Died for your Sins* (New York: Avon, 1970).

30. See, for instance, the novelist Leslie Silko's combination of personal and tribal memories in *Storyteller* (New York: Seaver Books, 1981), Ted C. Williams's use of autobiographical material in *The Reservation* (Syracuse: Syracuse University Press, 1976), and Gerald C. Vizenor's idiosyncratic fictional experiments combining earthdiver myths and autobiographical material, in *Earthdivers: Tribal Narratives on Mixed Descent* (Minneapolis: Minneapolis University Press, 1981), and 'I Know What You Mean, Erdupps Mac Churrbs: Autobiographical Myths and Metaphors', in Chester G. Anderson (ed.), *Growing Up in Minnesota* (Minneapolis: Minnesota University Press, 1976).

31. N. Scott Momaday: *The Way to Rainy Mountain*

32. N. Scott Momaday, *The Names: A Memoir* (New York: Harper & Row, 1976), p. 48.

33. 'The Man Made of Words', in *Literature of the American Indians: Views and Interpretations*, ed. A. Chapman (New York: New American Library, 1973).

34. *Hunger of Memory: The Education of Richard Rodriquez: An Autobiography*, (Boston: David R. Godine, 1981), p. 160.

35. Ibid., p. 19.

36. Ibid., p. 186.

37. Ibid., p. 187.

38. Two representative examples are *The Life Story of the Mexican Immigrant: With Autobiographic Documents* collected by Manuel Gamio (Magnolia Ma: Peter Smith) which has a sociological introduction and translates in a plain, unfussy way, brief life-stories intended to be seen as case-studies, and *Pablo Cruz and the American Dream: The Experiences of an Undocumented Immigrant from Mexico*, compiled by Eugene B. Nelson (Notre Dame: University of Notre Dame Press, 1977).

39. Ernesto Galarza, *Barrio Boy* (Notre Dame: University of Notre Dame, 1971).

40. Elaine H. Kim provides a bibliography and excellent brief accounts of these works, which I have relied heavily upon, in 'Asian American Writers: A Bibliographical Review', *American Studies International*, 23, 2 (October, 1984).

41. Maxine Hong Kingston, *The Woman Warrior* (London: Picador, 1977), p. 11.
42. Ibid., p. 22.
43. Ibid., p. 13.
44. Ibid., p. 49.
45. Ibid., p. 49.
46. Ibid., p. 53.
47. Quoted in Kim, op. cit., p. 66.
48. M. M. Bakhtin, *The Dialogic Imagination: Four Essays* (Austin: University of Texas Press, 1981), p. 276.
49. For an analysis of ethnographic texts in terms of dialogical and dialectical ideas see: James Clifford, 'On Ethnographic Authority', in *Representations* 1–2 (Spring, 1983): George E. Marcus & Dick Cashman 'Ethnographies as Texts', in *Annual Review of Anthropology*, 11 (1982): and Kevin Dwyer, 'On the Dialogic of Fieldwork' in *Dialectical Anthropology*, 2 (1977).

9

The Haunted House: Jewish-American Autobiography

by MICHAEL WOOLF

Like all the hyphenations through which Americans construe themselves—Afro-American, Italian-American, Polish-American and the like—Jewish-American involves a complex juxtaposition of notions. To be Jewish of necessity means to be conscious of some versions of an Ancient Regime, a history that includes concepts of prophecy and endurance, diaspora and holocaust. To be Jewish-*American* has meant to find a new way of being, a means of inventing a form of identity that achieves a synthesis of disparate notions which permit a sense of future and redemption. Thus throughout the major Jewish-American autobiographies of this century, the American Jew has appeared neither quite American nor Jewish enough to establish a simple, unambiguous sense of a self which is liberated from the burden of self-conscious dualism.

Yet in whatever way this radical ambiguity is explored, one factor has been recurrent: it involves a dramatic process of dialogue with the past both as a collective and utterly personal experience. The children return time and again to a haunted (and haunting) house of the past—to engage with, to contemplate and wonder at, to find bearings within, the worlds of their forefathers. Each generation seeks to interpret the experience of the previous generation, to understand its own process of reconciliation, adjustment and rise within an America which progressively has become a clearly more hospitable place. While the first immigrant Jewish experiences can be characterized by suffering and struggle, the offspring establish an increasingly more secure place at the centre of all American life—and its literary culture most especially—and in that security look back upon their forefathers (and mothers) as almost a myth of origin, a past which has succeeded a still older sequence of pasts.

A major part of Jewish-American autobiography, therefore, takes the form of extended dialogue between generations. Their creators negotiate with the voices of parents and grandparents, possessed of a deep problematic anxiety that, one way or another, they have in truth betrayed a legacy, a community of values, by acceding to the ease of present-day America. Writing in the 1960s, for instance, Norman Podhoretz, as the wholly successful Editor of *Commentary* and an essayist of wide acclaim, can describe himself as 'a problematic American and an even more problematic Jew'.[1] His story, and that of Jews generally in twentieth-century America, tells of extraordinary success; but it tells, too, of a moral and cultural ambiguity disturbingly inherent in that success itself. The generations which look back on the *shtetl* and the immigrant years find themselves tinged by a certain guilt, an awareness that their ease and comfort arise out of a past of suffering and fissure, be it the years of the first diaspora, or Russo-Poland, or Hitlerian Germany. To write of oneself, evidently, has been to write of one's ghosts.

This sense of a dialogue between generations is most clearly established in Charles Reznikoff's *Family Chronicle* (1963). It takes the form of three inter-connecting narratives that tell the story of immigrant experience through the eyes of Sarah and Nathan Reznikoff. Sarah Reznikoff's 'Early History of a Seamstress' (1930) recalls the struggles of immigrant Jews with a simple and understated clarity. She recalls experiences that are familiar as, for example, in Mary Antin's *From Plotzk to Boston* (1899) or Abraham Cahan's *Bleter Fun Mein Leben* (1926; translated, *The Education of Abraham Cahan*, 1969). Sarah Reznikoff captures precisely a sense of cultural dislocation and trauma which is allied to a persistent optimism for the future to be lived by the succeeding generation. It depicts, in other words, the almost archetypal Jewish immigrant experience that begins in the Russian *shtetl* of the 1880s and an environment that is characterized by marginal economic survival, disease and hostility from anti-Semitic neighbours. In that world, however, there is no fundamental challenge to religious faith. It is a landscape in which simple certainties co-exist with an uncertain future.

Her existence is represented in terms of a dual sense of hunger:

> Soon our life went on as before. It disgusted me. My mind was starving. I loved to read, but how could I when I had so much to do? I was too miserable to eat and wished to die.[2]

She is, however, sustained by a recurrent image, not of a religious Zion but of a dreamed landscape called America. As for Mary Antin, America becomes the secularized alternative to the myth of Zion. Before the disillusion of reality, frequently dramatized in versions of arrival in America, the idea of the New Land is profoundly, almost religiously, affirmative—a source of renewed hope: 'The thought of America was balm to me. I felt stronger than ever.'[3]

That is part of the archetypal engagement with the idea of America. The dream is enforced, strengthened by the symbol of the Statue of Liberty as seen from a distant perspective, and then undercut by the reality of disembarkation upon inhospitable shores. Emma Goldman, too, writing in *Living my Life* (1931) describes precisely the same process:

> We travelled steerage, where the passengers were herded together like cattle. My first contact with the sea was terrifying and fascinating. The freedom from home, the beauty and wonder of the endless expanse in its varying moods, and the exciting anticipation of what the new land would offer stimulated my imagination and sent my blood tingling.
>
> The last day of our journey comes vividly to my mind. Everybody was on deck. Helena and I stood pressed to each other, enraptured by the sight of the harbour and the Statue of Liberty emerging from the mist. Ah, there she was, the symbol of hope, of freedom, of opportunity! She held her torch high to light the way to the free country, the asylum for the oppressed of all lands. We, too, Helena and I, would find a place in the generous heart of America. Our spirits were high, our eyes filled with tears.

Gruff voices broke in upon our reverie. We were surrounded by gesticulating people—angry men, hysterical women, screaming children. Guards roughly pushed us hither and thither, shouted orders to get ready, to be transferred to Castle Garden, the clearing-house for immigrants.

The scenes in Castle Garden were appalling, the atmosphere charged with antagonism and harshness. Nowhere could one see a sympathetic official face; there was no provision for the comfort of the new arrivals, the pregnant women and young children. The first day on American soil proved a violent shock.[4]

Goldman's intense vision of a dreamed world in which freedom, hope and opportunity are available is brutally undermined by the truth behind the illusion of America's 'generous heart'. Goldman's narrative typifies the pattern of immigrant experience in which a mythic version of America is constructed prior to arrival. Her disillusion is part of an inevitable process where an idealized vision confronts social reality. The chasm between vision and reality leads, as Goldman shows in her narrative, to an inevitable ambiguity about life in America: 'Life in the new country, they said, was hard; they were all still possessed by nostalgia for their home that had never been a home.'[5] The immigrant exists, therefore, between two types of mythic construct: a dreamed America and an idealized Europe seen through the distorting lens of nostalgia. The reality can hardly avoid being pallid in the light of those rosy illusions.

Emma Goldman's alienation from America was extreme, and by 1919 complete, when she was deported to the newly formed Soviet Union, another version of a secular Zion that was in its turn to fail her. Sarah and Nathan Reznikoff's experience is the more familiar in that, despite the disillusionments brought on by American reality, they sustained a sense of hope, if not for themselves, then for the generation that was to follow. Sarah's chronicle ends with the burdensome legacy that the next generation carries into the future:

One day, one of our cousins who had just arrived from Russia, was in our house; and when it was nearly three o'clock, all the children came running out of school—so many of them—and his eyes filled with tears. I remembered how I, too, had longed for an education. 'We are a lost generation,' I said. 'It is for our children to do what they can.'[6]

Charles Reznikoff represents their pathway into the American promised land and carries the burden of Sarah and Nathan's frustrated ambitions. In 'Needle Trade' he establishes the manner in which parental ambitions, as projected onto the son, establish a hurtful schism between the generations. The son is alienated from the world of the parents precisely because it is part of their aspiration that the son should occupy a world radically different from their own:

> I was to have nothing to do with this business or any like it; I was to study and to make my living otherwise: my parents had always spoken of their business and all ways of making money by trade with distaste. And if it was their doom because they had come to the country penniless and ignorant, if they were to be worms and crawl about, their children should have wings.
>
> When I was in high school and used to go to the city on a Saturday afternoon, I never went to the shop if I could help it (they used to work all day Saturdays then), although my father would reproach me for it, afterwards. I did not want to run any errand; I did not want to meet those to whom my father would introduce me proudly and who would greet me with a friendliness I thought uncalled for by our brief acquaintance; I felt alien and clumsy there.[7]

Reznikoff, alien and clumsy in the world of his parents, personalizes a cultural condition that leads inevitably towards the alienation of generation from generation. The book itself, however, seeks to perform an act of reconciliation. It both records and gives value to his parents' struggles, a tribute to archetypal immigrant experience and a means of self-clarification.

Family Chronicle also offers a way of understanding the complex processes of acculturation and assimilation. It describes the beginning of a process by which American Jews were transformed from marginal existence to a place in the mainstream and its accompanying security and influence. Alfred Kazin's autobiographies equally testify to this process. His three volumes, *A Walker in the City* (1951), *Starting Out in the Thirties* (1962) and *New York Jew* (1978), create in effect a map of Jewish-American experience, at once deeply personal yet symptomatic, particular yet mythic and representative.

Like Reznikoff, Kazin carries with him the burden of his parents' ambition:

202

It was not for myself alone that I was to shine but for them—to redeem the constant anxiety of their existence. I was the first American child, their offering to the strange new God; I was to be the monument of their liberation from the shame of being—what they were.[8]

Thus the process of 'making it' in American society again involves, as an integral part of the act, an alienation between the first and second generation. The children were to 'move in' to America's beckoning world even as their parents were to be excluded from it by origin. Kazin's use of the word 'monument' precisely indicates the degree to which the burden of parental ambition imposes a profound pressure upon the identity of the following generation. The child is both sacrifice and memorial elevated, in both cases, way above the flawed humanity of the parents. To become a symbol for the aspiration of others is to be separated from them and diminished in terms of a sense of community with their human suffering. The price of failure is betrayal of their dreams. The price of success is betrayal of their humanity. These books, then, express an inevitable anguish, a powerful tissue of guilt and bewilderment. Kazin's *A Walker in the City*, like *Family Chronicle*, begins from the abandoned world of childhood in order to make an act of contrition, to pay homage to a past that cannot be painlessly discarded.

Much Jewish-American autobiography is, thus, a record of liberation from the limitations of the parents' world and, simultaneously, an expression of the impossibility of liberation. The past is carried heavily into the comfortable future and Kazin moves toward a sense that to be a Jew in America is inevitably to remain in the place from which one has travelled. For Kazin that place is Brownsville and the past: 'Brownsville is the road which every other road in my life has had to cross.'[9] This is precisely the place Norman Podhoretz, also, departs from on the road to fame and success as a New York intellectual: 'One of the longest journeys in the world is the journey from Brooklyn to Manhattan—or at least from certain neighborhoods in Brooklyn to certain parts of Manhattan.'[10]

A similar metaphor of journeying recurs in Jewish-American autobiography. There is a repeated sense of America as a foreign country, a far distant land to which the writer comes with the heavy baggage of parental ambition and from which he returns obsessively. Daniel Bell recognized that the preoccupation with the landscapes of the past is almost a defining characteristic of Jewish consciousness: 'For me, therefore, to be a Jew is to be part of a community woven by memory!'[11]

Kazin repeatedly returns to childhood and to memories of the family which persist in imposing moral questions in the present. As in Henry Roth's autobiographical novel *Call It Sleep* (1934), the figures of the father and mother are sources of profound emotional complexity. Kazin's mother might almost be a precise reflection of Sarah Reznikoff and Henry Roth's Genya Schearl:

> The kitchen gave special character to our lives; my mother's character. All my memories of that kitchen are dominated by the nearness of my mother sitting all day long at her sewing machine, by the clacking of the treadle against the linoleum floor, by the patient twist of her right shoulder as she automatically pushed at the wheel with one hand or lifted the foot to free the needle where it had got stuck in a thick piece of material. The kitchen was her life. Year by year, as I began to take in her fantastic capacity for labor and her anxious zeal, I realised it was ourselves she kept stitched together.[12]

The author returns to childhood to recall and interpret experiences that were misunderstood, or falsely understood, in the past.

Kazin's father similarly bulks large in these narratives often as a bemused, sometimes infuriated, frequently powerless individual. He is a victim of the transformed nature of Jewish experience in America. Nathan Reznikoff struggles against the vagaries of urban life and gradually loses both fortune and hope. Kazin's father, like the father in *Call It Sleep*, sees his son not in terms of his life but as a recorder of his death, a 'monument' to his engagement with America. The son is left with the pain that that rôle imposes:

> My father always introduced me around very shyly but with unmistakeable delight, as his *kaddish*. What an intense pride that word carried for him, and how it saddened me. *Kaddish* is the Hebrew prayer for the dead, read for a father by his son.[13]

Podhoretz's father engages in a futile, impotent struggle with America—an inevitably failing battle to retain the unproblematic Judaism that had been left across the Atlantic:

> He was . . . a Jewish survivalist, unclassifiable and eclectic,
> tolerant of any modality of Jewish existence so long as it
> remained identifiably and self-consciously Jewish, and outraged
> by any species of Jewish assimilationism, whether overt or
> concealed.[14]

With the inexorable secularization of American Jews, the rôle
of the father becomes increasingly ambiguous. No longer the
unqualified head of the household, his traditional spiritual
authority eroded, he begins to occupy a more and more
marginal (and impotent) place within the family structure. In
its extreme manifestation, this transformation becomes a source
for the comic inversions found in a succession of novels in the
1960s and '70s, particularly Philip Roth's *Portnoy's Complaint*
(1969), Bruce Jay Friedman's *A Mother's Kisses* (1964) and
Wallace Markfield's *Teitelbaum's Window* (1970). In all three
novels, the impotence of the father is measured against the
menacing and massive presence of the mother. The roots of that
satirical inversion of traditional family structure are found in
the real cultural dilemma described in the autobiographies of
Reznikoff, Podhoretz and Kazin.

Kazin moves out of his parents' world and into the intellectual
mainstream of American life but his books are both a record of
that experience and lyrical re-explorations of the past, acts of
reconciliation with a now by-passed and even abandoned
world. They are also part of a crucial discovery in Jewish-
American culture: that literature could be made out of domestic
experience and that the creative model need not be drawn from
a conventional W.A.S.P. world. Thus, by the 1950s, Podhoretz
was able to learn:

> that it was possible to achieve cultivation without losing touch
> with oneself, without doing violence to one's true feelings,
> without becoming pompous, pretentious, affected, or false to the
> realities of one's own experiences—without, in short, becoming a
> facsimile WASP.[15]

Podhoretz discovers that the path to intellectual success need
not be through High Art and Modernist Criticism. There was
another route to that taken by Lionel Trilling. You could be, as
Kazin's title boldly asserts, a 'New York Jew' and 'a man of
letters'. There had to be no intrinsic contradiction between the

two conditions. Similarly, Philip Roth speaks of the parallel lesson he learned from the work of Saul Bellow and Bernard Malamud:

> They pointed to a world that I could recognise and said this is the material of fiction . . . so I got the idea that I could look at what I knew. I could look at my Newark. I could look at my South Orange and that stuff qualifies as fiction.[16]

In another sense, therefore, imaginative literature offered the means by which the disparate worlds of Jewish childhood and American maturity could be reconciled, melded together and transformed into art. That, of course, was a necessary prerequisite for the creation of a body of literature, particularly the novels, which brought Jewish-American experience into the centre of American culture in the 1960s and '70s, creating what Leslie Fiedler called 'the Judaization of American culture'.[17] In short, domestic experience could be translated into art and myth.

Kazin's autobiographies also identify those moments of contemporary history that take on symbolic intensity in Jewish-American literature. In *Starting Out in the Thirties* he focuses on the Depression as a key period where material suffering was allied to a fervent socialism among Jewish workers and intellectuals. The history of Jewish socialism is well-documented, and it coheres around a succession of radical periodicals from Yiddish newspapers to *The New Masses* and *Partisan Review*. For the immigrant, the assertion of a socialist faith gave dignity and purpose to existence in America, as Abraham Cahan indicates: 'But in my heart I was proud of being a socialist. I was not just running away like an ordinary immigrant.'[18] The socialism of the Depression particularly and persistently nags at the consciousness of later writers. The religious certainties of the *shtetl* thus give way to the radical certainties of the '30s. They are symptomatically merged in Mike Gold's *Jews Without Money* (1930). Gold's concluding vision of revolutionary faith is expressed in terms of the Jewish Messianic myth:

> A man on an East Side soap-box, one night, proclaimed that out of the despair, melancholy and helpless rage of millions, a world movement had been born to abolish poverty.
> I listened to him.

O workers' Revolution, you brought hope to me, a lonely, suicidal boy. You are the true Messiah. You will destroy the East Side when you come, and build there a garden for the human spirit.

O Revolution that forced me to think, to struggle and to live.

O great Beginning![19]

The radical voices of the '30s, in turn, haunt those that follow. The voices of the Grandfather and Father combine to accuse the children of the 1960s with their images of lost Edens, destroyed Zions and abandoned faiths. Kazin, 19 in 1934, recalls the nature of his literary radicalism in the following way:

> What young writers of the Thirties wanted was to prove the literary value of our experience, to feel that we had moved the streets, the stockyards, the hiring halls into literature—to show that our radical strength could carry on the experimental impulse of modern literature.[20]

The period is repeatedly revisited in the fiction, for example, in the mood of Bernard Malamud's *The Assistant* (1957) or as a source of black-comic exorcism in Markfield's *Teitelbaum's Window*. This period, too, haunts the radical intellectuals of the 1950s, as described by Podhoretz, whose faith is under siege both from McCarthyism within America and Stalinism in the Soviet Union. What Kazin calls 'the radical confidence of the 1930s'[21] evaporates painfully in the complex and pained introspection, and emerging conservatism (as in Podhoretz's case), of the following decades.[22]

Inescapably, American Jews have also been confronted by images of the holocaust. In some respects like the memories of the '30s, the Hitlerian disaster assaults and undermines any assumed comfort and security in the post-war world. The fictional approach is, for the most part, oblique, but, as Philip Roth asserts, 'It's hard to be a Jewish writer or a writer who is a Jew or both and write something that doesn't reverberate and eventually touch these dead Jews.'[23] What is repeatedly described, however, is the failure to mould that experience into art. In 'Notes on the Working Day', Wallace Markfield typically sees the holocaust as a persistent pressure, a dream/nightmare that simply cannot be translated into a literary form:

> The clock gave him five more minutes, yet he knew that this dream of death would be with him always, carefully plotted out,

stamped within him like an economist's chart, rising higher and higher each day, yet never touching the heights of marginal utility.[24]

Markfield's story precisely captures the manner in which Kazin asserts the persistence of this particular memory: 'The war was over. The war would never end.'[25] The Jewish-American writer cannot but be locked into a permanent dialogue with the dead and, thus, the holocaust is sustained within the consciousness. It persists in raising the sort of question asked in Barbara Probst Solomon's *The Beat of Life* (1961): 'How do we get off so easily? Why do we call ourselves Jews?'[26] The same unresolvable issue is raised by Kazin. He sees it as creating a barrier of consciousness between the American Jew and the cultural mood of the 1960s:

> The holocaust would not go away, and so could be denied. The more 'Jewish' we became, the more we were open to the new horror: *the past did not exist unless you had lived it yourself*. There was no historical memory if you chose not to have one. The buoyant, the storm-laden, the tumultuously revolutionary sixties filled up the present. The pleasure principle mocked the 'atavistic' Jewish demand for a sign from one's fellow men.[27]

The persistence of Kazin's 'historical memory' alienates him from a period that sought to liberate itself from the past. Such an act of forgetful liberation is not within the moral options open to the Jewish-American writer who is locked into a past that is both historical and personal, that has as its landscapes the cruel rubble of Europe and the warm kitchens of childhood.

Thus, by the 1960s, American-Jewish autobiographical writing reflects a complex engagement with the recent and more distant past in both its American and European contexts. These versions of the past impose moral imperatives upon the present. Despite prosperity, security and secularization, the Jewish-American writer is unable, and often understandably unwilling, to discard some ancestral version of a sense of Jewish identity. The ambiguity lies in the fact that his or her sense of being historically marginal within American culture persists even as the writer increasingly gains status and influence. This manifests itself, for example, as an attitude to language in Cynthia Ozick's preface to *Bloodshed and Three Novellas*: 'It occurs to me that if only I had been able to write "Usurpation" in a Jewish language—Hebrew or Yiddish . . .—it would have been understood instantly.'[28]

Writing in the 1960s Barbara Probst Solomon evokes this paradox of being an outsider and insider as follows: 'I feel like a Jew, but I cannot *act* like a Jew'.[29] This feeling, the sense of remaining Jewish without a commitment to faith, is an aspect central to the ambiguity of all Jewish-American writing of the last three decades. The sense of marginality paradoxically co-exists with the process of transformation noted by Saul Bellow in his review of Philip Roth's *Goodbye Columbus*:

> For in the past what could money buy that can compare with the houses, the sinks, the garbage disposals, the Jags, the minks, the plastic surgery. . . . To what can we compare this change? Nothing like it has ever hit the world; nothing in history has so quickly and radically transformed any group of Jews.[30]

The money, prosperity and status does not, however diminish a sense of engaging in a dialogue with a Jewish past. Podhoretz called the New York intellectuals of the 1950s a 'Jewish family' and that feeling of being, sometimes reluctantly, part of an uneasy family is an integral aspect of Jewish-American consciousness.

A related aspect is the recurrent need to define the nature of a Judaism that persists without faith or religious commitment. The dilemma of identity recorded by Norma Stahl Rosen in *Joy to Levine!* (1962) imposes a need to invent and re-invent versions of Judaism that will encompass its paradoxical persistence in a secular world: 'A Jew not a Jew, with a longing to be a Jew and not a Jew'.[31] Such ambiguities lead, for example, to Leslie Fiedler's playful and apocalyptic projections of Judaism as a kind of symbolic stance where 'to be a Jew means to live on the margins of the world in failure and terror, to be in exile'.[32] That is precisely the margin at which Malamud creates a version of Judaism in *The Assistant*. There are, though, versions of Judaism that retain substantially traditional parameters. For Chaim Potok, for example, Jewishness derives from a belief in, and commitment to, the rational logic and justice he sees as implicit in religious practice and faith:

> I would rather live in what I take to be a meaningful world and be staggered by moments of apparent absurdity than in an

absurd world and be troubled by instances of meaning. I would rather try to discover some light in the patches of darkness than extend the darkness to wherever there is light.

The notion that the universe is intrinsically meaningful is, for me, a provisional absolute.[33]

Potok's concept of a world given meaning by faith is somewhat anachronistic, though appropriate enough for the Lone Rabbi of Jewish-American writing.

Nathan Glazer, writing in *Commentary* in 1985, represents an alternative view in which the processes of change will leave only a notional, diminished, secular Judaism freed from connection with the voices of the past. In this view, Judaism melts into the mainstream of American culture and persists, if at all, as a vaguely realized means of identification:

We have been told that Judaism in America is in a line of historic continuity and represents no decisive break with the past, that it is different but still the same. In my judgement this argument is too optimistic. Less and less of the life of American Jews is derived from Jewish history, experience, culture and religion. More and more of it is derived from the current and existing realities of American culture, American politics, and the general American religion. What this means for the future is that Jews will survive, yes, and perhaps even continue to identify themselves as Jews, but that little by way of custom, belief or loyalty will be assumed as a result of their identity as Jews.[34]

A more representative position than either of those is taken by Philip Roth. For him, the central issue is the effort to discover what imperatives Judaism, in its transformed state, might impose upon the writer. He finds himself still directly in tension with the historical experience of the Jews:

As I see it, the task for the Jewish novelist has not been to go forth to forge in the smithy of his soul the uncreated conscience of his race, but to find inspiration in a conscience that has been created and undone a hundred times over in this century alone. Similarly, out of this myriad of prototypes, the solitary being to whom history or circumstance has assigned the appellation 'Jew' has had, as it were, to imagine what *he* is and is not, must and must not do.[35]

The task, then, is to imagine, to invent and re-invent, versions of Judaism in the contemporary environment. This act continues to involve an exploration of the present in tension with the past; the child continues to inhabit some corner of his parents' house.

For Kazin, the tension is symbolized in the relationship of father to son, an explosive one in the newly radical '60s:

> The young en masse suddenly became revolutionaries against all fixed things. They were terrible, outrageous; they were outside of literature, they were even anti-literature. But since they were our children, children of the new middle class, they were perfectly equipped and ready to dynamite us.
>
> The sons were out to get the fathers—especially if the fathers had been 'radicals' during a certain ancient Depression. Although I was as much a target to my own son as my old friends were to *their* sons, I had a secret sympathy with the sons in general.[36]

The schism between generations is, thus, inevitably re-enacted. The rebellious son finds himself uneasily in the rôle of bewildered father.

Jay Neugeboren, in his autobiography *Parentheses: An Autobiographical Journey* (1970), traces the process by which Kazin's 'sons' become that angry, secularized, politicized generation. Religion in terms of faith and ethnic particularity plays little part in his childhood:

> My father, raised in an extremely Orthodox Jewish family, wanted his sons to be 'Americans': my mother had named me Jacob Mordecai (for my father's father) but three days after I was born, my father changed the name to an 'American' one— Jay Michael.[37]

The act of naming, as the act of removing earlocks for an earlier generation, asserts a new allegiance and a new sense of self—an attempt to define the self in relation to an American present rather than a Jewish past. The father's legacy to the son, as in Nathan Reznikoff's legacy to Charles Reznikoff, is the new American world and the illusion of liberation from history. Ironically though, Neugeboren traces the process of political education that leads to an alienation from the gift of America and a retreat, during the Vietnam war, to France: 'Life here, hopefully, has unfitted me for a return to American civilization'.[38] The American civilization that the sons of Sarah Reznikoff were to conquer is, thus, rejected by the grandsons. There is a major alienation from the world of the fathers, an awareness that the rebellion of 1968 'is the struggle of the young against the old'.[39]

Neugeboren also expresses a recurrent pattern in Jewish-American writing: the escape from an oppressive world and the pursuit of some kind of dreamed, alternative universe. Sarah Reznikoff dreams America and in due course escapes from the land of her fathers. Norman Podhoretz's journey is across the Brooklyn Bridge but into a vastly different cultural world. Neugeboren crosses the Atlantic, ironically in the reverse direction of Sarah Reznikoff, in search of his version of Eden and ostensibly discarding the values of the generation that preceded him. In his fiction, however, he returns again and again to those values, completing the obsessive cycle of escape and return, enacting the impossibility of escape. In both *An Orphan's Tale* (1976) and *The Solen Jew* (1981), Neugeboren engages with the problems of Jewish-American identity, examining the paradox of 'being a Jew but not practicing Judaism'.[40] Throughout those novels, Jewish motifs impose imperatives that cannot be fully accepted nor totally discarded. The father's legacy proves, in the end, to be a burdensome one.

Erica Jong, similarly, fails to achieve liberation from her sense of herself as a Jew tied in some imperative way to the Jews of the holocaust. Her particular failure of liberation begins ironically within the context of the rejection of male-assigned rôles. The achievement and enjoyment of sexual freedom does not, in Jong's work, co-exist with freedom from a burden of Jewish ethnicity. She raises, as does Barbara Probst Solomon, the sense that the European experience imposes upon the American Jew a persistent awareness of the accident of survival, a feeling, therefore, that existence itself is a problematic gift:

> I lived longer in Heidelberg than in any city except New York, so Germany (and Austria too) was a kind of second home to me. I spoke the language comfortably—more comfortably than any of the languages I had studied at school—and I was familiar with the foods, the wines, the brand names, the closing times of shops, the clothes, the popular music, the slang expressions, the mannerisms. . . . All as if I had spent my childhood in Germany, or as if my parents were German. But I was born in 1942 and if my parents had been German—not American—Jews, I would

have been born (and probably would have died) in a concentration camp—despite my blond hair, blue eyes, and Polish peasant nose. I could never forget that either.[41]

Jerome Charyn moulds many of the preoccupations apparent in Jewish-American writing into a series of fables and mythologies. His work expresses a radical use of cultural and personal history. In the novel *Panna Maria* (1982), for example, he traces the development of immigrant society through the turbulent first three decades of this century. The protagonist is mythologized into a 'tzarevitch' who assumes a magical status in the eyes of the other characters. There is a tension, however, between the figure as a heroic 'magus' and the figure as a poverty-stricken, alienated immigrant. The ambiguities of identity are given new forms in that novel. His first novel, *Once Upon a Droshky* (1964), coheres around the conflict between father and son in which the son is an agent of an inhuman, legalistic America. The novel, narrated by the father in a form of Yiddish-English, is an act of cultural retrospection—a means of revisiting, and giving moral worth to, the values of the past.

Charyn's autobiographical statements reveal both the process by which domestic experience is transformed into myth and the degree to which the son begins to echo the discordant, suffering voice of the father:

> I was born in the hour of the ostrich, 4am, when even the dark is confused as it awaits that first, false dawn. I haven't given up the ostrich hour, living with my head in the ground.
>
> I came from a family of ostriches. My mum and dad were part of some atavistic migration out of Sweden, Russia, Portugal, or wherever ostriches tend to cling. They stumbled upon this continent and never quite recovered from their journey. And I'm their offspring, an ostrich with dark hair.
>
> How could I have discovered English in the ordinary way when my father grumbled no language at all? It wasn't Russian or Swedish of the lower depths. It was a primitive cry of want. I woke to that cry and went to sleep with it. It was the sound I started to gurgle in my ostrich crib.[42]

Charyn takes the archetypal immigrant experience—and its resultant cultural dislocation—and transforms it into a personal mythology in which, nevertheless, the condition of parental confusion becomes the legacy of the bewildered son. The son breathes the same muddied air and carries the 'primitive cry of want' into the land of plenty. In *The Catfish Man: A Conjured Life* (1980), Charyn's most ostensibly autobiographical novel, 'all the changing colors the past can fling at you',[43] are brilliantly synthesized into a reinvention of landscape and memory. The reader again is made witness to a process of re-exploration and re-engagement that once more shows the degree to which the complex legacies of the past cannot be abandoned—thought they can be understood and harmonized by transformation into literature.

These autobiographies by Jewish-Americans, spread across time from the first major waves of immigration to the contemporary present, thus can lay claim to their own vision and idiom; yet equally they represent a confrontation with the burden of a wholly collective past. Theirs is truly a haunted house. It may be *that*, especially in a secular age, which above all makes it impossible not to think of Jewish-Americans as always to an extent distinct from their fellow American citizens. They are locked in a discourse with history, with ancestral voices. For as much as they may attempt to argue, cajole, reprimand or even honour as a way of coming to terms with that past and those voices, they can never wholly shut out the unsilent witness of the generations who have gone before. Loren Baritz's observation in a 1960s essay for *Commentary* on the ambiguity at the heart of all American-Jewish identity accordingly assumes a most representative quality:

> Because of America's rejection of the past, of the fierce commitment to the notion that this land will start anew, the American Jew is pulled apart. To be a Jew is to remember. An American must forget.[44]

NOTES

1. Norman Podhoretz, *Making It* (London: Jonathan Cape, 1968), p. 92.
2. Sarah Reznikoff, 'Early History of a Seamstress' in *Family Chronicle*, Charles Reznikoff (London: Norton Bailey, 1969), p. 28.
3. Ibid., p. 65.
4. Emma Goldman, *Living my Life* (1931; rept. New York, Garden City: Garden City Publishing Co., 1934), pp. 11–12.

5. Ibid., p. 12.
6. Sarah Reznikoff, op. cit., p. 99.
7. Charles Reznikoff, 'Needle Trade', in *Family Chronicle* op. cit., p. 274.
8. Alfred Kazin. *A Walker in the City* (New York: Harcourt, Brace and World, 1951), pp. 21–2.
9. Ibid., p. 8.
10. Podhoretz, op. cit., p. 3.
11. Daniel Bell, 'Reflections on Jewish Identity,' *Commentary*, 31, 6 (June, 1961), 474.
12. Kazin, *A Walker in the City*, op. cit., pp. 66–7.
13. Ibid., p. 37.
14. Podhoretz, op. cit., p. 30.
15. Ibid., p. 149.
16. Philip Roth interview in 'The American Philip Roth', B.B.C. Radio 3, 7 October 1985.
17. Leslie Fiedler, *Waiting for the End: The American Literary Scene from Hemingway to Baldwin* (1964; rept. Harmondsworth: Penguin, 1967), p. 74.
18. Abraham Cahan, *The Education of Abraham Cahan* (1926; rept. and trans., Leon Stein, Abraham Conan, Lynn Davison; Philadelphia: Jewish Publication Society of America, 1969), p. 205.
19. Michael Gold, *Jews Without Money* (New York: Horace Liveright, 1930), p. 309.
20. Alfred Kazin, *Starting Out in the Thirties* (1962; rept. London: Secker and Warburg, 1966), p. 15.
21. Alfred Kazin, *New York Jew* (London: Secker and Warburg, 1978), p. 4.
22. The evaporation of faith becomes, in some cases, a torrent of reaction in the 1980s. Norman Podhoretz has assumed an almost virulent pro-American, conservative position. There is, in that phenomenon, a sense that an area of Jewish opinion starts to move toward a total identification with mainstream American thought. See Norman Podhoretz, 'The Dialect of Blame; Some Reflections on Anti-Americanism,' *Encounter*, LXV, 2 (July/August, 1985), 6–8.
23. Interview in 'The American Philip Roth', op. cit.
24. Wallace Markfield, 'Notes on the Working Day', *Partisan Review*, XIII, 4 (September–October, 1946), 463.
25. Kazin, *New York Jew*, op. cit., p. 141.
26. Barbara Probst Solomon, *The Beat of Life* (London: Andre Deutsch, 1961), p. 110.
27. Kazin, *New York Jew*, op. cit., p. 258.
28. Cynthia Ozick, *Bloodshed and Three Novellas* (London: Secker and Warburg, 1976), p. 11.
29. Solomon's comment was in the context of a symposium in *Commentary* magazine: 'Jewishness and the Younger Intellectuals: A Symposium', *Commentary*, 31, 4 (April, 1961), 306–59. Throughout the 1960s and '70s, a number of similar symposia took place and the recurrent issue was precisely this state of cultural and religious introspection. The following are among the most interesting: 'My Jewish Affirmation—A Symposium', *Judaism* 10, 4 (Fall, 1961), pp. 291–352, 'The Meaning of *Galut* in America

Today: A Symposium', *Midstream*, IX, 1 (March, 1963), 3–45, 'Where do I Stand Now—A Symposium', *Judaism*, 23, 4 (Fall, 1974), 389–466.

30. Saul Bellow, 'The Swamp of Prosperity', *Commentary*, 28, 4 (July, 1959), 78–9.
31. Norma Stahl Rosen, *Joy to Levine!* (London: Michael Joseph, 1962), p. 116.
32. Leslie Fiedler, *The Second Stone* (London: Heinemann, 1966), p. 252.
33. *The Condition of Jewish Belief: A Symposium Compiled by the Editors of Commentary Magazine* (New York: Macmillan, 1966), p. 178.
34. Nathan Glazer, 'On Jewish Forebodings', *Commentary*, 80, 2 (August, 1985), 36.
35. Philip Roth, *Reading Myself and Others* (London: Jonathan Cape, 1975), pp. 245–46.
36. Kazin, *New York Jew* (op. cit.), pp. 258–59.
37. Jay Neugeboren, *Parentheses: An Autobiographical Journey* (New York: E. P. Dutton, 1970), p. 59.
38. Ibid., p. 23.
39. Ibid., p. 37.
40. Jay Neugeboren, *An Orphan's Tale* (New York: Holt, Rinehart and Winston, 1976), p. 83.
41. Erica Jong, *Fear of Flying* (1973; rept. London: Panther Books, 1974), p. 27.
42. Letter to the author, 17 October 1983.
43. Jerome Charyn, *The Catfish Man: A Conjured Life* (New York: Arbor House, 1980), p. 309.
44. Loren Baritz, 'A Jew's American Dilemma', *Commentary*, 33, 6 (June, 1962), 525.

10

Norman Mailer: Frontline Reporter of the Divine Economy

by ERIC MOTTRAM

1

America is the world's most advised nation. Bookstores are crammed with advice books on religions, diets, how to make friends and influence people, how to make money, keep fit, bring up children, how to preserve pot plants and what to do about death. Among these must be included biographies and autobiographies to be read for warning and hope, as acts of confession to keep society going. The United States came into initial existence just as self-consciousness began its force in definition of 'the modern world as "modern" ', in the words of the distinguished cultural historian, Warren I. Susman, condensing the necessary history of how excessive beliefs in 'human behaviour and destiny [are] felt to arise . . . *within* the individual' during the seventeenth century.[1] Biography and autobiography delineate ways in which we believe we can and cannot control ourselves, and what is to be inferred by this kind of statement, along the passage from Donne's 'An Anatomy of the World: The First Anniversary', *The Origin of Species* and Social Darwinism, and Freud's psychoanalytical relegation of responsibility. 'Surely', writes Susman, '*character* was a key word in the vocabulary of Englishmen and Americans', and this is demonstrated by the large amount of writings 'promising a way to character development and worldly success'.

In the early nineteenth century the most popular relevant quotation is Emerson's definition of character: 'Moral order through the medium of individual nature.' But that kind of idealism had to be modified with 'work as essential in a society constantly stressing producer values'. The twentieth century produced 'keen interest in the relation between social orders and psychological types'. Advice manuals register shifts from 'a culture of character to a culture of personality', setting up confused tensions between being different and being similar, being individual and being adjusted to current social norms, being masterful and being social. The culture star appears as an embodiment of advice; writers become stars of advice, and radio and television augment their audibility and visibility. They are produced as producers of behaviour.

But these presentations of self have shifted again under increasing late twentieth-century resentments against the corruptions of racism, imperialism, industry dedicated to careless chemical and nuclear production, and a rampaging spectator-consumer homogeneity. America's dissenting traditions have been strongly reasserted, and Norman Mailer is part of that necessity, from, for instance, his definition of the American outsider-existentialist as hipster, in the Summer 1957 issue of *Dissent*, to his identification of subway graffiti artists in similar permissive terms in 1974, interviewing his subjects in their homes in 'new journalism' style:

> You hit your name and maybe something in the whole scheme of the system gives a death rattle. . . . On the one hand, the police were getting tough, the beatings, when you were caught were worse, the legal penalties higher, and on the other hand something had happened to the process itself. Too many names had grown—a jungle of ego creepers. . . . 'The name', says Cay (CAY 161), 'is the *faith* of graffiti'.[2]

Mailer is the journalist-private eye investigating 'the mysteries of a new phenomenon', the Aesthetic Investigator, A-1. (In *Wild 90* he played a Mafia hood, in *Beyond the Law* an Irish cop, and in his third film, *Maidstone*, a film director running for president and a target for assassination.) As a writer and film-maker who watches himself create as an outsider for insiders, he appreciates the subway artist: 'There was panic in the act for you wrote with an eye over your shoulder for oncoming authority.' The ecstasy of risk, whether as army rifleman on patrol or embattled writer, has always energized Mailer, the prober of mysteries; the graffiti writer marries 'cool and style' in the mysteries of scripts with his heart 'hot with fear'. The enemy is Mayor Lindsay, who can 'live without faith if things were calm enough', the W.A.S.P. to whom graffiti is 'defacement' yet lives in a mansion itself an example of architectural obscenity (Mailer has consistently attacked official architecture since his articles for the *New York Times* and *Architectural Forum* in the '60s).[3] Lindsay and CAY 161 stand for the American city and its place in the metaphysics of the totalitarian: 'plastic above, dynamite below'. In 1964—the year of the attack on free speech at Berkeley, race riots in major cities, and the scurrilous Tonkin episode that enabled President Johnson to escalate the Viet Nam War—Mailer attacked 'the totalitarian impulse' manifest in America's daily technology,[4] and ten years later he still places it within a language of psychic theology—the need to make 'a clearing in the forest of the psyche free of dread'. He writes of the divine nebulosity of the mass like Jean Baudrillard in *In the Shadow of the Silent Majorities* another ten years later, except that Mailer's context is theological:

> . . . in our times man has disappeared into God. He is mass-man without identity, and he is God. He is all the schizophrenia of the powerless and all-powerful in one psyche.

It is that anti-oedipal impulse that guides Mailer through the labyrinth, as it guided Melville. Ishmael refused to be another Narcissus gazing in the waters below the Battery (Chapter One of *Moby-Dick*) by signing on as a lower-deck seaman, on a voyage which proves to be an investigation of power. Mailer signed on for New York. Alfred Kazin is right to draw the parallels:

> . . . he really gives and destroys himself with each hallucinatory subject . . . while fascinated with outlaws, murderers, criminals, people broken on the wheel of American disorder, he knows that his characters are *not* powerless and spiritually indigent. They are alive and fighting. . . . only Mailer had the solidarity with the

unknown vandals working through the night in the subway barns to imagine what they felt, what they wanted, what in their secret writing *they* are dreaming.

What Mailer recognizes, especially in the context of destructive and ferocious New York, is that Americans are drunk on a sense of power, induced by good money and the wars that bring good money. . . . Mailer, secretly obsessed with the ancestral idea of God as the only lasting power, has made this duplicitous American freedom the obsessive theme of his work . . . he has turned himself into an urban laboratory.[5]

In 1969 Mailer entered the stakes for mayor of New York, as if to enter and control what could have been his death as an urban Narcissus, and to enter one more battlefield of the eternal metaphysical battle. Four years before, he had dramatized the manichean war between God and Devil in New York in *An American Dream* (the battle between state law and the consequences of the Mormon version of these mataphysics appeared ten years later in *The Executioner's Song*). Stephen Rojack prepares to encounter Barney Oswald Kelly, the mafiosic embodiment of evil, in characteristic Mailer terms. He has married the Devil's daughter and killed her. The metaphysics continue: 'Comfortless was my religion, anxiety of the anxieties, for I believed God was not love but courage. Love came only as a reward. The metaphysics, however, was vast.'[6] The Waldorf Towers lobby is 'the antechamber of Hell', and Hell is Kelly's library inside, and, as in its earlier manifestation in Teppis's Hollywood tycoon office in *The Deer Park*, it inherits the aristocratic furnishings of power from the Middle Ages and the Renaissance in Europe. It is Kelly who expounds the metaphysics which Mailer himself proposes in his essays and interviews, the consistent bases of his autobiography:

Since the Church refuses to admit the possible victory of Satan, man believes that God is all-powerful. So man also assumes God is prepared to forgive every last betrayal. Which may not be the case. . . . God and the Devil are very attentive to people at the summit. I don't know if they stir much in the average man's daily stew, no great sport for spooks, I would suppose, in a ranch house, but do you expect God or the Devil left Lenin or Hitler or Churchill alone? No. They bid for favours and exact revenge. . . . you have to be ready to deal with One or the Other, and that's too much for the average man on his way. Sooner or later he decides to be mediocre.[7]

Rojack wants to be free from 'the patrols of the gods' but it is impossible, and exorcism involves the risks of madness or exile. Mailer's pre-Pacific self found it 'more attractive to conceive of oneself as (and to write about) a hero who is tall, strong, and excruciatingly wounded' (the advertisement for the 1942 story 'A Calculus at Heaven'),[8] and he recalls *A Transit to Narcissus*, based on a play called *The Naked and the Dead*, a novel drawing on his student experience of work in a state asylum. Narcissism and madness, courage and cowardice, risk within secular and religious controls: this is Mailer's world from the beginning. 'A Calculus at Heaven' imagines war in order to confront the issues of survival in extremity; the young battle hero uses 'God' to 'strengthen his mind', and becomes a member of all those Americans who 'wonder what the odds are on a heaven'. Work and death have to be justified if they are not to destroy essential dignity. For Mailer, seventeen years and the Pacific war later, Hilliard is 'sage'. He uses his fifteenth anniversary report to the Harvard Class of 1943[9] to write of his resistance to 'the wasting of the will, and the sapping of one's creative rage' by 'this totalitarian time, politely called the time of conformity'. What he calls 'running for president' is a resistance to disappointment with Kennedy, and mocking outrage confronted with Johnson and Nixon.[10] The model of honour and dignity is the American existential writer, Ernest Hemingway. The ambitious writer may 'wither from the high tension' and fall 'drunk or a burned-out brain'.[11] He must 'campaign for himself' with all the Hemingway dangers: the fear of thinking as well as feeling 'like a man'. Courage against cowardice is reinforced by presenting yourself to a public: 'advertize yourself'; and this calls for continual combat (developed in *Existential Errands* (1972), and *The Fight* (1976), with the danger of becoming 'punch-drunk', or succumbing to the fatigues of resistance to waste—'fights . . . sex, liquor, marijuana, benzedrine and seconal, much too much ridiculous and brain-blasting rage at the miniscule frustrations of a most loathsome literary world, necrophilic to the core'— which may be acts of waste in themselves. The resistant writer 'must defend courage, sex, consciousness, the beauty of the body, the search for love, and the capture of what may be, after all, an heroic destiny'.

In the 1964 interview, he recalls understanding as a young man, from Farrell's *Studs Lonigan*, that 'you could write about your own life.'[12] Reading Sabatini, Farnol and *Das Kapital* imbued him with a sense of the heroic man—and it is Marx's book that concludes his *Dissent* essay of 1957 with a typically individual reading of Marx and a characteristically energetic programme of resistance. *Capital* is:

> that first of the major *psychologies* to approach the mystery of social cruelty so simply and practically as to say we are a collective body of humans whose life-energy is wasted, displaced, and procedurally stolen as it passes from one of us to another— where particularly the epic grandeur of *Das Kapital* would find its place in an even more God-like view of human justice and injustice, in some more excruciating vision of those intimate and institutional processes which lead to our creations and disasters, our growth, our attrition, and our rebellion.[13]

Mailer's autobiographical texts constitute a record of 'this long patrol' against the 'collective condition', 'instant death by atomic war', 'the State as *l'univers concentrationnaire*', and 'slow death by conformity with every creative and rebellious instinct stifled'. But those were days of hope that he might influence American culture—and at least one of Mailer's establishment critics writes that, by 1971, 'So goes Mailer, so goes the nation. This is the form his genius takes.'[14] Mailer was conscious of the American tradition he belonged to—'the family tree' of dissenters, socialists, radicals, rebels, nihilists and anarchists— and, like both Wilhelm Reich and Scott Fitzgerald, of the necessity of making 'the radical bridge from Marx to Freud'. Mailer's God was, then, more like that dionysian force which energized plenty of American writing and music in the '50s[15]:

> . . . that God which every hipster believes is located in the senses of his body, that trapped, mutilated and nonetheless megalo- maniacal God who is It, who is energy, life, sex, force, the Yoga's *prana*, the Reichian's orgone, Lawrence's 'blood', Hemingway's 'good', the Shavian life-force; 'It'; God; not the God of the churches but the unachievable whisper of mystery within the sex, the paradise of limitless energy, and perceptions just beyond the next wave of the next orgasm . . . the oldest dream of power, the

gold fountain of Ponce de Leon, the fountain of youth where the gold is in the orgasm.

By 1964, he states as the aim of his fiction: 'the terror of confronting a reality which might open into more and more anxiety and so present a deeper and deeper view of the abyss . . . of being reborn as something much less noble or something much more ignoble'.[16] The image of a writer keeping 'in shape' like a single combat boxer gives way to the writer in 'a vast guerrilla war going on for the mind of man, communist against communist, capitalist against capitalist, artist against artist'. He campaigns for mayor as a 'left-conservative'[17] against the city of cancer and plague, short tempers in 'the hideous air', poverty like 'a layer of smog'. The old desire for the dignity of the heroic returns in a political platform:

> What can education be in the womb of a dying city but a fury to discover for oneself whether one is victim or potential hero, stupid or too bright for old pedagogical ways? . . . The old confidence that the problems of life were roughly equal to our abilities has been lost . . . we cannot forge our destiny.

Beyond his earlier hope, Mailer now proposes New York as the fifty-first state. But he is only too aware that American discussion of a possible future takes place in a void: 'The answers are unknown because the questions all collide in the vast empty arena of the mass media where no price has ever to be paid for your opinion.' Mailer has the nerve to tell the police at the John Jay College of Criminal Justice that violence arises from increased boredom and 'bad, dull architecture', but suggests that the New York police should be organized on the basis of neighbourhood control, along with education, fire-prevention, sanitation and the parks. In all his speeches he opposed current economic and political answers handed down by 'an antiquated political machine' which those who have caused the present breakdown 'helped to create themselves':

> If we have a massive application of law and order . . . what we will get in turn is a Vietnam in New York, because people are living lives that are so intolerable not only economically but spiritually that they cannot put up with the thought of being deprived any longer.

Mailer is in fact using positions established fifteen years earlier in a perceptive analysis of David Riesman in *Dissent*[18]—a criticism of academic refusal even to see, let alone to consider, the actualities of control in America. In 1954 he formulated a statement which recurs, with slight variations, as the basis of his stance as citizen and writer, his autobiographical seed, as it were, and the justification for his 'new journalist' reportage:

> It is men's actions which make history and not their sentiments, but the actions of a man, particularly his social and historic actions, are comparatively minute in relation to the whole man.

Mailer's finest strength is, with that basis, to grasp what survival in the United States means at any time:

> America is a social organism with a capitalist economy whose problems are deep and probably insoluble, and whose response to any historical situation must be a function of its need to survive as that need is reflected, warped, aided and impeded by countless smaller social organisms, traditions, and finally individuals who cancel one another out or double their force (so far as *actions* are concerned) until the result of these numerous vectors represents a statement of where the power in America rests and where the necessity.

And that power 'does not belong to nine-tenths of "the people" ', since 'what characterizes all pre-socialist history and may (let us hope not) characterize a socialist history if there be one, is that the mass of men must satisfy the needs of the social organism in which they live far more than the social organism must satisfy them.' (This opinion is so near to Freud's in *The Future of an Illusion* that he may well have read it at this time; an American edition had in fact been published the previous year.)

It is clear already in this essay that Mailer understood the necessity to write autobiographically, non-objectively, and to fuse where possible the usually separated fields of fiction, history, sociology and autobiography. *The Armies of the Night* (1968) would be subtitled 'history as a novel' and written, like *The Education of Henry Adams*, in the third person autobiographical mode, an investigative form and style carried through also in *The Presidential Papers* (1964), *Miami and the Siege of Chicago* (1968), *The Idol and the Octopus* (1968), *St. George and the Godfather* (1972) and *Some Honorable Men* (1976):

> There is finally no way one can try to apprehend complex reality without a 'fiction'. But one may choose the particular 'fiction'

224

which most satisfies the sum of one's knowledge, experiences, biases, needs, desires, values, and eventually one's moral necessities. And one may even attempt to reshape reality in some small way with the 'fiction' as a guide.

Riesman is the example of faking objectivity, the 'liberal' for whom

at last all things are equal, are justifiable . . . drawn to quietism and acceptance . . . the left liberal—for want of a better classification—who like everyone else has become progressively more exhausted by the neurotic intellectual demands of the Cold War; there is peace and attractiveness in the endless varied world of what-is where finally everything can be seen inside-out or right-side-back-again if so the need arises.

But the real need is to use the force of the existential investigator's being-in-the-world (Mailer had read Heidegger and Sartre by 1963). The position taken in *The Armies of the Night* is already present:

The radical political life in America has become difficult, and to hold the position of libertarian socialist is equivalent to accepting almost total intellectual alienation from America, as well as a series of pains and personal contradictions in one's work. . . . It is difficult for us to approach the liberal, to attempt to convince him, when we can offer no place to go, no country, no cause, no movement, no thing, and are ourselves exposed to all the temptations of circular thought, of reversals of emphasis, until far from obtaining the satisfaction of thinking ourselves martyrs, we are more likely to torture ourselves with such questions as our own neurotic relation to life. . . . the radical temper is often turned most radically upon oneself. . . . Yet, after everything else, there remains the basic core of socialism so deep in Western culture, the idea, the moral passion, that it is truly intolerable and more than a little fantastic that men should not live in economic equality and in liberty. As serious artistic expression is the answer to the meaning of life for a few, so the passion for socialism is the only meaning I can conceive in the lives of those who are not artists, if one cannot create 'works' one may dream at least of an era when humans can create humans, and the satisfaction of the radical can come from the thought that he tries to keep this idea alive.

American anxiety, synaptic with the metaphysics of dread, is caused by the state of the nation:

> covert guilt that abundance and equality remain utterly separated,
> and we have reached the point where socialism is . . . obvious
> enough to flood with anxiety the psyches of those millions who
> know and yet do nothing.

Claims for a society which ensures happiness are 'best left to
dictators'. However, Mailer still succumbs to the rather smug
view that socialism at least raises 'man's suffering' to 'a higher
level'—he is still in the archaic and religious harness of
'tragedy' as at least a progress from history as 'melodrama,
farce, and monstrosity'.

The Armies of the Night details Mailer's concurrence, at a
Pentagon demonstration against the Viet Nam War in October
1967, with a wide range of protesters: Paul Goodman, Noam
Chomsky, Robert Lowell, Dwight Macdonald, and the Fugs,
led by Ed Sanders, a poet and Egyptologist who had already
been jailed for sitting on a submarine by way of protest. In
Book 2, Mailer states the reasons for the form of his text: the
presence of himself in the historical event he both witnesses and
reports, and stationed in the tower of history, 'a tower fully
equipped with telescopes to study—at the greatest advantage—
our own horizon'.[19] The Investigator is once again left with his
anxiety and his autobiographical continuities: 'Dutiful alliances
are deadening' and those between Old and New Left and Black
Militants are 'sometimes near to unendurable'. But the hippies
offered 'a new style of revolution—revolution by theatre and
without a script'. Their act of exorcism of the Pentagon is
perceived as part of 'a growing sense of apocalypse in American
life'. Mailer is again combatant, this time in another stage of the
long American semantics of law and outlaw, but outside Army,
party and campaign. The demonstrators said: 'our country is
engaged in a war so hideous that we, in the greatest numbers
possible, are going to break the laws of assembling in order to
protest this impossible war.' The government replied: 'this is a
war necessary to maintain the very security of this nation, but
because of our tradition of free speech and dissent, we will
permit your protest, but only if it is orderly'. The result: an
'absurd' compromise of a little disorder and a little law-
breaking, somewhere between 75,000 and 90,000 American
civilians against about 4,200 police, security guards and

National Guardsmen, 6,000 82nd Airborne Division, military police units, and 20,000 troops on alert—drawn from Washington, North Carolina, California, Texas, Florida, Arizona, etc.

So the issue extends: 'American brutality' at home and abroad no longer 'contemplated' but 'confronted' in a 'military situation' again. 'Personal history' enters newspaper reports and 'the collective novel'; autobiography precisely intervenes:

> The novel must replace history at precisely that point where experience is sufficiently emotional, spiritual, psychical, moral, existential, or supernatural to expose the fact that the historian in pursuing the experience would be obliged to quit the clearly demarcated limits of historic enquiry . . . enter that world of strange lights and intuitive speculation which is the novel.

A-1 places himself in the collective with methods that will serve him in *Marilyn* (1973), *The Fight* (1975—Muhammad Ali's Zaire combat), *The Prisoner of Sex* (1971—combat with Women's Liberation), and the three films for which he starred, wrote the scripts and directed. But at no point does the sense of a wider metaphysical conflict relax.

2

In *Cannibals and Christians* Mailer offers himself as a knight 'to rescue civilization' in 'a time of plague' and the failure and assassination of Kennedy. He would be a 'noble physician' in a world, not of 'adventurers, entrepreneurs, settlers, social arbiters, proletarians, agriculturalists and other egocentric types of a dynamic society', but of 'Cannibals and Christians'. Christians sell creeds to save the world—Lyndon Johnson, Mao Tse-Tung, 'anarchists, socialists, Communists, Keynesians, democrats, Civil Righters, beatniks, pacifists, Teach-inners . . . new Africa nations'. But they also overlap the self-devourers. The doubt emerges—and it is the motivation of a short story called 'The Last Night'—'was there indeed a death in the seed which brought us here?'; 'was the country extraordinary or accursed?' In the débris of shattered certainties, revenge replaces justice, power replaces liberty; the Viet Nam War is so illogical 'that any attempt to deal with it is logically illogical . . . rational political discussion of Adolf Hitler's motives was illogical and obscene'. Mailer's earlier faith in 'the secret potentialities' of America, that the nation 'was finally good not evil', has become 'not even tragic or doomed, but dirty and misplaced'. He entertains the notion that 'liberal rhetoric was conceived by Satan to kiss the behind of something unspeakable'. America is 'insane with Christ, Pop art, Fibreglass, moonshots, race riots, and Hilton Hotel architecture'. Where Frank Cowperwood 'once amassed an empire', now the literary world chooses to love Herzog, 'his bastard great-nephew'. In 'engaging the congealed hostility of the world', the existential-crusading writer must risk 'the mysteries of the Self' where 'insanity prepares an ambush'; 'infantrymen of the arts' must storm through to 'where the real secrets are stored', and

> one of us homeless guns had better make it, or the future will smell like the dead air of the men who captured our time during that huge collective cowardice which was the aftermath of the Second World War.

The 'Kierkegaardian hero' of dread must come forth against 'the inability to create one's nature by daring, exceptional, forbidden, or socially impossible acts'. Sexuality has to be prepared as a moral necessity unless it is to 'turn literally to violence'; the need is for a behavioural skill which combines Lawrence's deep orgasm and Henry Miller's sexual pleasure. But

> 'as they emerge from adolescence into young manhood [Americans] are very much like green soldiers being sent into difficult terrain ignorant of the condition. A lot of virility immediately gets massacred'.

So the self-interviews of this book are interrogation rooms which avoid limited engagements with weak official interrogators, and can engage the vocabulary of 'God, soul, Devil, spirit, vision, eternal and universal'. The book concludes with an apocalyptic coding:

> Vision is the mind of God; soul, His body; and spirit is what He has left behind. Literally. It is His excrement. . . . The Devil [is] the echo of history, the lore of the past, the mansions of philosophy, the blunt weight of every problem which has been solved and every lie which has succeeded . . . the dead spirit of institutional life, as mass communication. . . . The passion of totalitarianism is to conceal its own process; so its passion is to abstract form into

monotony for monotonous forms are superior at concealing the sinister processes of their creation since it drains vitality to study them.

Then Mailer 'sways slightly' from fatigue: a slight self-mockery to steady a euphoria against decadence that itself edges into decadence; an ancient language must be vitalized so that the manichean battle cannot simply be explained away as psychology and drugs, 'a derangement of the senses produced by chemicals.'[20] In 1967 the Pentagon had to be wounded 'symbolically . . . as if a symbolic wound could prove as mortal as any other combattive rent',[21] to evoke 'the nutritive mysteries' of the absurd in the Fugs's magic. Again, Mailer has to mock his knight-errantry as an

> ambiguous comic hero . . . an egotist of the most startling misproportions, outrageously and often unhappily self-assertive, yet in command of a detachment classic in severity. . . . Such egotism being two-headed, thrusting itself forward the better to study itself, finds itself at home in a house of mirrors, since it has habits, even the talent, to regard itself. Once History inhabits the crazy house, egotism may be the last tool left to History.

The 'severity' is the product of the novelist and the theologian. The Fugs's magic is like the counter-magic against official America in Allen Ginsberg's 'Wichita Vortex Sutra' (1966)[22]; and Ed Sanders uses Mailer's own terms—'demons', 'cancerous tumours', 'the plague'. For Mailer this is 'the cutting edge of all primitive awe . . . the fuse of blasphemy', used 'to cast out the EVIL . . . the pentacle of power'.

But the representatives of American law and order also represent mass democracy in power in a 'no man's land between the old frontier and the new ranch home', 'the unredeemable madness' of small town America. The Enemy is present in a peculiarly American form:

> Beneath all these structures advertized as majestic in law and order there was this small carnal secret which the partners of a bust could share. . . . These Marshals had the dead eye and sour cigar, that sly shuffle of propriety and rut which so often comes out in a small-town sheriff as patriotism and the sweet stink of a crooked dollar.

So that 'each side is coming face to face with its own conception of the devil!' The class war becomes 'apocalyptic vision' in the 'crisis of Christianity in America [with] military heroes on one side, and the unnamed saints on the other!' The old American Adam is searching for totalitarian gods to obey, not to resist.

Four years later *Harper's Magazine* devoted its March 1971 issue to *The Prisoner of Sex*. Once again Mailer adopted his Adams third person, as prisoner of the Pulitzer prize and 'war as wedlock'. He retreats to his Maine house with his five children and 'an old love, his dearest old love', in danger of being 'incarcerated into larger paralyses'.[23] Hearing from a *Time* editor that Women's Liberation has selected him as 'their major ideological opposition', he embarks on a serious analysis of his position as male: 'better to expire as a devil in the fire than an angel in the wings'. His initial stance is classic: human beings, both women and men, exist between beasts and gods. His ludicrously macho aggression on T.V., always his Limbo of horror,[24] betray the main field of his life: 'revolution, tradition, sex and the homosexual, the orgasm, the family, the child and the political shape of the future. . . .' He recognizes the truth of a woman's refusal to be automatically taken as an object for male use:

> any man feeling so stripped of his skin would be suffering an unholy mix of narcissism and paranoia. Inner conditions like that were usually reserved for combat, for committing robbery (when even the furniture looks at you) or on the first day in jail.

The tough language of feminist writers, quoted at length as 'remedial reading', is necessary, as it is for blacks and homosexuals. Further, women were now 'writing about men and about themselves as Henry Miller had once written about women'; this constitutes another radicalism against fascism and degenerate liberalism. When Valerie Solanas counters penis envy with 'pussy envy', he recognizes 'a cultural revolution and a sexual revolution', and he accepts the bases of Friedan's *The Feminine Mystique* and other feminist writings as part of a needed revolt against 'this vast system of waste and exploitation', and an intervention into both Marxist class warfare and the assumptions of 'universal' male-female polarity. But the implications need investigation. Women are not in the categories of the Marshals, the Pentagon or the masses.

They are, in fact, 'a step, or a stage, or a move or a leap near the creation of existence', and 'contain the future as well as the present'. Therefore they are 'never free', and this appears to be a limit, in spite of sexual technology and a certain feminist's belief that 'sexual intercourse would have to cease to be Society's means to population renewal'. Technology, once again in Mailer's work, threatens both 'virility' and 'nature' (a relationship explored in a book he had just completed, *A Fire on the Moon*), which are taken to be universals, constants not in need of historicization. Generation and sexual pleasure, and the tyrannies of sexuality need reconsideration; Kate Millett is right, and Mailer admires her argument and uses the texts she quotes as contributions to 'the snarls between mind and groin'. But then he moves in to attack *Sexual Politics* from theological teleology. The orgasm is placed by 'the Lord, Master of Existential Reason' inside 'the act of creation' for a cause of 'the profounder sort', the future life of a child. The 'transcendant instant' of sexual love ensures that the new soul may 'live with more light later'. This is a sacred issue: 'Angels and devils are collecting in the embrace at Revolution Hall.'

It is no use for Millett to 'ignore forever what did not fit' her argument that 'men were guilty and women must win'—and his analysis of her methods and results stands. She misreads Miller because she cannot comprehend the nature of lust. Her revolution is incomplete and, at this point, hypocritical. Nor can she understand Mailer's own presentation of 'man's sense of awe before woman, his dread of her position one step closer to eternity', a source of men's need to revile and humiliate women, 'do everything to reduce them so one might dare to enter them and take pleasure of them'. In absence of these recognitions, Millett becomes one of Mailer's totalitarians, along with other 'literary technologists' and 'ideological mincers': 'It was the measure of the liberal technologist and the Left totalitarian that they exhibited the social lust to make units of people.' In a passage in the *Harper's Magazine* version, omitted from the book, Mailer allows his 'metaphysical drift' to speculate—'Who knew what dramas of selection took place in the first days of embryonic life?'—and in the course of a consideration of Jean Genet and homosexuality, he again tries to prevent idle dialectics from confusing an already complex issue:

a man can hardly ever assume he has become a man—he is on the way to becoming less masculine on the instant. So the cultural conditioning to be masculine or feminine may not be so much the arbitrary exercise of a patriarchal society as derive from some instinct or impulse of nature.

There is no certainty here; perhaps 'all men are homosexual but for their choice not to be', and prison life shows as much. Prison is punishment as radical loss of meaning, including a lust transaction 'as much leading to baselessness, and therefore insanity, as masturbation'. At which point Mailer knows that he had better explain himself carefully! The autobiographical stance of honest probing appears to enter the totalitarian it ostensibly assaults.

In *The Presidential Papers* Mailer argues with Paul Krassner that masturbation destroys

> everything that's beautiful and good in one . . . the ability to contemplate one's experience is disturbed. Instead, fantasies of power take over and disturb all sleep. . . . The ultimate direction of masturbation has to be insanity.[25]

Now, seven years later, he believes the 'metaphysics' here are right because 'the fuck' must be part of 'meaning which went to the root of existence':

> . . . try to decide there is design in the universe, that humans embody a particular Intent, assume just once there is some kind of destiny in the universe intended—at the least!—*intended* for us, and therefore human beings are not absurd, not totally absurd, assume some Idea (or at least some clash of Idea versus ideas) is in operation—and then sex cannot comfortably prove absurd. . . . and sexual rights become no more than a tricky species, some half-ass rights to property.

Today,

> a dread of the future oozed from every leak in the social machine—unless the future could be controlled. That wave of totalitarianism which had begun with the urge to infiltrate the life and control the death of millions had come to close upon every style and habit.

'Genetic engineering' is part of it, as contributory to making sex absurd as masturbation. In Millett's 'burned-out arid landscape', 'the scientist and the narcissist come together . . . to explore the exquisite possibilities of the single permissive sexual standard'. The baby produced would be a monster, possibly a clone: 'prognosis of sanity—low; narcissism—intact; capacity for incest —infinite'. In the city Mailer campaigned for in 1969, respect for sexual life, as a life 'to learn', might be 'the rationalized end of that violence' between women and men, the beginning of the liberation of the mutual search for 'the best mate' and an assurance that the baby 'came from the root of God's desire to go all the way, wherever was that way'.

Masturbation combines lust and narcissism, a fusion which blights creativity in Mailer's myth. In 1973 and 1976 he turns to Henry Miller[26] as a writer who mastered the autobiographical fictional form without the debilitations of Narcissus, and without that murder and suicide which had captured the heart of Ishmael, the outcast. Miller's is a psyche singularly 'free of dread', the writer as 'the ultimate definition of the word protagonist', 'just a little different from his work. But in that difference is all the mystery of his own personality, and the paradoxes of a great artist. And the failure'. Great artists fail in that they cannot fulfil 'their own idea of themselves'. Miller is 'a sage' who does not become 'more compatible with time . . . he evades our sense of classification. He does not become a personality, rather he maintains himself as an enigma.' The author-personality is like a movie star: 'Hemingway and Fitzgerald impinge on our psyche with the clarity of Bogart and Cagney.' *On the Road* is 'close to Kerouac, yet he gives a happier Kerouac than the one who died too soon'. After *The Sun Also Rises*, Hemingway 'set out to grow into Jake Barnes and locked himself for better and worse, for enormous fame and eventual destruction, into that character who embodied the spirit of an age'. But it is Miller who is the more 'self-regenerative', and 'without stoicism of good taste'; 'considering where the world was going—right into the world wide sewer of the concentration camp—Miller may have had a message that gave more life than Hemingway.'

Since one of his occupations is to project his entrances into religion, politics, technology and the arts with a media action far beyond anything these writers experienced, Mailer has to consider the possibilities of self-love and self-hate in the Narcissus character very carefully. 'Narcissism' (1976) condenses twenty-five years of his autobiographical modes,[27] 'the fundamental relationship with oneself. That same to-and-fro of love and hate which mates feel for one another is experienced within the self. A special kind of insanity always underwrites the narcissist, therefore.' Love between narcissists is 'fine tuning . . . the natural matrimony of the Stereo Century'. Miller, 'the last great American pioneer', pioneered its major text. But 'a narcissist is not self-absorbed so much as one self is immersed in studying the other . . . the scientist and the experiment in one.' To resist characteristic boredom, he engages in 'feverish, even violent attempts to shift the given . . . experience is poured into no vessels of the psyche, but seems to drain away.' Once more, the metaphysics have to be stated: in the manichean battlefield, Narcissus's gaze turns towards his society in order to survive as the alert patrolman or hipster-writer. To remain a Narcissus may be 'a true disease, a biological displacement of the natural impulse to develop oneself by the lessons of one's experience', a relationship parallel to onanism and copulation, cancer and 'the natural growth of tissue'. The utter Narcissus lives in a state of existential terror of isolation which results in 'real need' for another. Then Mailer moves into a characteristic development:

> To the degree that narcissism is an affliction of the talented, the stakes are not small, and the victims are playing a serious game in the midst of their scenarios. For if one can break out of the penitentiary of self-absorption, then there may be artistic wonders to achieve.

It is such issues that Christopher Lasch misunderstands in his sociological study of 'the new Narcissus'[28] as part of the deteriorations of self-regard in 'art and philosophy'. He produces Mailer as his example of self-advertisement which refuses what Lasch simply offers as 'reality' and 'the everyday artists in the street'. Felix Guattari is much more useful to show a constructive narcissism against an enforced national consensus sociology:

> Emergence from destructive narcissism does not mean that a subject has to go through a process of being repressed in reality or being castrated in phantasy: on the contrary, it means achieving greater potency and neutralizing the forces of alienation. It is therefore essentially a matter of gaining power over the real, never just of manipulating the phantasies or the symbols.[29]

234

For Mailer, this is a revolutionary act in America—and the chat-show is his Limbo punishment for yielding to the temptations of becoming what consensus requires—a personality rather than a human being. With some justification, Henry Adams and his 'autobiographical mode' appear as major, if unconscious controls, when Mailer looks back to *The Armies of the Night* from 1980 and 1981[30]; both men understand that 'education' must resist imposing culture and the power of an investigative intelligence. The personality becomes a self-ventriloquist in a personality-ridden culture—a form of crass obedience.

But the penetrating oedipal relationships of army, self and nature in *The Naked and Dead* (1948) remain, despite their transformations. Coercion and sacrifice remain the key dangers. *Ancient Evenings* (1983) still researches multiple oedipal interpenetrations, religious and military. The characters are controlled victims of that 'familialism'[31] which may penetrate dreams, immortalities and existences without end, those crises and violations which encroach on Rojack as the diabolic embodied in disease, international evil and the degeneration of sexuality in 1965. *Why Are We In Vietnam?* situates the oedipal transmissions within the parental urges to the hunt and war, inherited by the young in 1967, and present not only in Texas but within the polar circles of the Devil's totalizing enforcements. That seduction myth receives a governing and ambivalent treatment in *The Deer Park* (1955), in which the liberal victim, Charles Eitel, may contain both god and devil, and the 'magic' of the nuclear explosion in the Nevada desert, not long before Mailer published the novel, is the narcissist Mario Faye's god in action against the army and the press as they 'hide the world with words' (Chapter 13):

> So let it come, Faye thought, let this explosion come, and then another, and all the others, until the Sun God burned the earth. . . . Let it come, Faye begged, like a man praying for rain, let it come and clear the rot and the stench and the stink, let it come for all of everywhere, just so it comes and the world stands clear in the dead white dawn.

In Chapter 25, the origin of Faye's faith and anxiety, between orthodoxy and heresy as hangovers from the ages of faith and their polarizations of Christ and Anti-Christ, the spiritual and the carnal, appear in an ancient myth:

> . . . the priest who takes the Devil to save the world must use the
> Devil to destroy it . . . beyond, far beyond, was the heresy that
> God was the Devil and the One they called the Devil was God-in-
> banishment like a noble prince deprived of true Heaven, and
> God who was the Devil had conquered except for the few who
> saw the cheat that God was not God at all. So he prayed, 'Make
> me cold, Devil, and I will run the world in your name'.

In such a state of *Angst*, an American inheriting New England
beliefs in both the God of the Covenant and the manichean
conflict may end up being in an American *sparagmos* of dis-
membered hope, recalling 'The Dismantling of Lemuel Pitkin'
in 1934—the subtitle of Nathanael West's *A Cool Million*. In
1962, Mailer described himself as 'living in a no-man's land'
between being 'a mystic' and 'a rationalist',[31] and is therefore
fascinated with Jews 'obsessed in their unconscious nightmare
with whether they belong to a God of righteousness or a Devil of
treachery', and Negroes 'secretly fixed upon magic—that elixir
of nature which seems to mediate between God and Devil'—
neither having ever 'made peace with Christianity, or mankind. . . . As the Negro enters civilization, Faust may be his
archetype, even as the Jew has fled Iago as the despised image
of himself.' Then he uses Buber's *Tales of the Hassidim: The Early
Masters*, as he once again turns to the metaphysics of God,
Devil, narcissism, the combatant and that existential outlaw
figure he first conceptualized through Jean Malaquais.[32] The
oedipal need is for a God with a design:

> If there is any urgency in God's intent, if we are not actors working
> out a play for our salvation, but rather soldiers in an army which
> seeks to carry some noble conception of Being out across the stars,
> or back into the protoplasm of life, then a portion of God's creative
> power was extinguished in the camps of extermination. If God is
> not all-powerful but existential, discovering the possibilities and
> limitations of His creative powers in the form of the history which
> is made by His creatures, then one must postulate an existential
> equal to God, an antagonist, the Devil, a principle of Evil whose
> signature was the concentration camps, whose joy is to waste
> substance, whose intent is to prevent God's conception of Being
> from reaching its mysterious goal.

Reflecting on Jean Genet's *The Blacks*, in 1961, he criticizes
anyone who 'prefers to deliver his will to an institution or faith

outside him in the hope that it will absorb the rebellious hatred of his Being':

> Man turns to society to save him only when he is sick within. So long as he is alive, he looks for love. But those dying of inanition, boredom, frustration, monotony, or debilitating defeat turn to the Church, to the FBI, to the Law, to the *New York Times*, to authoritarian leaders, to movies about the Marine Corps, or to the race for Space. . . . The modern faiths appeal to mediocrities whose minds are too dull to perceive that they are offered not answers but the suppression of questions; the more sensitive turn to older faiths and shrink as they swallow emotional inconsistency. The cancerous who are inclined to the Fascist look to the police, the secret police, the *Krieg* against crime, corruption, and Communists.

Within Mailer's favourite sport, boxing, the Liston-Patterson fight is set up as another scene in 'the battle of good and evil, that curious battle where decision is rare and never clear'. The time is Halloween. The boxers are into 'the existential venture', 'a defense against the plague . . . which comes from violence converted into the nausea of all that nonviolence which is void of peace'. The Devil had struck Patterson down 'with vastly greater ease than the Devil had intended', but the reporter of the cosmic battle accepts his share of the outcome:

> for of course the fighters spoke as well from the countered halves of my nature: what more had I to tell myself of sex versus love, magic against love, magic against art, or the hustler and the infantryman? . . . I began in the plot-ridden, romantic dungeons of my mind . . . to see myself as some sort of centre about which all that had been lost must now rally.

Far from mere egotism, this is the writer's responsibility, beyond journalism and personality:

> To believe the impossible may be won creates a strength from which the impossible may indeed be attacked. Fidel Castro alone in the jungle, with a dozen men left, seven-eighths of his landing party dead, lost, or captured, turned to his followers in the sugar-cane and said, 'The days of the dictatorship are numbered.'

As he shakes hands with Liston, the Goat confronted, any foolish eccentricity is ameliorated:

> . . . some ghost of Don Quixote was laid to rest in me. . . . To shake the hand of the Devil must quiver the hole: who knew any

longer where Right was Left or who was Good and how Evil had hid? For if Liston was the agent of the Devil, what a raid had been made on God, what a royal black man had arisen.

The narrator of the 'broken fragment from a long novel' in the final section called 'On Waste', certainly speaks for this Mailer. Sartre, he claims,

> had no sense of evil, the anguish of God, and the possible existence of Satan. That was left for me, to return the rootless disordered mind of our Twentieth Century to the kiss *sub cauda* and the *Weltanschaung* of the Medieval witch.

Mailer's nervous poise between self-conscious eccentricity and urgent necessities of the crusader emerges:

> . . . as a rule of thumb (since one is hardly so divine oneself as to speak with authority of the Divine Economy) God must raid upon evil to recover it, even as the Devil lusts to capture love. . . . Thus, at last, a hint of my style and the character of my mind.

Mailer's is a metaphysical version of Guattari's definition of the necessary self in any serious discourse: 'the whole fabric of my inmost existence is made up of the events of contemporary history.'[33] He had, from the first, to find out how to live in his time—how to be an engineering student, budding writer and Jew at Harvard; how to be a soldier in a Texas regiment in the Pacific; how to be the centre of the best-selling novel racket, and the target male in a macho society from the late 1960s onwards; and, above all, how to act within the Divine Economy: God 'needs us—those of us, at least, who are working for Him.' Since the Devil could be either

> a creature of the first dimension engaged in a tragic monumental war with God or . . . a species of nonexistence, like plastic . . . every single pervasive substance in the technological world that comes from artificial synthesis rather than from nature.[34]

The place of the Bomb and the Space Rocket is therefore theologically clear in *A Fire on the Moon* (1970). The Faustian urge remains active within the astonishing technological achievement. Malign magic for power edges the project into the diabolic. The doctor's confrontation with 'a cancer plague' and the technologist with the twentieth-century Machine both produce dread. The latter:

knows that technology, having occupied the domain of magic, now has a tendency to invade every last social taboo. . . . So the century feels a profound anxiety. . . . Technologists and technicians know their work is either sufficiently liberating to free man from the dread of his superstitition-ridden past, or their work smashes real and valuable taboos, and so becomes sacriligious acts upon a real religious fundament. Could this not yet destroy the earth as it has already disrupted every natural economy of nature? That is the primary source of the great anxiety of the technologist as he stands before the idea that a machine may have a psychology.

So Aquarius 'explores the depths of his own ability to perceive crisis and react to it . . . ultimate modes of existence in sex and in violence, in catastrophe and in death'. The gaze of autobiography and the test in combat fuse in the halls of N.A.S.A. Self-named after his zodiacal sign of 'the scientist-universalist whose garnered treasures of ideas are applied to the service of all',[36] Aquarius descends into the underworld:

> So the real substance of a dream was a submersion into dread. One tested the ability of the psyche to bear anxiety as one submerged into deeper and deeper plumbings of the unknowable until one reached a point where the adventurer in oneself could descend no longer, panic was present—one was exploded out of the dream. But the dangerous shoal had at least been located.

The reporter-artist returns to his work

> as a mediator between magic and technology, between the world of instinct and scientific fact. . . . his central impulse is to create a spell equivalent to the spell of the primitive felt when he passed the great oak and knew a message deeper than his comprehension of things was reaching him,[37]

This is the evaluating moment:

> I would come near to arguing that civilization came out of man's terror at having to face dread as a daily condition . . . a civilization which would insulate us from the exorbitant demands of existence.

Beyond a self-adventure lies the issue of *kharma*, added in the 1970s—a 'peculiar calculus' which is 'that we're not only acting for this life but for other lives. Our past lives and our future lives. Paying dues, receiving rewards.' This may be God's artistic dialogue with other 'cosmic artists'. At the age of 50, Mailer observes: 'Perhaps human souls represent some of the most poignant notions of God.' The beauty of human relationships, however absurd, is that, under 'all that spleen and waste and brutality, there's a blocked aesthetic conception'. Sex and marriage can therefore be part of 'a transcendent vision', part of how you may 'earn your reincarnation'.

Reincarnation, central to Gilmore in *The Executioner's Song* and the three lives of Menenhetet in *Ancient Evenings* (1983), gains reinforcements from Africa in *The Fight*. Norman, the narrator, separates his 'vice' of writing about himself and 'his own small effects on events' from 'egotrips' and 'the unattractive dimensions of his narcissism'. By 'luck' he discovers, in a New York bookshop pile, *Bantu Philosophy*, by a Dutch missionary in the Belgian Congo, and finds that 'the instinctive philosophy of African tribesmen happened to be close to his own', with 'humans as forces, not beings', 'forces that came to inhabit him at any moment from all things living and dead'. A man is himself and the karma of past generations, 'not only a human with his own psyche but a part of the resonances, sympathetic or unsympathetic, of every root and thing (and witch) about him'. Ideally, this could enrich the *muntu*, 'the amount of life in oneself'. It is a belief not dissimilar to 'the Calvinism of the chosen' and its 'primitive sinews of capitalism', but less primitive in its concept of dread: 'it takes bravery to live with beauty and wealth if we think of them as an existence connected with the messages, the curses and the loyalties of the dead.' When Muhammad Ali is knocked out in training and says jokingly from the floor, 'Now, a defeated Ali leaves the ring. . . . He's had his mouth shut for the last time', the watching Africans are appalled: 'A silence, not without dread, was rising from them. . . . Ali had given a tilt to the field of forces surrounding the fight', since 'every word reverberates to the end of the earth, a weak word can bring back an echo to punish the man who spoke; a weak action guarantee defeat'. Both Ali and Norman, the reporting witness, cannot resist the force field with egoism. The writer and the fighter have challenged the karma.

Looking back in 1980 to *Advertisements*, he sees it as a 'watershed' of 'personalized journalism' which enabled him to move beyond being simply 'successful and alienated'. He needed to speak of a protagonist named 'Norman Mailer' in *The Armies of the Night*, but thereafter became 'less interested himself as protagonist . . . half-heroic and three-quarters comic'. In 1981: 'After a while you walk around your own life as though it were a piece of sculpture', thinking less about yourself, and remembering 'there's nobody any more . . . who can tell us how to live.' But he continues as a passionate investigator. He still signs himself in the register of respected outlaws in a state of risk:

> Journalism is bondage unless you can see yourself as a private eye inquiring into the mysteries of a new phenomenon . . . ready to take up your role in the twentieth-century mystery-play.

Mailer belongs with those artists who took part in the extraordinary cultural risks in the United States during the 1940 to 1980 decades, not only in writing but in the civil rights and anti-war movements, in music and in the visual arts; we can recall Mark Rothko speaking in 1943 for the new American expressionists: 'To us art is an adventure into an unknown world, which can be explored only by those willing to take risks.'[38] And Mailer also shared with Kerouac, Charles Olson and Robert Duncan, Elliott Carter, Jackson Pollock and Rothko the need to be absorbed as artists into mythical universals. As a Harvard engineering student, Mailer, almost certainly unaware of it then, was already part of that tradition established by Charles Pierce and his Metaphysical Club, with its varied intelligentsia of the 1870s. They were American experimentalist professionals for whom the sciences, metaphysics and pragmatism came together as essential social investigation: William James, John Dewey, Chauncey Wright and Oliver Wendell Holmes were members.[39] James, in particular, was like Mailer obsessed with cohesion and falling apart: 'The world is One just so far as its parts hang together by any definite connection.' And in a celebrated passage in *Pragmatism* he opts, as Mailer does, for 'the restlessness of the actual theoretic situation'. In the 1940s both the *Advocate* staff and the members of the Signet Society, to which Mailer belonged, may still have inherited some of the spirit of the Metaphysical Club.[40] But, as Mailer would be the first to acknowledge, manichean beliefs give dangerous permissions to a range of advisers to the Nation: fundamentalists, creationists, born-again salvationists, pop singers manipulating the masses by yelling 'With God on our

241

side' into their amplifier systems, and a President who holds that Evil emanates from the Kremlin. As Djuna Barnes once said: 'Too great a sense of identity makes a man feel he can do no wrong. And too little does the same.' In 'The Last Night', the American President and the Soviet Premier, heading the forces which have polluted the Earth, decide to blow it up in order to rocket one hundred best people to set up a new colony somewhere in the Universe. In her painful deathbed, the President's wife warns him: 'You would destroy the world for a principle. There is something diabolical about you.' As he presses the apocalyptic button, and hears her voice saying 'You will end by destroying everything', all he can reply is: 'May I be an honest man and not first deluded physician to the Devil.'[41]

NOTES

1. Warren I. Susman, *Culture as History* (New York: Pantheon Books, 1985), pp. 271–85.
2. Norman Mailer, 'The Faith of Graffiti', *Pieces* (Boston: Little, Brown and Company, 1982), pp. 132–58.
3. Norman Mailer, *Cannibals and Christians* (New York: Dial Press, 1966), pp. 233–40.
4. Ibid. p. 239.
5. Alfred Kazin, 'New York from Melville to Mailer', M. C. Jaye and A. C. Watts (eds.), *Literature and the American Urban Experience* (Manchester: Manchester University Press, 1983), pp. 81–92.
6. Norman Mailer, *An American Dream* (London: Andre Deutsch, 1965), pp. 206–9.
7. Ibid., pp. 238–57.
8. Norman Mailer, *Advertisements for Myself* (New York: Signet Books, 1960), pp. 24–6.
9. Ibid., p. 16.
10. Norman Mailer, *Some Honorable Men: Political Connections 1960–1972* (Boston: Little, Brown, and Company, 1976).
11. *Advertisements for Myself*, pp. 18–21.
12. 'The Art of Fiction XXXII: Norman Mailer: An Interview', *Paris Review*, 31 (1964), pp. 29–58.
13. *Advertisements for Myself*, pp. 322, 304, 328, 316–17.
14. Wilfred Sheed—Hilary Mills, *Mailer* (Sevenoaks: New English Library, 1983), p. 345.
15. See Eric Mottram, 'Dionysus in America', *Other Times*, 1 (1976).
16. 'The Art of Fiction', pp. 45–58.

17. Peter Manso (ed.), *Running Against the Machine* (New York: Doubleday, 1969), pp. 44–5, 6–9, 14, 51, 89.
18. 'David Riesman Reconsidered', *Advertisements for Myself*, pp. 173–85.
19. Norman Mailer, *The Armies of the Night* (New York: New American Library, 1968), pp. 219–54.
20. *Cannibals and Christians*, pp. 2–4, 71–9, 87–130, 158–201, 365–78.
21. *The Armies of the Night*, pp. 54, 79, 120–25, 137, 144, 148, 256–79.
22. Allen Ginsberg, *Planet News* (San Francisco: City Lights Books, 1968), p. 119.
23. Norman Mailer, *The Prisoner of Sex* (London: Sphere Books, 1972), pp. 7, 9, 16–25, 30ff., 65–90, 95–170.
24. *Pieces*, p. 81.
25. Norman Mailer, *The Presidential Papers* (London: Andre Deutsch, 1964), p. 141.
26. *Pieces*, pp. 86–93; *Genius and Lust* (New York: Grove Press, 1976).
27. *Pieces*, pp. 106–14.
28. Christopher Lasch, *The Culture of Narcissism* (New York: W. W. Norton, 1978), pp. 91–2.
29. Felix Guattari, *Molecular Revolution* (Harmondsworth: Penguin Books, 1984), p.80.
30. Norman Mailer, *Pontifications* ed. Michael Lennon (Boston: Little, Brown and Co., 1982), pp. 149, 150, 186–87.
31. *The Presidential Papers*, pp. 148, 189–206, 247–71.
32. *Advertisements for Myself*, pp. 323–29; *Mailer*, pp. 94–116.
33. *The Molecular Revolution*, p. 26.
34. *Pontifications*, pp. 37, 49–57, 88–102, 145–78, 134.
35. Norman Mailer, *A Fire on the Moon* (London: Weidenfeld and Nicolson, 1970), pp. 131–34.
36. Ralph Metzner, *Maps of Consciousness* (New York: Collier Books, 1971), p. 137.
37. *Pontifications*, p. 54; *The Fight* (London: Granada Publishing, 1977), pp. 32–8, 67.
38. Dore Ashton, *About Rothko* (New York: Oxford University Press, 1983), p. 79.
39. C. Wright Mills, *Sociology and Pragmatism* (New York: Oxford University Press, 1966), Ch. 5 and pp. 178, 227.
40. *Mailer*, pp. 53–4.
41. *Cannibals and Christians*, pp. 389, 396.

Notes on Contributors

WARREN CHERNAIK, born in New York and educated at Cornell and Yale, is Reader in English Literature at Queen Mary College, University of London. He is the author of *The Poet's Time: Politics and Religion in the Work of Andrew Marvell* and of other studies of seventeenth-century English literature, and has lectured on American literature in Spain, Austria, Turkey and elsewhere. He regularly reviews for the *Times Higher Education Supplement* and recently lectured on Robert Lowell for the Poetry Society.

DAVID ELLIS teaches English at the University of Kent at Canterbury. He has translated Stendhal's *Souvenirs d'Egotisme* and his articles include work on Jane Austen, Coleridge, Barthes and D. H. Lawrence. His most recent publication is *Wordsworth, Freud and the Spots of Time: Interpretation in 'The Prelude'* (1985).

BRIAN HARDING teaches American literature at the University of Birmingham and is the author of *American Literature in Context*, 11, 1830–65 (1982). He is currently preparing World's Classics Editions of Hawthorne's *Young Goodman Brown and Other Tales* and *The Scarlet Letter* for publication in 1987.

ELIZABETH KASPAR ALDRICH has taught American literature at Yale University, the University of Geneva and the Claremont Graduate School. She has written (under the name Elizabeth Davis) on such subjects as Samuel Richardson's early American imitators, Benjamin Franklin and John Berryman's use of Anne Bradstreet. She is currently at work on a book-length study of formal properties and cultural uses of secular 'saints' lives' entitled *American Hagiography*.

A. ROBERT LEE is Senior Lecturer in English and American Literature at the University of Kent at Canterbury. He is editor of the Everyman *Moby-Dick* and seven previous collections in the Critical Studies Series: *Black Fiction: New Studies in the Afro-American Novel Since 1945* (1980); *Nathaniel Hawthorne: New Critical Essays* (1982); *Ernest Hemingway: New Critical Essays* (1983); *Herman Melville: Reassessments*

(1984); *Nineteenth-century American Poetry* (1985); *The Nineteenth-century American Short Story* (1985); and *Edgar Allan Poe: The Design of Order* (1986). He is the author of B.A.A.S. pamphlet No. 11, *Black American Fiction Since Richard Wright* (1983) and has published recent essays on Chester Himes, Richard Wright, Emily Dickinson, Mark Twain, Herman Melville and Robert Penn Warren. He is a regular broadcaster for B.B.C. Radio and a book-reviewer for the *Listener*.

ERIC MOTTRAM is Professor of English and American Literature in the University of London, at King's College. He has written extensively on nineteenth- and twentieth-century American Literature, most recently on Pound, Ross Macdonald, Poe, James and Science Fiction. He has published books on Faulkner, William Burroughs, Paul Bowles and Kenneth Rexroth, on literary theory in *Towards Design in Poetry*, and is the co-editor (with Malcolm Bradbury) of the *Penguin Companion to American Literature*. He also writes on contemporary British poetry and his own most recent poetry is in *Elegies, Interrogation Rooms* and *The Legal Poems*.

DAVID MURRAY is Lecturer in American Studies at the University of Nottingham and has written on Pound, the New York poets and Poe, as well as a B.A.A.S. pamphlet *Modern Indians* (1983), essays on critical theory and a forthcoming full-length study of American-Indian culture.

FAITH PULLIN teaches English and American literature at the University of Edinburgh. She is editor of *New Perspectives on Melville* (1978) and has published essays on D. H. Lawrence, Afro-American literature, Hemingway and Muriel Spark and is currently completing a critical study of the fiction of Elizabeth Taylor.

DAVID SEED teaches American literature at the University of Liverpool. Among his recent publications are articles on Henry James, Thomas Pynchon, I. B. Singer, James Fenimore Cooper, Henry Roth, Ernest Hemingway, J. D. Salinger and William Faulkner. He has just completed a book-length study of Thomas Pynchon and is currently at work on a study of Joseph Heller.

MICHAEL WOOLF's Ph.D. was on contemporary Jewish-American literature. He is a Lecturer in Literature at Tottenham College of Technology in London and a writer on cultural affairs for B.B.C. Radio 4. His other current research interests include expatriate writing, the work of Henry Miller and the contemporary American novel.

Index

248

Critical Studies Series

FIRST PERSON SINGULAR:
Studies in American Autobiography
edited by A. Robert Lee

Of all literary forms, Autobiography might well be thought – as Wallace Stevens said in another context – the Supreme Fiction; for it offers a self, a version of the self at least, at once real and invented, historic and fictive. Has not, too, Autobiography always been a hospitable but testing genre able to encompass the Confession, the Memoir, the Apologia, the Diary, the Journal, even the Life unfolded as a sequence or exchange of letters? What, in addition, do we make of the explicitly 'fictive' narrative or poem which assumes a first-person, autobiographical stance, a self-acknowledged persona? And as readers, do we not almost always from the outset concede that Autobiography will be subject to the tilts and uncertainties of memory and to the editorializing one way or another of the author?

In the case of American autobiography, is there not furthermore a quite unique dispensation to be reckoned with, a culture which from its Puritan beginnings through to the present age has by its newness and ideology of 'Americanness' acted as a call to self-declaration in its citizenry, a profession of contributing identity? Few nations at least have quite literally produced as much autobiography – estimates run to nearly 10,000 volumes – evidence, were it needed, of the unabating American urge to name and perpetuate the individual self.

The present collection opens with a reconsideration by Elizabeth Kaspar Aldrich of the autobiographical impulse in Puritan culture, the interrogation of self within historic New England. David Seed, in turn, compares the autobiographies of Jonathan Edwards and Benjamin Franklin, presenting, on the one hand, a Puritanism urged in all its Calvinist intensity and, on the other, a Puritanism socialized and made over into the secular work-ethic. Brian Harding takes up this legacy in his account of Transcendentalist autobiography, the 'home-cosmography' of Ralph Waldo Emerson, Henry David Thoreau and